p Dostoevsky

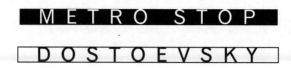

METRO STOP DOSTOEVSKY

■

Travels in Russian Time

■

INGRID BENGIS

NORTH POINT PRESS

A division of Farrar, Straus and Giroux

New York

North Point Press
A division of Farrar, Straus and Giroux
19 Union Square West, New York 10003

"Requiem," from *Poems* by Anna Akhmatova, translated by Lyn Coffin. Copyright
© 1983 by Lyn Coffin. Used by permission of W. W. Norton & Company, Inc.
"He Did Love," by Anna Akhmatova, from *Modern Russian Poetry: An Anthology with
Verse Translations,* edited and translated by Vladimir Markov and Merrill Sparks. Indi-
anapolis: Bobbs-Merrill, 1967. Used by permission of Merrill Sparks.

Library of Congress Cataloging-in-Publication Data
Bengis, Ingrid.
    Metro stop Dostoevsky : travels in Russian time / Ingrid Bengis.— 1st ed.
    p. cm.
    ISBN 0-86547-672-1 (alk. paper)
    1. Russia (Federation)—Description and travel.   2. Bengis, Ingrid—
Journeys—Russia (Federation)   I. Title.

DK510.29 .B46 2003
947.086'092—dc21
[B]   2002042598

Designed by Abby Kagan

www.fsgbooks.com

1   3   5   7   9   10   8   6   4   2

To my mother and father, who didn't live to read this,

and to Edouard, who can't

Russia is a Sphinx! Exultant and afflicted,
Drenched in blackest blood,
She gazes, gazes, gazes into you,
Yes, with hatred and with love.

    —Alexander Blok, "Scythia"

Metro Stop Dostoevsky

■

I t was two o'clock in the morning of February 3, 1990, when the phone rang next to my bed. "I can talk for only two minutes," B said, shouting over the crackling line to make herself heard. "I'm calling from Siberia. I have my passport, and they just gave me an exit visa. There's a ticket available to America from Leningrad this Saturday, or else one for next August. Those are the only two dates available. I have to decide now. Do you still want me to come?"

"Take the ticket for Saturday," I said, trying to remuster the bravado I'd seemed to have in excess when we were last together in Russia, but which had somehow evaporated in the clear Maine winter light. "I'll drive to New York and pick you up at Kennedy. I'll be there waiting." There was no need to ask which airline or which flight. There would be only one.

I didn't have time to ask her why she was calling from Siberia instead of Leningrad, but she probably wouldn't have been able to answer anyway, with the Russian operator listening in. Nor had anything been said about how long she planned to stay. This was her first trip outside of Russia, and I knew from her last letter that she and her husband had just separated. Under those circumstances anything could happen.

By then, of course, I already knew about invitations, knew that you can't just say to someone in Russia, "I'd love to have you come visit me in America," and then forget about it. An invitation is an official gesture, requiring official documents, not just an invitation, but an Invitation, a *Priglashenie,* presented to the local Russian-government passport office as a request for an external passport, which, if granted, then becomes a request to the American government for a visa to enter the United States, and is followed by another request to the Russian government for an exit visa. Invitations are coveted trophies, particularly since Russians can receive permission to travel to the West only if they have a notarized invitation. People forge invitations, or buy them for astronomical sums, or agree to rent their apartments to people who are willing to give them invitations. Invitations are to Russians what green cards are to foreigners in America. This was true then, and it is still true now. Although many things have changed in Russia, the invitation has not, and Westerners who offer invitations in a general sort of way often have little idea of the leaps of heart produced by the gesture, nor do they have any idea of what they are potentially getting into.

But while I had known B for four years, she had never asked for an invitation or hinted at a desire for one. When I finally asked her to come to Maine, she didn't immediately jump at the chance, but just said calmly, "You'll have to do an official invitation," and then seemed to forget about it. Three days before I left Russia, I made the offer again, and then wrote up the letter of invitation in a rush. I had never really expected her to come.

Conversations that involved direct demands for help and immediate irreversible decisions had come to seem normal to me in Russia, a function of Russian realities, but in America, things were different. Now I had to remind myself how B had risked coming to see me at my hotel in Russia when Russians were still not allowed to set foot in hotels for foreigners, had given me her only travel bag and only pair of French stockings when my luggage was stolen at the train station and invited me to stay overnight at her and her husband's Leningrad apartment when doing so could have put both of them in jeopardy. By then we had sat up many times in her kitchen until five o'clock in the morning, drinking tea with raspberries and talking endlessly "soul to soul," and sometimes in pantomime. As the child of Russian émigré parents who spoke Russian, French, Romanian, German, Polish, and some Spanish, though no English when I was born, I'd thought that I had lost irretrievably any memory of the Russian they had spoken to me as a child. But that eventually proved to be an illusion, as did so many other beliefs, which collapsed one after another in astonishing sequence over the coming years.

At any rate, like many people in rural Maine, I had a seasonal job that left me without a rigid schedule in the middle of February, or even much of a schedule at all, so there was nothing to prevent B from coming and staying as long as she wished. Nothing except the American mentality I didn't think I had.

In the end, she stayed for what turned out to be three months. When I returned to Russia again in the fall to sing *Boris Godunov* in the chorus of the Surry Opera Company, an amateur opera company from Maine that had annual exchanges with Leningrad, she was ready with her own invitation for me. Just as we had never talked about how long she would stay in America, we never talked about how long I would stay in Russia, or even when I would come. Whenever possible. That was all that needed to be said. With an invitation, I would be allowed to stay at her house for as long as six months. The invitation was good for a year.

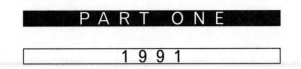

PART ONE
1 9 9 1

∎

o n e

■

The train from Helsinki to Leningrad's Finland Station leaves Helsinki at 1:00 p.m. and arrives in Leningrad at 8:00 p.m., crossing the Russian border after a two-hour customs delay at Wiborg, once part of Finland but incorporated into the Soviet Union at the end of the Russo-Finnish war in 1939. There is no change in the landscape between Finland and Russia; on both sides of the border, it is almost interchangeable with the landscape of coastal Maine, even down to the scattering of islands offshore, and the rose-granite ledges at the edge of the Baltic. But the barbed wire is still there, going off at a ninety-degree angle from the landward side of the border and stretching as far as the eye can see up over the spruce-covered hills. It testifies that, although these are times of profound change in Russia, the watchtowers and the barbed wire have not yet been taken down. You are the same, the train is the same, the landscape is the same. The only difference is that you are crossing into Russia.

It is February 28, 1991, and the fifth time that I have come to Leningrad on this train, the same one taken by Lenin when he was returning to Russia from Switzerland in April 1917, and was greeted at the Finland Station by swarms of supporters: soldiers, sailors, workers. It was, in fact, from this train that the Russian Revolution was launched, with Lenin addressing the crowds at the station: "Dear comrades, I am happy to greet you in the victorious Russian Revolution, to greet you as the advance guard of the international proletarian army. . . . The hour is not far when . . . the people will turn their weapons against their capitalist exploiters. . . . Not today, but tomorrow, any day, may see the general collapse of European capitalism. The Russian Revolution you have accomplished has dealt it the first blow and has opened a new epoch . . . Long Live the International Socialist Revolution."

The ticket counter where you purchase tickets for the train to Russia is in a shabby little room, no more than a cubicle, hardly noticeable when you walk through the Helsinki station, where tickets to Everyplace Else But Russia can be bought in a big shiny ticket office with orderly lines of people paying their money and starting off on their journeys. But the door to the Russian ticket office is closed, and when I open it, there are only two people inside, a Filipino couple from California on their honeymoon, sitting on plastic chairs. They want to go to Russia for a few hours to have their pictures taken in the Finland Station, or maybe in front of the Winter Palace, just so their friends will know they were really there, and they can't understand why no one will give them permission to do this, why they must stay for at least one day when they don't want to, why they need a visa and can't get it on the spot, why Russia is so, well, different from all of the other countries where they've had themselves photographed. They are traveling all over Europe for three weeks, and they've never experienced this before, being told no so absolutely. Crestfallen, they go out of the office and take each other's pictures in the grand waiting room of the Helsinki train station. At least they can tell their friends that they were in Helsinki. Wouldn't it have been nice, though, to say that they were in Russia?

The two young Russian women behind the counter are wearing red lipstick and flowery dresses. They are carefully, elaborately made up, and when one of them comes out from behind the counter I see that she has on spike heels. They have neither the sloppy informality of Americans and many Northern Europeans nor the casual elegance of the French or Italians, but, rather, a certain mixture of determination and wistfulness, which seems to say, as women in Russia do, Life may be hard, but I'm still a woman. They carry their femininity like a badge of courage, wanting to look like European women but not succeeding, only because you can tell how hard they are trying. Yet they are lovely, in a particularly Russian way. No one would ever mistake them for Finns, even though they may be wearing clothes from Finland or are living temporarily in Finland, even though clothes like these can be found in Russia, purchased at great expense to make Russians feel European. The most insulting thing you can say to Russians these days is that they are not Europeans, not really, even if they are, geographically speaking. It is because they are caught in a time warp, because their lives, their experience, shows in their faces, and because theirs is not a European experience. Still, they want to be really European. There is nothing they want more.

The ticket agents are always faintly surprised when I ask for a second-class ticket on this afternoon's train without a reservation and then produce the necessary visa. Foreigners don't usually do things like that. Either they travel in groups with a guide, or else they try to buy a ticket but don't have a visa, or they have already bought their tickets ahead of time, paying in a foreign country in foreign currency and carrying with them only travel vouchers. What they are not used to is someone who acts like going to Russia is no different from going anywhere else, as the Filipinos did, but who has a visa, travels alone, and isn't afraid.

It's true that I'm not afraid. I never have been. Fear wasn't bred into me the way it was bred into native Russians who lived with the system all of their lives. Nor was the typically American cold-war fear of Russia and Russians bred into me, since my parents were both "Russian," and, growing up in America, I always felt the ambiguity produced by recognizing oneself in the enemy.

In 1988, at this very same ticket counter, after an unsmiling man in a gray military uniform with red stripes on the shoulders and a red star on his cap told me that there were no tickets available on the Leningrad train for a month, I simply boarded a Finnish train going in the same direction, traveled two hours farther down the line to Lahti, and waited for the Leningrad train to pull into the station, presenting my visa to the conductor and climbing aboard when he waved me on and seated me in a car where I turned out to be the only passenger. I never could understand why they preferred having an empty train to selling seats on that train, or why they lied about it, but after that, I always approached the ticket counter with confidence. Because I knew already that the sternness was a sham, and that in Russia there is a way to do everything if you persist. *"Terp-yenye y trud fsyo peritrut"* roughly translated as "With patience and work everything will come to you"—still applies. On the other hand, there is another popular saying that might apply as easily: "Without papers, you are shit. With papers, you are a human being."

In either case, I don't care that Russians never smile when they say yes (or no). Nor does it matter that the American habit of smiling under stress is something Russians find irritating.

What matters is getting on this train. And the knowledge that B, wearing her white fox fur coat and hat, will be waiting for me at Leningrad's Finland Station. In her arms will be red carnations.

An enormous white banner flutters from the ceiling near the swinging doors that open onto the platform from which the Repin, the daily train to Leningrad, will soon be leaving. I look up at it. It reads:

WAR IS OVER
IF YOU WANT IT
LOVE AND PEACE FROM JOHN AND YOKO

Last night, while I was flying across the Atlantic, my mind already leaving America behind, focusing tightly, intently, on Russia, the war in the Persian Gulf ended. Cheers went up all over America as Stormin' Norman Schwarzkopf appeared on TV wearing his camouflage fatigues and boasting about how the Allies had tricked Saddam Hussein into believing that an amphibious attack was imminent, when in fact a land-based attack was sneaking around his troops to victory. How uncomfortable I am with this upsurge of superheated patriotism, this emphasis on rubbing Saddam's nose in the dirt. Humiliation rarely leads to improvement of character, but acts as a corrosive agent, breeding a hypersensitivity to one's condition and a continuing desire to settle scores. No people can long stand being made to feel inferior; it was, after all, humiliation and economic disaster that led from World War I to World War II. But today, the Berlin Wall is down, Germany is reunited, Iraq is defeated, and socialism is everywhere collapsing. Does this mean that, after almost fifty years, World War II is finally over, or has it just sprouted new, as yet invisible shoots? Today is America's hour of triumph.

Why, then, do I feel such treasonous relief to be leaving behind this glorious New World Order for the safety of Russian uncertainties? Perhaps it's because deep down, I suspect myself of still being Russian.

The Repin is now in the station, ready for boarding. I walk out onto the snowy platform, breathing in the Russian winter, even though it is still on the other side of the border, wheeling my overloaded luggage cart unsteadily across the packed whiteness. We all know, every newspaper in America has said so, that these are hard times in Russia. Chances are that there will be nothing to eat. For safety's sake, I have brought along five boxes of De Cecco spaghetti, two pounds of sun-dried tomatoes, Moroccan olives, anchovies, and several heads of garlic, as well as two liters of extra-virgin olive oil. Not exactly proletarian fare, but also things I'm not likely to find in Leningrad. Anyway, sitting all afternoon or all night around B's kitchen talking, I will probably forget about food. My mother once told me that after she and her family escaped from Russia in 1921, when she was twelve, she never again met anyone with whom she felt she could talk soul to soul. The Russian writer Tatyana Tolstaya once recounted that when she used the word *soul* in a lecture at an American university, the audience laughed. B doesn't laugh. People don't laugh about the soul in Russia. They just worry about losing it.

Almost fifteen years ago, on my first trip to Russia, during the Brezhnev years, I went searching for my mother's dacha by the sea in Odessa, with its miniature theater where the officers of the White Guard performed during the summer, its cherry orchard and fountain and avenue of lime trees that before the Russian Revolution led to a wide field and then a beach on the Black Sea shore. What I found was a *dom otdykha*, a vacation house, for families with tubercular children. I hadn't expected that. I hadn't expected to find the dacha at all, and in fact, following my mother's directions, had stumbled on it by accident. When I told an old babushka who lived there that it had been my mother's summer house before the Revolution, she insisted that I take a handful of earth with me to give to my grandmother in America. I did, but somehow along the way I must have lost it, and didn't even realize that it was gone. My mother shrugged. My grandmother didn't. This was what happened to souls in America. I had to come back to Russia to find mine.

During my last trip to Russia in June, I went to Odessa with B again, but I couldn't remember the exact directions to the dacha and never was able to find it. Was it possible that it had simply disappeared? I spent three days looking for it, looking at places that resembled it but weren't it. I finally gave up. On the train back to Leningrad, we shared our compartment with a young painter, twenty years old. We were traveling illegally, without a visa for Odessa, and B had warned me against speaking either English or bad Russian, so I remained mysteriously silent despite his hearty *Z'drastvuite* and friendly-puppy manner. He began talking immediately, however, with none of the wariness of a Russian from Moscow or Leningrad. There was paint under his fingernails, and he carried a bag with a paintboard and pad. Instantly, he fell in love with B, and when he realized that my silence was not exotic but practical, he fell in love with me as well. He could not believe that B was Russian and I was American, and that we were traveling together and she had stayed in my home. He thought that she could not possibly be Russian. Where did I live in America? he asked. Where did she live in Leningrad? Impossible! It was all impossible! And then he asked me, "Do you know that we are a socialist country? Do you know what is socialism?" A few minutes later, he asked, "Do you think Bush wants peace or war?" and then, "Please, what are the words for this song 'Glory, Glory, Hallelujah'?" He was working in an Odessa theater, designing sets for a Tennessee

Williams play, and was on his way to Leningrad, having decided to take the examination for admission to the Institute for Theater and Cinematography in acting; for the exam he would have to recite one poem, do one scene and one improvisation, dance, and sing. He planned to recite Trofimov's monologue about philosophy and kindness from *The Cherry Orchard*, a poem of Krillov's called "The Rich Man and the Poet," some Japanese haiku, and Nikolai Tikhonov's World War II song about a soldier going to war. In preparation for the trip, he had brought with him *pirozhki* made by his grandmother, Odessa sausage (famous throughout Russia, he said fervently), and cucumbers and tomatoes from his family's garden. Later, he bought tiny strawberries in a newspaper cone from a peasant woman selling them at a Byelorussian station platform uncomfortably close to Chernobyl. We shared with him smoked ham from the Odessa farmers' market ("so expensive," he said) and blueberries and little sweet cherries, but kept for ourselves the five-kilo bucket of sour cherries we planned to use in Leningrad to make jam for the coming winter—if, of course, we could find enough sugar, which was always in short supply during jam-making season, but was in especially short supply prior to this winter of Leningrad's anticipated discontent.

"Do you like realist art or abstract art?" he asked.

"Good art," I said.

"Yes, but which? There are only two styles. In Russia, we have the realist tradition. In the West, you have abstract tradition. Which do you like better?"

"Too difficult to answer," I said. "Though I probably feel closer to the Russian tradition."

"We in Russia don't need what you in the West call democracy," he said, giving up on that subject. "We need a good strong leader. This is also our tradition, and our problem is that we don't have one now. But the catastrophe is happening so quickly. It is maybe too late already. The greatest experiment in kindness in the history of the world is dead. Socialism is finished. Every man has part of himself which is like an animal—only for himself, an egotist. The animal in man has finally won over the God in man."

Only eight months have passed since that conversation. This time I am not just visiting Russia, biting into watermelon slices of my past history and spitting out the seeds. This time it will be seeds and all. In less than three short weeks, everyone will be voting on whether or not to maintain the Soviet Union as a union. The second question listed on the ballot will be whether or not Russia should have an independent president of the Republic. Everyone in Russia knows what this means. It means Yeltsin, a vote for Yeltsin, who has promised all things to all people, everything with the exception of socialism. For this, he has become a hero. A vote for Yeltsin probably does mean the end of socialism. "The greatest experiment in kindness in the history of the world" or a prison for the Soviet people? Or perhaps, yet again, an experiment that has never really been tried, at least not here?

I remember Edmund Wilson's phrase from the 1971 preface to his classic 1941 study of the Russian Revolution, *To the Finland Station:* "It is all too easy to idealize a social upheaval which takes place in some country other than one's own." Last year I taped this sentence to the mirror above B's kitchen sink, which doubles as a bathroom sink, so that I could see it every morning when I brushed my teeth. Just to be sure I didn't forget.

What I want to know now, though, is what has socialism (or its simulation) killed in the Soviets, and what has it created? What has capitalism killed in Americans, and what has it created? I need to ask these questions now, before socialism disappears altogether.

As I struggle through the snow toward the platform for the Repin, three men approach me and offer to help with my things. I gladly accept. The man who takes over my luggage cart begins to speak to me in Russian. He wants to know if I would mind taking a letter with me and mailing it from Leningrad. He puts his fingers to his lips and pleads with me in a whisper as we trudge through the snow. "Hide it in your pocketbook," he says.

"Of course," I say immediately, taking the letter, which I know would need a month to get from Helsinki to Leningrad by mail, even though the cities are only four hours apart by train, not counting delays at the border. But why the whisper? Why the secret?

He kisses my hand after he has brought my things to the train, and once I am inside the compartment, I see the three of them standing outside the window waving at me, like old friends. I close the compartment door, then lower the window shade and hold the letter up to the light, thinking that maybe it contains money which he is sending to his family in Leningrad. But there is nothing visible through the envelope aside from a letter. So why did he seem afraid? Is this the memory of censorship or its perpetuation? The address on the letter is in Yalta, the Crimea. Maybe he's a Crimean separatist? Yalta, of all places, just when the Persian Gulf War has ended, and all of Eastern Europe is once again being recarved.

Someone knocks at the door. Instinctively, I put the letter under my skirt. The compartment is filling up. As the train pulls out of the station, my co-conspirators wave at me until the train is completely out of sight. I sit back in my seat and look out the window at the spruce trees heavy with snow. Each car has its own conductor, and the woman who is responsible for this one comes by to ask if anyone would like some tea. Within an hour, we all know each other: an Estonian psychologist, a Korean student studying in Leningrad, a West German computer scientist going to a conference on semiconductors in Sverdlovsk, and a heavy Russian woman who sits directly across from me and keeps wiping her brow anxiously and sighing, *"Kakoy koshmar"* ("What a nightmare"). The tea finally arrives in a glass, with an ornate nickel-plated holder that commemorates the launching of Sputnik, and two sugar cubes, which I save.

The letter is still tucked under my skirt when the Estonian starts to speak about Estonian independence, which, if all goes well, should be achieved in two years. He talks about it as if Russia is somehow irrelevant to all this, as if Estonia has gone beyond thinking about Russia. The Russian woman sighs heavily again and again. Who has died? Who is suffering? But never, throughout the entire journey, does she reveal the source of her nightmare.

As the train pulls to a stop at the Finland Station, B appears in front of my compartment window, standing so close to it that her high aristocratic cheekbones, translucent complexion, and classic profile reminiscent of Akhmatova are framed by the dusty glass like a prerevolutionary sepia photograph. Her unsmiling face is luminous with feeling, but there are no flowers in her arms, and instead of her white fox fur coat and hat, she is wearing a dark-gray wool tweed coat, a red fedora, and a red woolen scarf that make her seem, if anything, more elegant than ever.

Out on the platform, she apologizes for having come to the station empty-handed; the friend of a friend who promised to bring her to the station in his private car never showed up, and after standing in the street for half an hour, hoping for a ride in a taxi, car, or anything else on wheels, she finally gave up and took a bus to the station instead of stopping for flowers. "So much for that beautiful Russian soul you're so romantic about. People don't care about each other at all now."

What about her fur coat? I ask. She shrugs and says that she doesn't wear it anymore. "No one goes out now anyway," she says. "Only prostitutes and speculators. After eight o'clock the city is empty." Besides, in these difficult times, it is provocative, dangerous, and perhaps immoral to show that you are okay, or at least appear to be. She is acutely aware of the distinction, and hardly needs me to remind her that her conductor husband bought the coat three years ago for two hundred dollars while on a performance tour in Greece, at a time when she is quite certain that he didn't have two hundred dollars. She wore it anyway, almost as an act of defiance. From her perspective, the homecoming present was a form of what she would call "protection money," and in this way no different from any of the thousand acts of bribery that pockmark everyday Russian life like a case of the measles; it was clearly intended, along with a sewing machine from Germany that she had long coveted, to help ease his passage through the rocky shoals of their marriage to the safety of a new marriage to a "woman from the West." Who, after all, but a woman from the West would pay two hundred dollars for her lover's wife's fur? Now that B and A are finally separated, however, the coat has to some extent lost its raison d'être, and B, who cares little about material possessions, is sincere when she says, "It doesn't matter," speaking as much of the marriage as the fur coat. "For what do I need a fur coat anyway?"

In front of the Finland Station, she negotiates strenuously for a taxi, finally settling on a two-dollar fare with the driver of a private car who recently had a heart attack and needs extra money. Moments later, under the watchful eye of Lenin's statue urging the workers forward across the Neva to the Winter Palace, we cross the bridge into the city center, with its faded but still-ravishing beauty, like a former grande dame fallen on hard times who nonetheless cannot help comporting herself with her customary sense of dignity.

Along the way to B's apartment, we pass the wrought-iron gates of the Summer Garden, its naked statues safely ensconced in their winter wooden enclosures, the Field of Mars, where in June the profusion of hundreds of varieties of lilacs exhaling into the white midnight sky is so intoxicating that it lingers in the imagination long into February, and the Winter Palace, now the Hermitage, all pale blue-green and dazzling white, facing out onto the vast openness of Palace Square. Across the river, on the shore of the icebound Neva Embankment, the gilded spire of the illuminated Peter and Paul fortress, where the tsars are buried and Dostoevsky once languished in prison, pierces the sky with a sharpness rendered all the more acute by the absence of anything taller in the vicinity, for in this city, unlike any other European or American city, there are no skyscrapers, no neon, no steel or glass or glittering storefronts. Just the naked, unblemished city itself, with the pastel hues of the palace façades built during the time of Catherine the Great reflecting in the icy river. A city that, visually at least, remains untouched by any of the confusing jumble of twentieth-century progress.

A wave of nostalgia washes over me, despite my awareness of the rutted streets dug up in anticipation of needed repairs, and then, as perestroika's promise turned to poverty, abandoned to their asphaltless fates, the shops with their dirty windows behind which there is virtually nothing to show, and the crumbling courtyards of the center city, within which most people still live in communal flats. But I am too much enamored of this city to see its faults as anything other than a manifestation of its suffering, and I suspect that I might love it less were it more perfect, and thus, in some sense, more ordinary. Besides, I have always been reluctantly dragged along by progress, and if there is one thing communism has done for this city, it is to stave off progress. Russia lives in a time warp where every element of life moves at a lumbering pace, a pace all but destroyed by the modern world, a knotty, tangled, intractably conservative pace. Will the capitalism now waiting so impatiently in the wings turn all that into something merely archival, a fossil imprint left behind by the onrushing sweep of the glacier, or will it endure, as it has endured every other onslaught for centuries, with its customary patience and stoicism? Napoleon and Hitler couldn't conquer Russia. Can Pepsi? Sure. Only a privileged Westerner can afford to think this way, but I still can't help begging the future to wait just a little bit longer, to spare this city from the turmoil of contemporary times, to let me climb quietly back through this window from the West in peace.

We met in 1986, when I was on tour for the first time in Russia, singing *Boris Godunov*. She was in the audience with her sister and her niece. It was November. At the end of the opera, they came up to the stage and spoke to me. I had no idea who they were, nor did I know that her husband was a musician at the Kirov Theater and that he had been the first person to initiate contact with our opera company. I certainly didn't know that he had been Communist Party vice-secretary for ideology for the musicians at the Kirov and had been forced to resign his position as a result of having friendly relations with Americans, or that her mother had spent ten years in the Gulag. She spoke in a low, soft, musical voice that suggested an unusual inner calm, and her cool, appraising gray eyes seemed to register, like some powerful magnetic field, everything that passed before her gaze. There was something catlike about her, and I have always been afraid of cats, with their strange compressed energy threatening to break out unexpectedly, their claws ready to scratch out my eyes in a second. They stare at me. I stare at them. There is no question which of us would win in a staring contest. Every cat that looks at me knows that I am a hopeless case, a dog for life.

I looked away from B and asked her niece if she knew the Russian lullaby my mother had sung to me throughout my childhood; kneeling at the edge of the stage, I sang it to them in Russian. Then B invited me to come back to their apartment for tea. She met me in the lobby of my hotel. I didn't know that she wasn't allowed to come in. She never said anything about it, and I didn't ask, though I knew that other people were cautious about how and where they met me, and about telephone calls, which I was told to make only from pay phones on the street. Americans find Russian friendships demanding. "They give so much, but they expect so much," I have heard Americans say. I have even heard Russians who have been living in America for several years say about Russians who haven't, "They have no sense of limits." But as far as B is concerned, Americans don't know what friendship is. I wonder if this judgment includes me.

We are woken up at noon the day after my arrival by B's brother-in-law Pavel, ringing the doorbell, bringing carnations and champagne and enough food to get us through the first few days in Leningrad, since B has been in Moscow for the past week. Pavel works as the manager of a hotel restaurant, and in Russia this is as advantageous a job as it is possible to have. It means that you have permanent access to good food. Pavel has brought us a vacuum-packed side of smoked salmon, produced by a Soviet-German joint venture. The Russians provide the salmon, the Germans provide the packaging and handle the distribution in the West, they split the profits fifty-fifty. I am reluctant to comment that I think this is a lopsided deal, since what counts most is the salmon. On the other hand, if you don't have vacuum packs and can't produce them, what good does it do to have the salmon? In any case, it is superb. We will eat it for breakfast, lunch, and dinner, alternating it with some sausage that Pavel also has brought for us, and bread from the corner bakery—good, heavy Russian bread, the kind B dreamed about so often when she was visiting America.

But Pavel has not only brought us something. He is waiting for something too. I look down at his shoes, dove-gray slip-ons with thick crepe soles, very soft and beautiful leather. The shoes surprise me, since B had told me that he had no shoes for spring and asked me to bring him some. But the ones he is wearing look like the shoes I couldn't afford to buy for him in New York, the ones reduced from $200 to $126. I thought I was being extravagant with what I brought: three pairs of Italian shoes from Sym's in New York, intended to astonish him with the revelation of beauty wedded to craftsmanship. Now I'm not so sure.

While I am in the other room, B gives him the shoes. I don't hear a word of reaction, nothing but complete silence. I spent so much money, and he doesn't like them. It's true that one pair is size fifteen, and he wears size thirteen, but they were Ballys, on sale, reduced from $180 to $20. I've learned from being in Russia that you should always buy what is available if the price is right; if you don't need it yourself, someone else will, and then you can exchange it for something you do need. In this way, having an extra pair of shoes is like having money in the bank.

I come into the living room, and ask if I can take a closer look at the shoes he is wearing, and if he can tell me where they come from. They are Salamanders, he says, from Germany.

"What are Salamanders?" I ask.

He and B look at me as if I must be slightly retarded.

"They're the best," B says. "We used to have a lot of such shoes from Germany and Italy and Spain. Our stores were full of them. And they were only sixty roubles. Now it is impossible to find them, and if you can, the price is five or six hundred roubles. This is why our people are angry. It is the result of our perestroika."

So I understand why Pavel is not overjoyed with the shoes,

which for him are only a bitter reminder of how things used to be. The irony, however, is that most Americans can't afford German or Italian shoes like the ones he is wearing either. Except most Americans probably could never afford them, and never expected to, whereas he feels entitled to them, the most dangerous legacy of socialism. As they say, it's easier to go up than to come down. Yes, I agree: people should be entitled to a good education and medical care and a decent place to live and a job and enough food to eat and security in their old age. But these things to which all people should be entitled are things that many Americans have never had, things they only dream of or hope for in the future, if they even consider them to be possibilities for themselves. In Russia, however, the romance of "having," the raw, exotic exposure to Western consumer goods (perhaps of dubious usefulness, but nonetheless imbued with dazzling panache) flooding in from the West, or displayed to Russians when they travel to the West, is beginning to take its disorienting toll, producing a kind of frenzy, a consumer madness that makes them covet everything they see, especially if it comes in an appealing package. All their lives they have been hoarding snippets of what is necessary, what is available, and now they see places in the West where everything is available, and they're still hoarding, buying until they collapse from exhaustion and indigestion. This frenzy for having is much more powerful for them right now than the drab, unadvertised, unglamorous fundamentals to which they have always felt entitled, and which they take for granted in much the same way that we take for granted the right to express our opinions. The Russians, I'm afraid, are in for a rude awakening. German shoes are just the tip of the iceberg.

Late in the afternoon, in waning silvery light, we go for a walk to the farmers' market across the Neva on Vasilevsky Island. We cross the Potseluiev Bridge over the Moika River, from which I can see the gilded dome of St. Isaac's Cathedral in one direction, and in the other, the pale-blue confection of Nikolsky Cathedral, its three domes transforming themselves as the light shifts, sometimes seeming to be silver, sometimes silvery blue, sometimes platinum, ringed with a silver halo so delicate that it appears to merge and dissolve into the sky above it. Behind it is the cobalt-blue dome of the Troitsky Cathedral, really quite far off, on the opposite bank of the Fontanka River, but from here it seems to be pasted onto the back of Nikolsky's dome, echoing it like a half-moon in eclipse. Nikolsky is a working church; the Troitsky is not. For the past thirty years, like Cinderella dressed in rags, it has been used for storing potatoes, though the penetrating blue of its dome never fails to draw attention to the beauty of its true identity.

The Russian Orthodox Church is steeped in a sense that beauty itself is redemptive, and every time I glimpse Nikolsky out of the corner of my eye, or face it head-on, or sit in the park that surrounds it, I am drawn in by its splendid yet intimate harmony, at once joyful, playful, and serene. But I am often embarrassed by its effect on me. After all, I am a practicing Jew, and all around me, Jews are in flight from Russia. Every week, tour buses pull up in front of the synagogue near B's apartment. The surprise is that the buses contain not only American Jews but non-Jewish Russian tourists visiting churches of various denominations and learning about Judaism from their tour guide. I never go to the synagogue. Instead, I turn to Nikolsky Sobor and its park, which have always been my retreat, soothing as a baby blanket. I am ashamed to admit this, but it is true. I will never be anything but Jewish, yet I cannot imagine living here, in a neighborhood where it would be impossible to see the Nikolsky.

At the market, it is late in the day and long stretches of metal countertop are already bare. Under the outer arches of the market is a stall selling beer, and the line in front of the stall is long, rowdy, and bleary-eyed. We walk past it into the courtyard that houses the market complex, going into the warehouse-sized "root-vegetable room" to buy potatoes, cabbage, beets, and onions, and passing on from there into the next huge building. Here, pork and beef are butchered from whole animals on huge chopping blocks directly behind the counters, the ax-strokes resonating with great thumps throughout the high-ceilinged room. Women stand longingly in clusters before the meat counters, asking, "*Pochom?*" ("How much?"), then lapse into silence and wander away. On the other side of the room, they sample the farm women's fresh sour cream from little slips of paper dipped into buckets, and chunks from the wheels of farmer cheese covered in muslin. Again, "*Pochom?*" followed by silence. At one counter, someone is selling rabbits, but a rumor has been going around that hundreds of rabbits injected with cancer cells were stolen from a lab. Despite the strict controls on what comes into the farmers' market, no one is buying rabbit today, and the farmer selling them, who has only a few rabbits, is standing alone and silent.

The market is crowded, but B says that people shop here only when someone in the family is sick or a child is on a special diet or they have guests or it is a holiday. Here is the finest in fresh food, without nitrates or chemical filters or stabilizers. Food bought outside, on the street surrounding the market, is cheaper, but also riskier. Maybe it came from soil contaminated by Chernobyl and couldn't be certified to be brought into the market. The people who live around Chernobyl are trying to survive just like anyone else; they sell what they can to whoever is willing to buy.

"It used to be cheaper in the farmers' markets than in state stores," B says. "But now you have to be either rich or desperate to buy anything here."

"Well, I'm not rich and I'm not desperate," I say.

"You're a foreigner. *Chuzhie. Ni nasha.* Not one of us."

"Thanks," I say. "It's always nice to feel welcome."

B looks at me and then looks away. She says nothing.

"You don't understand what I love about this market," I insist. "The tomatoes from Azerbaijan that we bought last spring made American tomatoes taste like rubber balls. The pork you get here can only be found in America on small family farms, where the pigs are fed apples and natural-food garbage. The slop pails on the second-floor landing of your building, where we deposit all of your food garbage for the trucks to collect and use as pig food—things like that don't even exist in America. There are a lot of things you have here that we don't have in America."

"Why are you telling me this?" B says.

"Because I'm sure that everyone here isn't rich or desperate."

"You can think whatever you want," B says coolly. "It's a free country."

That throws me. Of course she knew it would. I wish she would argue with me. It might make me feel better. I know she has food coupons for sugar, meat, sausage, kasha, and macaroni that she gives to her mother. I know she gives her coupons for wine and vodka to her upstairs neighbors. But why should that make me feel ashamed of my love for Azerbaijani tomatoes, or the fact that I can afford to buy our groceries?

All around us, I hear snippets of conversation about the price increases that went into effect at the beginning of the year. Ryzkov, Gorbachev's premier, who has a gentle, intelligent face like so many of the other people around Gorbachev, has just gone on TV to announce a doubling of the official price of meat. He always takes the time to explain the reasons for what he is doing. Then there is a storm of protest, and the price hikes are retracted. He can't seem to bear the prospect of causing pain. He is an *idealist*, the Russian word carrying the Russian contempt reserved for anything associated with ideology. People here are allergic to ideology. It was idealists who thought they could make Russia a better place, idealists who believed in the "New Soviet Man." Hah! Look at him, this New Soviet Man. That's what our idealism has produced. Besides, how can an idealist like Ryzkov reform the economy?

The price of meat has been the same throughout the entire Soviet Union ever since the 1960s. So has the price of bread. You get used to it being that way, to giving day-old bread to the birds, to buying eggs that are more than three days old at a reduced price. Russian doctors recommend eating eight times a day. Meat and potatoes. Whatever time of day you walk into a Russian home, there is always something on the table. B says that Americans don't know how to eat, that in America she was always hungry. What do you mean? I say. How could you have been hungry? We ate so well. No normal bread, B says. No normal soup. No normal tea. What do you Americans have against meat? Don't you know that pizza isn't food? Wait a minute, I say. We never ate pizza. And you cried when you went into that New York meat market with me and saw what they had in the case. I remember you crying. I was crying for a different reason, she says. What reason? I say. Never mind, she says. I don't want to talk about it.

Before she left Maine to return to Russia, an American woman we knew asked if she could send a food basket for a friend back to Leningrad with B. The basket had macaroni in it, split peas, packaged Kraft cheese, and miniature smoked sausages. B said that she would be embarrassed to give someone such a present. Cheese like rubber. Split peas and macaroni that we get for coupons. Sausages that taste like I don't know what, maybe sweetened cardboard. How could this woman think that Russians eat worse than that? Better to send ten dollars, or maybe some aspirin, the kind that fizzes up when you put it into a glass of water. Or, just for fun, how about those little blue bars that you put in the toilet tank to turn the water blue?

We walk back through the snow to B's apartment with a week's worth of groceries packed into her sturdy Soviet rolling cart with its built-in canvas shopping bag. It is four o'clock in the afternoon and already close to dark. The street lamps reflect in the canals as the full tramways make their arching turn at the edge of the Moika, where it meets the Kriukov Canal, and snake around onto the straightaway to the Kirov Theater and Nikolsky. Alongside the stage entrance to the Kirov, the tramway bedding and rails have been dug up, abandoned by a crane that seems to be idling permanently in midair. Everywhere are mountains of crushed rock delivered to the site a year ago, left unused through a winter and a spring and another winter, diminished only by slow but steady theft. Is this the decay of neglect or the decay of trauma, of shell shock, of "the transition period to capitalism," its rosy future imbued with the same lingering sweetness as once was signified by its predecessor red star? The statues, with water dripping down their necks from widening cracks in the classic surrounding masonry, look down on us sorrowfully. All around us are houses that have been gutted, though their façades have been left intact. B says that they're waiting for the city to have enough money to fix them. She remembers the days when Leningrad's houses were painted every year, when the streets were clean, the roads repaired. But what is the point? she says. It only makes one crazy to think about it.

A musician carrying a cello case and a dancer from the Kirov who recognize B stop to speak to her. They evidently know who I am, but don't speak to me or even acknowledge me. B is silent on the way back home. "We were good friends," she finally says. "*Bivsheh.*" Formerly. Before. That has become the saddest word in the Russian language to me, signifying memories of a life that is vanishing from one day to the next. Was it better or worse? When B says "before," does she mean before perestroika? Before her separation from A? Before her trip to America? Before A began his romance with a Western woman? When did "before" end and "now" begin? B's sorrows balloon into the courtyard as we wheel the shopping cart up over the entry step and close the apartment door behind us.

t w o

∎

t is after eleven-thirty when the telephone rings. Nina, B's upstairs neighbor, wants to know if B is busy. B says no.

"Are you sleeping?" Nina asks.

"No."

"Are you alone?"

B pauses for a moment and then answers "no" again, in a slightly suggestive tone.

Nina hesitates. "Is it all right if Oleg comes down to you for just a few minutes?"

B deliberately doesn't answer right away, encouraging Nina to think that maybe she is with a lover.

"Oh, maybe it's better if he doesn't. He can come tomorrow."

"It's okay," B says. "He can come. Why not?"

Within a few moments, Oleg is at the door. B, wearing her long red bathrobe, opens the door, and he comes in, a little nervously. He is surprised when he walks into the kitchen and sees, instead of B's mysterious lover, me, cooking dinner. He doesn't know what to think, though the hooligan in B has clearly been at work here, deliberately stirring up a hornets' nest, and now he is trying to decide whether he should behave like a guest because of me, or whether he should simply sit down in the kitchen, as he usually does, and have tea.

Immediately B starts to pour, but he interrupts her.

"I really should go back upstairs," he says, shifting his feet. "With this new job, I work twice as much as before. There was another meeting in Palace Square today. Small, but still a meeting. Take my advice: if you don't want to get into trouble, stay away from meetings. Who knows what can happen at them? It's dangerous. If you hear about one, walk the other way."

"She loves meetings," B says, indicating me. "She's always asking me about them. She doesn't want to miss any."

I look at her in astonishment. Why is she telling him this? After all, Oleg is in the militia, and it's best, as far as I can tell, not to discuss things like this with him, though I understand that B is worried that I might not listen to his advice. He knows what's dangerous and what isn't, and he always does whatever he can to protect her—telling her when to stay home, or which way to walk, giving her a special number to call in case of trouble. There is clearly no need to warn B about attending meetings, or about participating in them. She would never go to a demonstration anyway. As far as she is concerned, the best way to deal with politics is to stay away from it, to sniff the prevailing winds and adapt to change as it comes, using the most finely calibrated antennae to determine what will be expected from you next. Being smart means being attuned to all of this, attuned to nuance, to the change of emphasis in a phrase, the change of wording in a required document, whereas politics, at least as it is understood in the West, is the very opposite of sifting through nuance. Protest? Against what and for what?

"Ever since Yeltsin made that speech asking Gorbachev to

resign, all of us have been nervous," Oleg says. "He was wrong; it was irresponsible, a provocation. I think he did it because his popularity has declined; he needed to do something dramatic to regain it. But the speech backfired. He lost more support, because everyone could see that it was just a question of egotism. Most of the people who go to these meetings are hooligans, speculators, Mafia. You never know when some spark will start an explosion. All it takes is one person to set it off. People are angry now, tired and angry. A lot of them have guns. And if they use these guns, we also will have to use our guns."

His face is pensive. He seems like a soft man in some ways, and he didn't expect that this would become his job, dealing with demonstrations, with people armed with guns. The responsibility of the militia is supposed to be to stop crimes and help people, not to get into political crossfires. So far the demonstrations have been peaceful. But who knows what will happen next time? Everyone is prepared at any moment for the possibility of a coup.

"I work all of the time now," he says. "I'm exhausted. I haven't had a day off in months. Not since I came back from California."

The last time I saw Oleg, he was sitting in a restaurant in Santa Cruz. He had just arrived in America three days before, and had spent his first night on the beat as a guest of the New York City police force, riding around Times Square in a squad car for the graveyard shift. He couldn't get over it, the technology, the squad cars, the paddy wagons. "They have things we never even dreamed of," he said, sitting down at the table next to us with his friend David, a former Berkeley student turned mounted policeman who had invited him to be his guest in California, to spend a week with him on the beat in San Jose. But the next day Oleg would have to put on his militia uniform and participate in a funeral ceremony for David's best friend, who had been killed when he stopped a car for speeding. His first day in America, and already he was going to a funeral. Even here, in America, policemen get killed.

David himself looked like the all-American boy. He had two female roommates in the country house, which he had recently bought. Oleg didn't quite understand what the relationship was among all of them. David had a girlfriend, but she didn't live with him. Instead, two other women did. David was getting married in June. What would happen to the other two women then? David explained that he needed help with paying the mortgage on the house. That's why he had roommates. Oleg couldn't get over the size of the house. But he also couldn't get over the fact that David was living in a situation not so very different from being in a communal flat.

I asked Oleg what he wanted to eat, and he said whatever they had. An opening reception for an artist who created environmentally conscious food art was in progress in the restaurant we'd wandered into, attracted by the gallery-restaurant-garden combination. A scene depicting the pollution of California's environment was laid out on a large square table: a parched hummus landscape crisscrossed by a river of mashed avocado, with black-olive purée belching from a factory smokestack and sour-cream clouds sailing through the sky. The garden was filled with women wearing expensive ethnic clothing talking earnestly with men in ponytails who clustered around the artist to congratulate him on his delicious and politically correct creation. People scooped up the river of avocado with big chunks of six-grain bread and washed it all down with apple cider. I contemplated how to explain to a Russian who had recently been spending sizable chunks of his day trying to locate sour cream that he should try some of the sour-cream clouds across the room. Or perhaps we could order some shrimp with lemon grass and coconut milk for him? How about meat? he asked. Is there any meat? I scanned the menu, but didn't see any sign of meat.

"It doesn't matter," he said, "I'm not hungry." And then he turned to B, speaking to her in rapid, agitated Russian, filled with sighs and grimaces. The problem was that he didn't know what to do in David's house, which contained so many beautiful things that he was afraid to touch anything. He felt that, as David's guest, he should be helpful, but what if he broke something? "It's not like a house," he said. "It's like a museum."

Now Oleg is back in Russia, with Nina in the real world, and America already seems so far behind him that sometimes he thinks he must have only dreamed about it. B has persuaded him to stay for tea, and while he is drinking it, he looks at what I am cooking, a sauce with sun-dried tomatoes and black olives. His face is filled with misgivings. He remembers the restaurant in California, the strange food all over America, and turns his head away.

When he has finished with his tea, B goes to her refrigerator and opens the minuscule freezer compartment, to give him what he has come downstairs to get, a kilogram of meat she has been keeping for him, since there was no room for it in their freezer.

He cups the hunk of meat in his two large hands. Now that he has his meat, he is eager to go, to escape from the memory of America, from too many questions, too many difficult impressions.

"Don't forget," he says as he heads for the door. "Stay away from meetings. Remember what I told you."

Almost as soon as the door closes, I say to B, "What exactly is Oleg's job now? I know he's in the militia, but he's not an ordinary policeman, he's some kind of chief. At one point, I thought he was the Leningrad chief of police, but now I understand that he isn't. So what does he do?"

B is obviously uncomfortable with the question. She looks away. "He's one of several chiefs," she says.

"Responsible for what?" I ask, persisting.

"I don't know. And I don't care. It's his business, not mine."

"But he and Nina are your friends, your closest friends. You've known them for twelve years. You and Nina have walked your dogs together twice a day for years. What if he's like the police in the Lyubyanka, what if he tortures people? And you say you don't care? How can you not care? Don't you know what made the Nazis successful? It was the fact that people didn't care, they didn't want to know."

A flush rises in her face, and her tongue, viperous, lashes out at me. "I never asked, and never will ask about his job. He told me some months ago that he had a new job, but he never spoke about it before. This is a new department they have, like riot police, but until now I didn't know about it, and he never spoke about it. In our country we never asked such questions. You are from a free country not like our country. In America, people have no sense of privacy. They ask anything that comes into their minds. They don't care if it's right or wrong to ask. I forgot about this. I forgot that you are not Russian, that you are real American bull in china shop."

She looks at me with a mixture of envy and estrangement.

"You will never get in trouble yourself," she says, "because you are American, and people will try to be civilized with you, to make you think that in our country we are also civilized. But for me, there will be trouble. Or, if not for me, for my mother or my niece. I don't care about being embarrassed. You can say anything you want that's embarrassing. But it's different if you endanger someone else's life. Do you understand?"

"Yes," I say in a small voice. "I'm sorry. I really am. Forgive me. I'll try to be careful. I promise."

"Do you know that, until five years ago, Nina also never spoke to me about her job? She never said what her work was, and I never asked. Now I know about her work, that she works with disturbed children, and I've even been to the school where she works. But until five years ago, she didn't speak to anyone about it. Why? Because no one was willing to admit that we have disturbed children in our country. They only have disturbed children in capitalist countries, because of capitalist society. But not in our society. Not in socialist society.

"I want you to promise me one thing. Please don't get involved in any meetings. Don't be selfish. Please."

"All right," I say, feeling as if the ground has been cut out from under me. No meetings, no questions. Or at least none of the wrong kinds of questions. How can I possibly live that way? I, who would have been a dissident if I had lived in Russia before glasnost. I, who would have known how to stand up for my rights. But would I have? Am I so sure?

I remember traveling with B by train to U—sk, the village forty kilometers from Leningrad, not far from Komarovo, where Akhmatova spent her last days and is buried at the end of a long road. U—sk is where B was born, where she grew up as a wild child, picking and selling mushrooms and berries from the forest. As for their house, right next to the railroad tracks, I am only free to imagine it, since it has been torn down, and now there is only a crumbled stone foundation and a pile of rotting lumber near the spot where they tethered the family goat until Khrushchev forbade anyone who lived within sixty kilometers of Leningrad to keep domestic animals. Until the house was torn down, and B's mother moved into an apartment in nearby Z—sk, she had never had to depend on stores for food. She was shocked to find out how much it cost, and compensated by unplugging the refrigerator when she wasn't using it, to save on electricity.

B's family wasn't allowed to live inside the city limits of Leningrad. No one who had been in the Gulag could. Much of the population of the villages all around the city consisted of former prisoners who would never have the propiska to live in

Leningrad itself. Although B lived in Leningrad with her husband for twelve years, her official residence is still in Z—sk with her mother.

In school, she was spotted as a potential ballet student, and her teachers urged her to apply to the ballet academy. But her mother refused, because she was afraid to fill in the information on the application, afraid that they would realize she had been in the Gulag. So B, with her completely artistic nature, became a topographer instead of a dancer. But the life of a topographer was too much like life in Uva, living in villages in difficult conditions, working outdoors in rain and sleet and snow. At the age of twenty-six, she decided to become a designer, because she had always loved to sew and create things with cloth. But at the Institute for Design she was told that she was already too old to become a designer. So instead she became a "secret seamstress," designing and making performance clothes at home for musicians and singers at the Kirov.

It has always been that way. There have always been obstacles to entering any of the professions she and her sister dreamed of. What counted in the family was to keep a low profile, not to make any mistakes, not to stand out. Who knew what had made her mother stand out so many years ago. Who knew what she had said or done, or why she had been arrested and sent to cut trees in the forest for ten years. No one ever told her. No one ever told a lot of people. Self-censorship was the surest route. And not standing out. But B, with her sharp tongue and sharp mind, always stood out, even when she was determined not to, even when it was just a matter of wearing an unusual hairpiece she had designed herself.

But she's right. She chose me as her friend. She took that risk. It was enough. I reach over to clasp her hand. And for reasons I don't understand at all, I start to cry.

t h r e e

■

B and I are still asleep in her Leningrad apartment when her ex-husband calls from Siberia. It is four hours later in N—sk, and even though A knows that B is a night person, and that in the morning he should expect only growls, it is nonetheless his habit to call at eleven his time, just before he leaves for rehearsals. His apartment, given to him by the theater, is across the street from it, and he usually spends a few minutes talking with B, hangs up, takes the dog for a walk, and goes to work. Every time he mentions the dog, B plunges into depression. They don't have any children, and the dog has become, literally and figuratively, the biggest bone of contention between them. Who will have final possession of the dog? A skirts the question, focusing instead on his invitation. He wants B to come to N—sk for the opening of his new production of *Boris Godunov* in two weeks. What about his girlfriend, I ask, the one from Holland, the one he was planning to marry? Why isn't she coming? I ask these questions. B doesn't. She almost never asks questions. That's one thing she doesn't like about people from the West, always asking questions, always thinking there must be answers. What is going to happen to Russia? they ask. What will the future be? How should I know? B says. What will happen with your marriage? What will happen with A? What will happen with his Dutch girlfriend? Will he marry her? How should I know? B says again. We will see. For me, this would never be enough. I want to know definitely. But nothing is ever definite in Russia. Besides, people who have grown accustomed to reading between the lines never ask direct questions. People who are used to being overheard in restaurants or even in their own apartments certainly never do it. What about the famous Russian directness? I ask. Ah, that is different. That isn't asking questions. That is saying what you feel. Americans don't say what they feel. Instead they ask questions.

I have a question, though. An important question. What if she goes to N—sk for the opening of *Boris Godunov* and there is a coup while she is gone? After all, the referendum on whether or not Russia should have an independent president, and the fate of the Union, is scheduled for March 17, and everyone is talking about the military stirring. Just last month, there was a severe crackdown in Vilnius. And I've already heard that a big demonstration is planned in Moscow before the referendum. It would be the perfect opportunity for the military to seize the moment and declare a state of emergency. People almost seem to be waiting for them to do that, to take some kind of action that would avert chaos, stop the strange changes dead in their tracks, end the confusion. Sometimes I think that B wishes the military would intervene. She's not the only one who feels that way; it's an undercurrent in conversations, something dreaded and wished for at the same time. If they stage a coup while B is in Siberia with A, I would be in Leningrad alone, with all communications cut off between us. I would die of worry. I would be asking endless questions, of anyone I could find. I would get in a lot of trouble.

There is only one solution, I say to B. If she goes, I have to go with her. We could take the train to Moscow, and then another train to N—sk. We would need three days to get there, along the route of the Trans-Siberian Railroad, and we would see all of Russia. It would be an experience. If we travel by train, I could probably get away with not having a visa, I say, just the way we did on the train to Odessa. True, N—sk is a closed city, but I could do what I did then, keep my mouth shut. B does not agree. Siberia isn't Odessa. It's big and snow-covered, and you can disappear there without a trace. There are different customs in Siberia. The military has a voice of its own there, and if I vanish in Siberia, no one will care. Besides, it would be my own fault for going without a visa. Better to apply for a visa and then go. A could do an official invitation for me. He could send a telegram requesting permission for me to come. I could write about his production of *Boris Godunov*, an opera that is particularly relevant these days, with its theme of subversion of the traditional order, the struggle for power, the torment of the existing leader over his failings, and the plotting of the false Dmitri for Boris's overthrow. I would have interesting things to say about it. A's invitation, in any case, wouldn't be wasted.

On the other hand, what about my teaching job, the one I don't have yet, the one that B, along with numerous friends and acquaintances, has been making strenuous efforts on my behalf to find? Isn't that an important question too? It isn't enough for me just to write and sing. I need some real work too. Wasn't that part of our plans when I came back to Russia, to stay in Leningrad and for me to teach? The problem, though, is that, until now, all of these efforts have produced no discernible results. Everyone has said, "Oh yes, that would be wonderful, and I have just the right school in mind for you," but that seems to be as far as it goes.

Russians by and large do not have methodical minds (they some-times thank God that they are not Germans), and their enthusiasm and big plans fall easily into entropy when it comes to the tedium of trying to translate a plan into action, particularly in a climate in which bureaucratic maneuvers have been raised to the level of an art form, and stasis rather than motion is the norm. As the thermometer plummets, so does the Russian vision of produc-tive activity, and for Russians with a genetic predisposition to *Oblomovtshina* (Oblomovitis, coined after the sedentary, socially superfluous hero of Goncharov's nineteenth-century novel), it of-ten seems so much sweeter and easier to dream than to do.

"Success and Failure in American Life as Seen Through Contemporary American Literature." I can't imagine anyone not jumping at the chance to take a course like that, or to offer it. But even though I composed a letter several months ago ex-plaining to various academic institutions who I am and describ-ing the course, no one has shown any interest until now. True, "American" has a different meaning for Russians than it has for me, stirring up among them every possible fantasy of fulfill-ment, making their minds glaze over with the seductive power of the dream. And God forbid that I should be responsible for puncturing anyone's dream.

Yet, every time I see the glow in some Russian's eyes, when I say that I am American, the image of my father comes between me and those Russian eyes, and I find myself trying to explain something to them of what America can be like even for decent, hardworking, principled people who somehow end up on the short end of the American dream. Like a sailor whose ship has been smashed up on the rocks, I have become obsessively deter-mined to warn others of the unmarked hazards in the channel.

Does this mean that we should go to N—sk, or stay in Leningrad? It doesn't matter what we decide, B says. In Russia, you can't decide anything anyway. We should wait and see what happens. What do you mean, wait and see? I say. If you want something to happen, you have to do something to make it happen. That's a typically Western way of looking at things, B says. You're in Russia, not America. Here, you wait and see. Anyway, she thinks that the real reason I don't want her to go to N——sk isn't that I'm afraid of a coup, it's because I'm afraid that she won't come back, that she and A will get back together. Why did I invite you to come here, she says, if I wanted to go back to live in N——sk with A? It is finished between us. But A never finishes any of his relationships with his former wives, I point out. One of them is visiting him in N——sk right now, staying at his apartment, crying about her terrible life. That isn't the same, B says. What she needs is to get back some of the things she left behind when she and A separated. She left with nothing. Even her fur coat is still there. Sooner or later, she will have to go back to recover her belongings. It's impossible in Russia to make decisions, but, still, why not go there when he has an opening, when he's feeling proud? Why not be the wife of the conductor, at least for one brief moment of glory? I look at her in astonishment. Former wives. Former husbands. Six of them between the two of them, and an almost infinite number of combinations among them, even though B claims that she always forgets about her husbands as soon as she's done with them. "Don't be stricken," B says. "It's just that I'm not so romantic as you are. I'm more practical. If we find a teaching job for you, I'll go and you'll stay. If we don't find a job for you, we'll go to Siberia together."

"Promise you won't go without me," I say.

"I never promise anything," she says. "It's like making decisions. You can't do it in Russia."

It is a time of waiting. Waiting for A's invitation to N——sk, which will require the signature of the theater's director; waiting for a job; waiting for the arrival of our humanitarian-aid shipment. Now, wait a minute. Which humanitarian-aid shipment? The one we sent from America, of course. The one we organized before I left, the one that was supposed to arrive the day after I did. The one that has mysteriously disappeared. But the Aeroflot chief who was responsible for humanitarian aid, the one who promised me that my shipment of used children's clothing from Maine, gathered together from the assorted treasures of friends and neighbors, would be shipped free of charge, is in New York, and I am in Leningrad. The distinction means everything. Words spoken in New York have the capacity to evaporate in the thin air over Russia. Humanitarian-aid shipments have the capacity to evaporate along with them.

B spends hours on the phone, trying to locate the shipment. What is it? a bureaucrat at the airport asks. "Used children's clothing," B says. "For an orphanage just outside of Leningrad." "Do you have an airbill number?" he asks. "Yes," B says and gives it to him, though, conveniently, at that point the line goes dead, and when she calls back, no one answers. The next time she calls, she is connected to the dispatcher, who asks the same question: What is it? When she tells him, the dispatcher asks if it belongs to her. No, she says. It belongs to the orphanage. It was sent by my friend from America. What is your interest in it? he asks suspiciously. If it's not your clothing, why do you care what happens to it? The round continues, from one official to another. But the clothing doesn't appear. Maybe it will show up when we return from N—sk, if we ever get there in the first place. Maybe, like my mythical teaching job, it will become a mythical piece of humanitarian aid.

B's apartment is around the corner from the Kirov Theater, and while we wait, I walk. As it happens, our neighborhood is also the neighborhood in which most of Dostoevsky's novels take place. Dostoevsky himself lived not far from here, and it is only a short walk along the Griboedova Canal to the apartment house in which Raskolnikov killed the old-woman pawnbroker. The canal, the apartment, the entire ensemble are virtually unchanged from what they were then, and Dostoevsky's characters flit along the nearby streets and canals with a ghostly intensity, often merging with and becoming indistinguishable from their present-day counterparts.

Our courtyard, like most courtyards here, has a play area for children, with shabby but functional swings, a jungle gym, and benches with missing slats, where mothers and babushki gather to gossip. Sitting on those benches, I learn of quarrels in the kitchens of communal apartments across from ours, quarrels that can take the form of spitting (or worse) into a neighbor's pot of boiling soup on a collective stove; of couples who continue living together even though they are divorced, because one or the other can't find another place to live; of the lone drinker, the rotten apple in the communal barrel, who throws the communal balance out of kilter. Husbands beat wives; wives sometimes do the same to their children; wars erupt over the use of the toilet or the telephone; neighbors irritated by a late-night call say that the person sought is dead or never lived there or is gone for good. People don't hold their feelings in; they boil over and forget about it five minutes later. B, not surprisingly, does the same. And the more I see of this, the more I hear of it from the sounds drifting through open windows, or the pounding above our heads from the upstairs apartment, the better I understand that Dostoevsky's characters are not exaggerations; they are ordinary Russians. Even the courtyard of the apartment in which Raskolnikov is supposed to have killed the old-woman pawnbroker is as dank and run-down as it was when the crime was committed. In fact, it isn't much different from ours. Why should it be? B says. Nothing ever changes in Russia.

Squeezing onto a crowded bus one day, I catch my arm in the door. The passengers shout and swear at the driver. By the time I extricate my arm, the sleeve of my mother's forty-year-old fur coat has a huge rip in it. "*Svoloch*," the woman next to me says of the driver. "Swine. They do it for pleasure. To show their power." On the same bus, B is crushed in the mob. A woman's voice behind her warns, "Don't lie on me," which in Russian has the double meaning of "Don't lay me."

"Please," B says politely, "can you turn around so that I can see your face?" "What?" the woman snarls, turning her head toward her antagonist. B looks her over. "Uh-uh," she says. "You. Never."

Under such circumstances it is normal, natural, and perhaps even inevitable to turn into a Dostoevsky sleuth, and I do. Whenever anyone is testy or spiteful or irritable in a bus or a store or a restaurant, I just think, *Aha*, there's a real Dostoevsky character for you, easily humiliated, grandiose, socially powerless, filled with spleen as well as surprising bursts of warmth, humility, kindness. Sometimes, while waiting for my rendezvous with literature, I think that I have died and gone to heaven and am living in Dostoevskyland.

I am not so surprised, therefore, when our journalist friend Olga calls one evening and asks if I would like to meet Dostoevsky's great-great-granddaughter, who has a problem and wants to talk about it with me. Olga thinks that maybe I can help her. After all, you never know who can help whom. Can we come for dinner tomorrow? I try to be nonchalant about the invitation. In Dostoevskyland, I tell myself, why shouldn't you meet Dostoevsky's great-great-granddaughter? She has to live somewhere, so why not here, in the city of her forebears? She has to know someone, so why not me? The biggest question on my mind is what to bring to Olga's house for the event. Armenian five-star cognac would be fine, if I could find some. Or carnations that are sold from street stands enclosed in Plexiglas with rows of lit candles inside them to keep the flowers from freezing. I learned from a mistake I made some years ago, when I brought what I thought was a scarce copy of Bulgakov's *Master and Margarita* to an administrator at the Moscow Writers' Union: lipstick or a shiny polyester blouse is a better present. But Dostoevsky's great-great-granddaughter? Is it possible that she also likes polyester? How old is she, anyway? Olga didn't say.

In the morning, I go on an expedition to the Dostoevsky museum, where I bone up on his margin notes and sketches for *The Idiot*, wondering what the fate of literary museums such as this one will be now that computers have begun to replace the pen, and writers no longer revise their manuscripts by hand.

From there I go to the *banya* just down the street from the museum, on a corner where one of the many churches blown up during Khruschev's time once stood. B doesn't have a shower or bathtub in her apartment, and since I, like most Russians, regard the Russian baths as a felicitous marriage of luxury to necessity, I happily spend several hours once a week luxuriating in the collective pleasure of being in an almost excruciatingly hot room together with naked women and children of all ages, as an old babushka urges her peers to drive the temperature up even higher by throwing buckets of cold water into the blazing woodstove, sending up billowing clouds of steam, and driving the younger and less hardy women back into the comfort of the shower room.

Afterward, wrapped in a sheet, I fall asleep on a cot in a room lined with cots, drink tea from a samovar in a corner of the room where women cluster together, comparing cosmetics, gossiping, and watching TV, and then have a massage. A week ago at another *banya*, friends of the masseur wandered in and out of the room while he worked on me, and he occasionally interrupted the treatment to go into a back room. B sat in a corner watching. The people coming in and out were his friends, but also his customers. He sold vodka as a sideline. Would we like to buy some? He shrugged at my surprise, not even bothering to point out the relationship between vodka and rubbing alcohol, and he recommended that I have a massage twice a week for six months to remove all the toxins from my body, and undo the damage that had been accumulating inside of me for most of my life. He was surprised when I said I didn't have the time to pursue a complete course of massages. How can a person not have enough time to take care of their health? Everything here takes time, a lot of time, amounts of time that are inconceivable to a Westerner. No one in Russia has yet come up with the idea that time is money. Availability is the issue. If you need a massage and can get one, do it.

After I leave the *banya*, I walk down Nevsky Prospekt, feeling like a new baby and speculating on the possibility that someday my skin will glow like the skin of Leningrad women. There is new snow on the ground, and, as always, despite the snow, fresh flowers are scattered at the base of Pushkin's statue. In the intense early-afternoon brightness, the city's proportions, its perfectly harmonized colors balanced against the whiteness surrounding them, are breathtaking. Life is beautiful, life is sweet, I think. But what should I get for the great-great-granddaughter of Feodor Mikhailovich?

Babushki standing in front of Dom Knigi, the House of Books, are selling copies of Dale Carnegie's 1936 best-seller, *How to Win Friends and Influence People*, out of copious handbags that can be stuffed full again if the militia pass by to ticket peddlers, but I don't think that she would want that, or the prominently displayed copies of Dr. Spock's *Baby and Child Care*, which became popular here during the 1970s, when, to the apparent delight of the Soviet government, Spock's child-raising techniques were found to be the natural concomitant of his anti-war activism. And although I am happy to stand in line for some of Leningrad's rich vanilla ice cream, the kind I remember from my childhood in New York, it is clear that ice cream in a cone is too perishable to consider as a gift either.

A year ago, Russian opera singers visiting Maine for the first time went with members of our opera company to an American ice-cream parlor. We asked them what kind of ice cream they wanted. A hurried, intense conference in Russian followed. "Ice cream," was the final, universally agreed-upon answer. "But which kind?" one of the Americans persisted. "Doesn't matter," the Russians said. "But you have a choice," the American insisted. B looked him straight in the eye. "For what?" she asked, by which she meant, "For what reason?" It was the end of the conversation. Everyone ate vanilla.

There is no Howard Johnson's, Baskin-Robbins, Häagen Dazs, or Ben & Jerry's on Nevsky Prospekt. The boulevard remains blessedly devoid of the trappings of the late twentieth century, and as I walk in the direction of the Admiralty, I find it easy to imagine Dostoevsky's Underground Man being ignored by his superiors or insulted by strangers gathered under the arched portals of Gostiny Dvor, the avenue's most important department store, or having his toes stepped on by irritable hussars near the door of the Europeiskaya Hotel, currently closed for renovations.

The atmosphere along Nevsky is electric, not, as on similar boulevards of Western capitals, because of the throngs devoted to acquiring an endless abundance of goods, but because of the opposite. Here the entire spectrum of Russian society converges from all directions, and the chase, the hunt for an elusive quarry, assumes its most intense form. You never know what will appear in a store on Nevsky, and as soon as it does appear, you want to be prepared to grab it. Lines form in front of stores that have been closed for lunch but will soon reopen, in expectation that something new might be found that wasn't there three hours ago, and won't be there three hours from now.

Yeliseyev's is a nineteenth-century food emporium with the kind of mahogany paneling, chandeliers, and elaborate decorative embellishments that could be at home in any one of Leningrad's seemingly endless number of palaces that have been converted into schools, cultural centers, and museums. During the nineteenth century, you could find oysters from Paris at Yeliseyev's, as well as every imaginable Russian delicacy fit for the tables of the old St. Petersburg aristocracy. After the Revolution, Yeliseyev's became the Central Market without the produce from Paris, though everyone continued to refer to it as Yeliseyev's.

One side of the store now deals in meats and fish. The other, separated by an outdoor passage that leads to the State Comedy Theater, carries sausages and smoked meats, candies, cakes, and whatever else happens to surprise the unsuspecting, though it is safe to say that no one alive today remembers seeing any oysters there.

Yeliseyev's is crowded, as always. The cashier is regally ensconced in the center of the store in an enclosure that resembles an opera box. Tendrils of lines form all around her, and at the counters within her imperial view. The women working behind the counters are brisk, matter-of-fact, methodical. They wrap the orders in butcher paper, on which they write the price; the customer goes to the cashier, who does the calculations on a modern calculator as well as an abacus, and then comes back to reclaim the package. The lines sometimes inadvertently mingle, resulting in the usual explosive exchanges in a Russian rich in expletives.

At the cake counter, I spot a beautiful fruitcake, covered with glazed halves of pears and plums. I have never seen anything like it in Leningrad before. I get in line, convinced that by the time my turn comes they will have run out. But this time I am lucky. The fruitcake is packed up in a box covered with pictures of apples, peaches, and pears painted in muted shades of yellow, orange, and brown, and tied up with string. I walk out of Yeliseyev's and continue down Nevsky, displaying my treasure with its label—*Fruktovy Tort*—outlined in bold script. What a triumph! What a joy! But then, suddenly, someone comes up very close to me, saying in a low, urgent voice, "Where did you get that? Was it near here?" His intensity is a little bit frightening, as if his Eureka has a darker coloration than mine. I suspect that he is accusing me of something, that I have inadvertently done something wrong. Well, of course I have. Just as Russians tremble at the thought of going into a *Beriozka* hard-currency store, because they don't have the right to possess the currency that would enable them to buy anything, I tremble at the thought that I have now disrupted the social balance by buying something intended for an honest Russian housewife, not a miserable foreigner who isn't entitled to buy goods subsidized by the sweat of Soviet workers. As a result, I'm about to be arrested for buying a fruitcake.

I think that maybe I shouldn't tell him where I got it, that I should just ignore him. Two years ago in Yeliseyev's, I photographed a display case full of chickens, and was immediately surrounded by a throng of agitated women. Why was I taking pictures of second-quality chickens? Just to show the West how terrible life was in Russia? "We don't need people like you here," one middle-aged woman said, "people who are interested only in taking pictures of our awful lives. We're just fine without you, thank you very much." But then another woman chimed in and said, "Why shouldn't she take pictures if she wants to? What's wrong with it? Our chickens aren't so beautiful. Why shouldn't people know about it?" By this time, at least ten women were involved, pressing in against me, arguing with me and among themselves. I argued back, saying that I thought the chickens were fine, that I appreciated that their feet weren't cut off because they are so good for soup, and that in fact I liked Russian chickens a lot better than American chickens, which are pumped full of hormones and antibiotics. Of course, the minute I said that, they lost interest in me completely. Perestroika or no perestroika, glasnost or no glasnost, they didn't believe a word of it. I was either a liar or a fool, and in either case hardly worth bothering with.

Maybe this man who wants to know where I have gotten my fruitcake is just suspicious of why I, a Westerner, who can buy anything I want, wherever I want, have chosen to buy a Russian fruitcake. Maybe I should just shrug it off. I try ignoring him altogether, and walk away as fast as I can. But a few blocks later, the same thing happens, only this time it is a woman asking, and I can't ignore her. "Yeliseyev's," I whisper in a conspiratorial voice, and she scuttles off, saying *spasibo*. The third time, I am prepared, and when I notice an old babushka eyeing my box and see her heading in my direction, I just say "Yeliseyev's," quite boldly, before she even has a chance to ask the question. She looks at me appreciatively, but also with sorrow. It is clear that, by the time she gets there, none will be left. I understand now that I have accomplished the impossible. I have stood in line at Yeliseyev's and in all innocence bought something that B later confirms hasn't been seen in Leningrad for at least a year. Or perhaps it has been seen, somewhere, by someone. But not by her. It is the perfect thing to bring to Dostoevsky's great-great-granddaughter.

I walk all the way back to the beginning of Nevsky Prospekt, at Palace Square, on the banks of the Neva, and then turn off near the Hermitage, heading for the Central Post Office. I am supposed to meet up there with B, who has gone to mail a certified packet to A in N—sk, a transaction which she calculated would probably take several hours, giving me plenty of leeway.

The bird's-eye view of the post office is dazzling: light

spilling down from a two-story atrium onto marble writing tables with scratchy fountain pens and inkwells sunk into bronze
dividers, and lots of people sitting in deep concentration as they
prepare letters and packages. A pot of glue with a brush stands
on a separate table. The feeling here, once again, is of another
time, or, rather, of time suspended altogether.

It does not take me long to find B, who is walking from one
window to another, still carrying the packet for A without an
envelope. The problem, apparently, is that the post office doesn't
have the necessary envelopes, or, rather, they don't have any envelopes at all. They are cutting pieces of brown wrapping paper
behind one counter and making them into envelopes suitable
for whatever needs to be sent, cutting and folding and pasting.

Not surprisingly, a long line has formed at this counter, since
there are no envelopes anywhere else in Leningrad either, and if
you want to send a package or letter, no matter how improvised
its packaging, this is the place to do it. When B finishes standing
in this line, she will have to go to another line to get the necessary
"brown form" to paste on the envelope. The brown form will be
fitted out with all of the necessary information about the contents
of her shipment. At a third counter, she will receive a second
white form, which will contain virtually the same information,
although this form must be enclosed inside the package, and is the
recipient's guarantee that none of the documents indicated has
been tampered with or removed by you-know-who or anyone
else. Behind the counter, a typist works with serious concentration, typing with two fingers. B is obliged to go back and forth
from one counter to another several times, since each time she is
given different information about the whereabouts of the necessary documentation. When I arrive, she is still waiting for her envelope to be constructed, and half an hour later, the line has
advanced by only five people, although ten people have left, saving their places, and gone off to do something else, anticipating

that they can wait in line somewhere else for half an hour before retrieving their places in this line. Russian lines are different from Western lines. The crucial question when you get in a line is *"Kto posledny?"* ("Who is last?"). Once you know where you belong in the line you can go anywhere and do anything, just so long as you keep track of the person in front of you, who can also go anywhere and do anything so long as he or she keeps track of the preceding person. Theoretically, the line could disappear altogether and still function properly, though I have never seen this happen. Most people take advantage of the time to read any one of Leningrad's eight or ten daily newspapers, or a book.

When I show B my fruitcake, I can see that she is impressed, even though the scope of her enthusiasm is limited by her struggle to accomplish yet another miracle: getting her certified letter into the mail. While she waits, I wander off to explore the post office, my eye suddenly caught by a counter at the far side of the room, which is piled high with books. As I come closer, I see that several counters are similarly covered, and there are boxes and suitcases and bags of books everywhere. The line in front of the nearby window for International Packages is filled with people carrying books, who keep moving back and forth from counter to line. At one of the counters, two couples seem to be working in tandem, unpacking books from soft suitcases, stacking them high on the counter. Near them is a balance scale, and they are carefully weighing the books in small lots of five or six books at a time. Trying not to be too conspicuous, I strain to scan the titles, discovering among them *A History of Russian Dramatic Theater from the Beginning to the 18th Century*, two volumes of Sergei Yesenin's poetry, *Alice in Wonderland* in English, *Reminiscences of the Decembrists*, writings of Pushkin, Paustovsky, Sholem Aleichem, and Omar Khayyám, an *Atlas of Human Anatomy*, a book of macramé, and several cardiology textbooks.

It dawns on me rather slowly that what I am watching is a

Jewish family preparing to emigrate, and that they are sending the books accumulated over a Russian lifetime to Israel. They quickly become aware of my looking at them and at the titles of their books, but they deliberately ignore me, trying not to seem nervous about the intrusion. They know by now that it is futile or even dangerous to show what they feel, that they must simply concentrate on the task at hand, daunting enough in itself, without reflecting on meanings and consequences. All this shows clearly enough in their faces, which register as well recognition of what must be a stricken expression on my own face, for it has never occurred to me that my first encounter with emigrating Jews would take place here, in conditions of such extreme intimacy, at the moment of severing ties with their homeland, surrounded by words, by the literary life I have been so assiduously courting throughout the city.

One of the women is blonde and perhaps forty-five years old. She doesn't look Jewish, though the man who is clearly her husband does, with his thick glasses and dark fringe of hair around an otherwise bald head. As she prepares and weighs the stacks, he walks back and forth to the counter, carrying each stack to the posting station and registering it. Several times he is told that his packages are too heavy, even though he and his wife have weighed each one to be sure, and he has to bring the package back and change one of the books in order to reduce the weight by a few ounces. The woman behind the counter takes noticeable pleasure in sending him back, and the man and his wife frequently exchange glances, trying to sustain each other in the face of what is evidently a torment for them.

When it becomes obvious that I have been standing there too long for my presence to be merely coincidental, I approach them hesitantly and ask the woman if she speaks English, thinking that she is more likely to trust an American stranger than a Russian one. She looks up.

"Badly," she says.

I switch to Russian, asking if she is Jewish and if they are emigrating.

"Yes," she says. They applied for their exit visa only a short time ago, and received permission to leave very quickly. They will be leaving almost immediately for Israel, although they have no idea where they will live or what they will do for work. They have been coming to the post office every day since they received their exit visas. Each package of books must weigh two kilograms and eight hundred grams, or it won't be accepted and may even be discarded. So far, they have sent more than five hundred books, four or five to a package.

"I saw books on cardiology," I say. "Are you a doctor?"

"Yes," she says, and for a moment I see her eyes flickering forward anxiously into the future. Her eyes are lively and compassionate, the eyes of a doctor you would trust, a doctor who reads poetry and literature as well as medical texts. Her husband, she says, is an engineer, and the other couple are her sister and brother-in-law, who are also leaving. They have one child.

"Boy or girl?" I ask.

"Girl," she says. "Also in medical school."

"I'm glad it's a girl," I say.

She looks at me thoughtfully. "We wouldn't go if we had a son," she says.

"Yes," I say. "Of course not."

I wish them good luck and say goodbye, first in Russian and then in Hebrew. When I find B, who is still standing in line waiting for her white paper to be stamped, there are tears in my eyes.

"What's the matter?" she says.

"I've just been talking with Jews who were sending all of their books to Israel," I say.

"*Nu?*" she says. "Don't be sentimental. Much worse things happen in our country."

I look at her in surprise, feeling uneasy and estranged. Fleet-
ingly, the thought passes through my mind that Dostoevsky was,
after all, an anti-Semite, no matter how "universal" his characters. Maybe his great-great-granddaughter is also an anti-Semite.
And what about B? She's a "real Russian," not a Russian Jew.

On the way back to B's apartment, I am newly conscious of
the nearby synagogue. Do the people who were mailing books
come here to pray? Are they believers? And the intense young
boys in their yarmulkas who gather every afternoon in the synagogue courtyard, are all of them planning to leave the country
as well? But why? For what? It's still their country. This isn't
Germany in 1933. Or is it? I put my fruitcake on the kitchen
table and go into the bedroom to change my clothes, sickening
suddenly. When I come back into the kitchen, I open the box of
fruitcake, carefully carve out a large slice, and stuff it into my
mouth. Then I close up the box again so that B can't see what I
did, and as she locks the door behind me, I carry it out to the
street.

So what do you want to know? First, about the fruitcake, of
course. The box was received with oohs and aahs and saved to
be opened at the very end of the visit, at which point B's eyebrows went up, our friend Olga stared in disbelief, and Dostoevsky's great-great-granddaughter turned to stone. In the end,
the fruitcake went back into the kitchen. Who knows what happened to it after that?

As for D's great-great, she was as poor as a church mouse and
much angrier than one, which is to say she was a poor relation.
Why didn't she receive a pension commensurate with her status
as a Dostoevsky descendant? She suffered from arthritis, and her
brother was ill and unable to work. They were obliged to live
from hand to mouth, in the same kind of poverty that had

cursed Dostoevsky himself. It was a disgrace for them, a disgrace for Russia. A year ago, however, she had met an American woman, a university professor, at a Dostoevsky conference in Leningrad she had attended, though she had not been given official permission to speak. The woman visited the great-great's brother, who had given her a collection of letters, correspondence between Dostoevsky's first wife and her son Andrei Feodorovich—not a direct Dostoevsky correspondence, but still of considerable interest to someone who claimed to be a Dostoevsky scholar. Neither brother nor sister knew where in America the woman taught. They weren't familiar with American universities, but they thought it was somewhere around Washington. They had no idea how to get in touch with her, and though she had promised to write to them, they hadn't heard anything from her since. The letters, she had said, would be placed in an archive. But which archive, and where?

"You gave her the letters just like that?" I say.

"She was writing about Dostoevsky. We thought she needed them, and they would be helpful. We thought . . ."

At this point, Olga interrupts. "This is why she needs your help. Of course she can't ask to have the letters back, it wouldn't be right, but the woman made a lot of promises, all kinds of promises, and then she just disappeared. Not one word. She stole those letters, if you ask my opinion. Why else didn't she ever write to them?"

"Letters like that could be worth quite a lot of money, I imagine," I say. "It isn't every day that someone gives you Dostoevsky family correspondence, just like that."

"Money?" Dostoevsky's great-great-granddaughter says, red spots forming on her puffy white cheeks. "Of course we couldn't think about money. It wouldn't be right. We did it with a different idea in mind. What do you think, though? How much money?"

"I have no idea," I say. "I've never been involved in something like that before. I'm not a biographer. Did you have anything in writing, some sort of an agreement?"

D's great-great-granddaughter shakes her heavy head. "She was a very nice woman," she says. "She invited us to the Pribaltiskaya for dinner. My brother didn't think about an agreement, I'm sure. You know how it is in Russia. Money for us is never a question. We're generous people. But the government isn't generous with us. This could never happen in America, that the government wouldn't support members of the Dostoevsky family. In America, we would live well, not like we do now, poor and miserable, without enough money even for medicine."

"I hate to tell you," I say, "but the American government isn't terribly interested in writers. They probably wouldn't give money to Dostoevsky himself, let alone his great-great-grandchildren."

D's great-great looks at me in astonishment. She doesn't believe me. It isn't possible.

"We have no money," she says, the pitch of her voice suddenly escalating. "Absolutely no money. The woman who took the letters said she would help us. But she never did. When you get back to America, speak to her. Tell her we want the letters back, that my brother made a mistake. Or else . . ." Her voice drops again, and she hesitates.

"How can I speak to her if I don't know who she is?" I say. D's great-great is astonished. "But you are also a writer, aren't you?" she says.

"Yes. But there are many writers in America. And I don't know all of them. I could try to find out, but I can't promise anything."

This time her voice is shrill. "Well, the government must know who she is. The government must be responsible."

"Responsible for what?"

"Doesn't the government know who people are? If someone does wrong, the government is responsible. They must do something about it. They have to help people. That's their job."

"In America," I say, "the government doesn't care about things like that. The government doesn't get involved. Every day of the week, someone buys the Brooklyn Bridge."

"What?" Olga says. "I don't understand."

"People cheat each other all the time," I say. "I don't know whether or not you were cheated, but if you were, it isn't unusual."

"But it's immoral," our friend Olga says. "Doesn't the government care about that?"

"The government only cares if it's illegal, but then you have to prove that it's illegal, and that's hard to do."

Everyone is stunned into silence.

Finally Olga says, "So the American government doesn't care about what happens to Dostoevsky's family? If they're poor, or if they're cheated, or if they don't have medicine? What kind of government is that?" Her childlike face, with its light-blue eyes, is acutely troubled now.

"It's the one we have. The individual in America is responsible for himself; the government isn't responsible for him."

All of them exchange glances. "I think that our government is better," Olga says. "Maybe it does wrong, but we expect it to do right. We expect our government to be moral and to help people."

There is another long silence.

"What you're saying is that you can't help us," D's great-great finally says.

"I'm saying that I'll try. But I'm not sure what I can do."

Suddenly she shifts gears. "How will I get home now?" she says irritably. "The metro is already closed. I thought you could help, but I see that you won't. I don't have enough money for a taxi."

It is not a statement. It is a demand.

I reach into my pocket, but B glares at me from across the table. How much should I give her? I have no idea. All I have on me is ten roubles. That's enough to pay for a taxi, but it's clear that she wants more than a taxi. After all, I'm an American.

"I'm sorry," I say, taking the ten roubles out of my pocket. "This is all I have."

For a moment, she looks as if I have insulted her. But is it because I offered money, or because I didn't offer enough?

She takes the ten roubles, without saying thank you.

We all stand up and start to go for our coats. Maybe B and I can still find a bus. Or at worst, it will be a forty-five-minute walk home, since our taxi money is in D's great-great-granddaughter's hands now.

As we are walking out the door, I turn and ask Dostoevsky's great-great-granddaughter whether she wants the letters back, if I do succeed in making contact with the American woman. Her face becomes very red, and a flash of panic momentarily lights up her eyes. "Oh no," she says hurriedly, "please don't do that. My brother would be angry. Maybe it's best to forget about the whole thing altogether. Forget I ever said anything about it to you."

"Are you sure?" I say.

"Absolutely," she says.

"If you change your mind," I say, "please don't hesitate to let me know."

Out on the street, B says she thinks Dostoevsky's great-great grandson sold the letters to the American woman, and didn't tell his sister about it. The reason we were invited, she says, was so that his great-great-granddaughter could figure out whether or not this is true.

I don't answer her. In the darkness up ahead, where the Anichkov Bridge crosses over the Fontanka Canal, I am watching Dostoevsky, deep in thought, walking quickly away from us.

f o u r

The kitchen curtains B made for the N—sk apartment are covered with little felt hearts sewn onto a red-and-white-checked background. From the eighth floor, the double south-facing kitchen window with its cocoon of hearts looks down onto the plaza in front of the Opera Ballet Theater, where A is preparing his premiere of *Boris Godunov* for its Saturday opening. Hearts are B's symbol, her specialty. She once made a pair of heart-shaped pot holders for me. They had red piping around the edges, but the piping was singed one day when I let it get too close to the flames on the kitchen stove in Maine. After that, the heart looked as if it had had a chunk eaten out of its side. I never used the second one, so it remained pristine. B sees no contradiction in her attachment to hearts and the fact that she never sleeps with any of her husbands after the first year of marriage. As far as she is concerned, there are enough problems in marriage without adding sex to them. Sex begins in the realm of fantasy, and that's where it should stay. As for sleep, who can sleep with a man who snores?

We arrived in N—sk at 5 a.m. after two days and three nights on a train from Leningrad, with a one-day stopover in Moscow, where militia were posted at all of the subway exits onto Red Square and no one was allowed to pass, to "prevent incidents." A's friend Vadim picked us up at the station and drove us to his apartment. It annoyed him that he had to go so far out of his way in order to get around the anti-Gorbachev demonstrations. I wanted to see them. Vadim said, "For what?" and kept right on driving. "These demonstrations are all provocations anyway. You need to relax before your trip. Rest and eat with us at home." Since he was at the wheel, I was his captive, a captive of the legendary Russian kitchen where everything of consequence, which is to say real life, takes place. What could I say? That I wanted to be a witness to history? Having a good breakfast and spending the day with his mother and son was enough history for him, he said. He'd had all the history he could stomach for one lifetime. He wouldn't mind if it paused for half a century. So, just as almost always happens, I was somewhere else during the big events, somewhere drinking tea and talking.

Vadim is a high-level bureaucrat in the Moscow Coal Ministry. His and A's family lived together in Sverdlovsk after they were evacuated from Leningrad during the blockade. That particular piece of history is theirs and can never be taken away from them, unlike my furtive embrace of a history not my own, a history shaped by an alien imagination. The miners are striking, demanding that the government resign. Vadim thinks that they don't know how good they have it, that they have been spurred on by Western provocateurs who have convinced them that they have terrible lives just because for a while there wasn't any soap in the coal regions. Of course soap is important, but so is being able to work only six months of the year, and spend the other six at a pension on the Black Sea. It is hard to weigh one thing against the other. Coal miners are the Soviet Union's privileged class. Everyone is on their side, sending them care packages during the strike. People are starting to agree with them that Gorbachev should go. It's a big mistake, Vadim says. His mother agrees. She likes their life. Why would anyone want to change it? They fill up the metal pots which we have brought with us for the journey with cutlets and cabbage and sausages and potatoes. By the time they take us back to the train station, the demonstrations are over. If you didn't happen to be near Red Square at the time, you might never have known that they had existed.

At the door of his N—sk apartment, A kissed me first, and then, when B reached out her hand to shake his, kissed her as well. He looks almost the same as he did when I saw him in June, shortly after his operation, a little bit heavier and with less hair, combed Napoleon-style. According to B, she left him in order to give him his freedom, so that he could spend the last days of his life with his Dutch love. It was an act of supreme nobility. The only problem with this version of history is that, like most versions of history, including mine, it is tailored to fit with subsequent events. In fact, B left A, or A left B, many months before his illness was diagnosed, and it was for the sake of her own freedom rather than his. Or was it? Depending upon who left whom . . . But, of course, all this is trivia. What counts now is that A has surprisingly come back to life. It looks like nobility is about to take a walk.

In the kitchen, dirty dishes are piled up everywhere, and A's clothes are strewn all over the apartment. B clears off space on the kitchen table for breakfast, and after we have eaten enough meat and potatoes to satisfy my quota for a month, she settles in for a long bubble bath. I go into the living room, where a thick layer of dust covers the shiny veneer of the living-room wall unit. I look into its glassed-in display cabinets, where A has installed what looks like a semipermanent exhibition that includes a photograph of himself and his Dutch love, various medicines, videocassette tapes, a Venetian scene in a box with a gold pop-out statue of a gondolier and his gondola, an empty but decorative cardboard box of Dutch coffee, shaving lotion, a Sharp megabass dual-cassette recorder, a big smiling plastic cello with a gloved finger extending out of its side to play it, a copy of the Sierra Club Home Planet postcard collection, a VCR, a couple of Russian icon postcards, and an open box of Trojan condoms, Economy Pak, $9.99 from McKay Drugs in New York. I look inside the box to check: twenty-one of the thirty-six are still in the box, which B brought him as a present when she returned from America nine months ago. A once said to B over the phone, when the subject of his Dutch girlfriend was raised, that since his chemotherapy his penis had virtually disappeared. B suspects that her sex has atrophied altogether, and mine is dormant. The open box is therefore a reminder of unfulfilled possibilities. But the question remains: what happened to the missing fifteen condoms?

It is almost midnight in N—sk. A sits at the kitchen table under the heart-strewn curtains, smoking and drinking vodka and going over the score for *Boris Godunov*, his right hand rising above the table to conduct a few bars from the scene of Tsar Boris's descent into madness. The doorbell rings constantly, and people stream in and out to discuss the usual calamities that befall a production two days before its opening. B asks what happened to their electric samovar. A says that his former wife, the one who spent a month taking care of him after his operation while B was in America, burned out the element. He has a new electric coffeemaker, which his Dutch girlfriend (no one ever mentions her name) brought him along with several tins of Dutch coffee the last time she stayed there. She has already called twice from Holland during the twenty-four hours since we arrived. B answered the phone the first time and hung up on her, even though she and A are separated, and he has every right, etc. "It's a shame about the samovar," I say. "It's so beautiful." "Here," B says. "Take it, it's yours."

They are deciding who is going to sleep where. A says that he will sleep on the living-room couch. B and I can sleep together in the bedroom. A's doctor, the surgeon who performed his operation, calls. No one finds it unusual that he has called after midnight. That's when everyone calls. The surgeon will come to give A a checkup tomorrow and stay for dinner. B and I will buy food at the farmers' market in the morning. It is improper to give doctors money but essential to cook for them. By the time we go to bed, it is four a.m. At eight, A's girlfriend calls again. B is furious, not because she called, but because the phone is in the bedroom and it woke her up. A walks noisily into the bedroom and starts to talk on the phone as if no one is in the room, even though we have both been asleep. He charges around the house, bellowing and snorting and growling, then stomps back into the bedroom and sits down on B's side of the bed to talk. I turn over on my stomach and bury my head in the pillow. A is upset. His best friend's son has just decided to defect while at a cello competition in Holland. Of course his first step was to call A's "future wife" and ask if he could stay in her house for the night. Already the one night has turned into four, in the usual Russian style, and she is getting angry. That is why she keeps calling. The Dutch government does not look at such defections kindly, and A is nervous as he confides in B about the situation. What if this unexpected act has dreadful consequences for him?

While I get dressed, A goes into the kitchen, where he consumes a large portion of meat and potatoes and soup with meat.

All day long he wolfs down more, walking in the door and eating almost without pause. Meals slide invisibly into each other. A is immensely proud of being able to afford all of this. When he gives B money for the farmers' market, he says, "If you like it, buy it."

Dishes are still piled up all over the kitchen. B ignores them. I have never seen A empty an ashtray, put the shells from a peeled egg into the garbage, hang up his clothes, or put dishes into the sink, let alone wash them. B says that this is his "character," the character of a typical Russian male. None of her friends or neighbors understand her decision to leave him: after all, he isn't a drunkard, he never beat her, he's a respected conductor, and she didn't have to work. What more can she ask?

Still, someone has to do the dishes. When I try, B stops me. The dishes are not our problem, she says. Yes, but we also have to eat from them. A is getting ready for his premiere. He's still undergoing chemotherapy. Is this the moment for a confrontation? Apparently the answer is yes. When A suggests that maybe B could wash some dishes, she shouts, "What do you think I am, your slave?" He doesn't answer, and doesn't seem bothered or surprised by her reaction. After all, they have been warring with each other for years. But I am ashamed for her, even though I too have become used to her temper.

"Don't look shocked," she says, kissing me on the mouth. "If I make him angry, it will give him strength. Otherwise, he will just feel sorry for himself and he'll never get better." I had been thinking that she talked to him that way because of his Dutch girlfriend, or because of everything that went wrong between them during twelve years of marriage. But now I see, or am supposed to see, that it is really in his best interests.

"America is a puritan country with simplistic ideas about happiness," B says. "Russians prefer to suffer. It is what we are used to, and it makes life more interesting. A would be bored to death with me if I treated him too well. This way he never knows what to expect. Sometimes he hates me, but he says that I am never boring. His Dutch girlfriend is boring. She is too uncomplicated. She fusses over him and he loves it for a little while, but then it starts to seem dull. He starts craving his own life, his own craziness. In the West, life is too predictable. Here it is never predictable. You have to improvise every minute. We can enjoy the West way for a while, because it's so unfamiliar, but then we feel suffocated and want to return to our own miseries, our own wildness. There is no wildness in the West, not real wildness. That's why people in America go insane and kill each other. They play at being free, but they're not. We have nothing, but we're much freer than they are. They are all prisoners of their cars and their mortgages, their things."

A agrees. He loves his Dutch girlfriend. She is a wonderful woman. But there's no madness in her life, the kind of madness Russians take for granted. She wants his madness, Westerners always do, but it's not something you can give away.

B says that she and A should never have gotten married. It ruined their relationship. They both knew it right away. It is a comfort for me to consider that I am not the only person who recognizes early on that a relationship is doomed but stays with it anyway until the bitter end, through every conceivable form of misery. When my father got angry, he threw tomatoes, occasionally plates, more rarely glasses. My mother took it in stride. After all, they were both Russian, and she too would probably have been unable to get used to American-style happiness. She wanted it, but she fled from it. Extremity was happiness. It always would be. I got the message.

A takes off his shirt so that B can give him a massage. She tickles his back with her perfect oval nails. He loves to have his back tickled. When she stops, he begs for more. The three of us sit in the kitchen together all afternoon after A's rehearsal is over, drinking tea the way we did when we first met in Leningrad, and looking out the window at the hard, bright snow in the plaza, talking about the permutations of love. B even consents to do the dishes, while I remember how whole afternoons in their kitchen simply vanished in this way, how B murmured to A in a mellow and soothing voice, and how they seemed, at the time, to be a perfect couple. Now, in N—sk, with the refracted light from the snowy street filling the room, and the profusion of little hearts on the curtains, we are in Russian time, which is to say outside of time, and I momentarily surrender to B's idea of happiness, the illusion that she and A and their dog, Elvira, and I are, for just this short instant, the "strange little family" A says we are. The family romance, in any case, has always been a triangle.

In Siberia, in winter, you often have the illusion that you are walking on a snow-covered sidewalk when, in reality, the sidewalk can be up to three feet below you, under packed layers of snow and ice. It affects your sense of proportion. So does the fact that the N—sk Opera Ballet Theater, smack in the middle of Siberia, is the largest opera-ballet theater in the Soviet Union, with seating for up to three thousand under a huge dome with a stage bigger than the one at the Kirov or the Bolshoi. Who comes? Children with ribbons in their hair. Pensioners. Soldiers on their day off. People who live at Academe Gorodok (Academic City), the perfect town for perfect people, half an hour away from N—sk, where the Soviet Union's top research scientists live, the streets and sidewalks are immaculate, there are musical and theatrical performances of the highest quality, and in the surrounding fields and orderly greenhouses, experiments in advanced agricultural techniques are performed.

At Academe Gorodok, there is a museum of Siberian life and culture. I went there on my first visit to N—sk, last June, bringing medicine and lemons for A. I flew in on a tourist visa and stayed in N—sk for a week. In the guest book, I wrote that I had always thought of Siberia as being nothing but tundra and labor camps and was glad to find out I was wrong. I didn't tell B what I had written and, fortunately for me, she didn't ask. Since I wrote it in English, I preferred to think that no one understood it anyway. In that too I was probably wrong. There are people who see danger everywhere in Russia. I am not one of them. This is not always a virtue. The biggest mistake you can make here is assuming that no one is paying any attention to what you do. They are . . . whoever they are.

Once, when I was having problems getting a visa, I sent a telegram to Gorbachev, explaining my situation and asking for help. That was during the time when everyone wrote letters to Gorbachev, because it was the easiest way to solve problems. Having difficulty with your apartment, your job, getting medical treatment for a life-threatening illness? Not to worry. A wave of Gorbachev's magic wand, and everything was taken care of. The letters poured in from everywhere. This was Russia's idea of democracy: a letter to the Good Tsar, who could produce instant results. My telegram was effective. The next day, my visa request was granted. The Intourist guide assigned to my group subsequently tiptoed around me so cautiously that she obviously took me for a person of international significance. I have no illusions that Gorbachev himself read my telegram. But why quibble? What counts is results.

During Stalin's time, some of the most brilliant members of the creative intelligentsia, who found themselves condemned to labor camps, took comfort in the fact that they had a direct line to Stalin's ear. It was just a matter of finding the right approach, combining adulation and obeisance, looking inside one's soul to find the worm in the apple that any Russian of more-than-average intelligence knows is there. If you wrote a letter to Stalin, he read it. If you were a great artist, you knew that you were important enough to the future of the Soviet Union that your mistakes counted for something, that you weren't a nobody, like artists in the West, to whom no one in the government (or anywhere else) paid any attention. You were someone worth sending to a labor camp, someone dangerous enough to be killed. What higher attention can a poet get than the acknowledgment that poetry is subversive?

The great Russian poet Marina Tsvetaeva, who, along with Akhmatova, Mandelstam, Pasternak, and Gumilev, belonged to the extraordinary pleiad of Russia's prerevolutionary poetic "Silver Age," left Russia in 1922, after the end of the Civil War and during the Red Terror, to live in Prague, Berlin, and Paris. She returned to Russia in 1939, shortly before the outbreak of war. Pasternak came to visit her in Paris in 1937, and, knowing of her plans to return, was apparently afraid to tell her the truth about what was happening in Russia then (the purges, among other things), and said nothing. Tsvetaeva's life in exile was a torment in part because people in the West didn't care about poetry. In Russia, she said, poetry was bread. In the West, it was, at best, dessert. Soon after her return to Russia, Germany invaded Russia, and she was evacuated from Moscow. Her daughter Anya had already been sent to the Gulag. In 1941, she hanged herself.

Anna Akhmatova, whose son was also sent to a labor camp, couldn't risk keeping copies of her poems during the thirties, so trusted friends committed them to memory. To this day, millions of Russians who learned her poems through word of mouth can still recite them by heart. I've heard them do it, at two in the morning, when most of the vodka bottles are empty.

This happened when only the dead wore smiles—
They rejoiced at being safe from harm.

And Leningrad dangled from its jails
Like some unnecessary arm.
And when the hosts of those convicted
Marched by—mad, tormented throngs
And train whistles were restricted
To singing separate songs.
The stars of death stood overhead
And guiltless Russia, that pariah
Writhed under boots, all blood bespattered
And the wheels of many a black maria.

Is this what lies buried under three feet of ice and snow in Siberia? Or is it really the new frontier, the land of opportunity, like Alaska? Is Siberia really Academe Gorodok? Is *Boris Godunov* just an opera? Where am I, really?

While A is out walking the dog, B conducts a search of the apartment, taking the opportunity of his absence to start packing up the things she defines as hers. This obviously involves rummaging in drawers, and the first drawer she rummages in yields more than expected (or perhaps not, since she begins the rummaging with A's desk), a pile of photographs of A and his Dutch love in Holland, Germany, and Russia. She studies the photographs carefully for revealing information, finding the chess set which she bought for his birthday resting on the coffee table of "Her" living room in Holland, as well as a *matryoshka* doll, a book about the Hermitage, and assorted other items she claims A has stolen from her and given to "Her" as presents. B dates the photos by the coat or scarf he is wearing—"Yes, he had this scarf five years ago"—but she cries out only once, at a photograph of the two of them standing in front of Catherine's

Palace in Pushkin. "He's with her in Pushkin! I could never get him to go there with me."

The photos show them together with friends, with "Her" entire family, on an estate in Germany where A is seen cooking ("Cooking—my god, just look at him") in a high-tech kitchen, and at Christmas, together with an eminently good-looking German bourgeois family, with red candles on the table and a heavily laden Christmas tree, in restaurants with friends ("Our friends—so everyone knew except me"), at "Her" condo in Amsterdam, feeding a duck on the canal in front of "Her" house, walking the dog on the streets of Amsterdam.

"Why did I waste five years?" she says. "I could have left him five years ago, when I was thirty-six and still had a good chance in life. I see now that I had no idea what his life was really like. Once, he even went down on his knees, crying and swearing to me that, yes, he made a mistake, but now it was over, because he saw that he couldn't live without me, that he never loved anyone as much as me. Why did I believe him? Why did I want to believe him?"

She starts to tackle a pile of papers in the living room, searching for letters, but then she hears his key in the lock and rushes to stuff the photographs back into his desk drawer, just in time to catch the dog in her arms as she tumbles excitedly into the living room with A following close behind.

"Let's go to rehearsal," B says after we have all had lunch together and A has returned to the theater.

At the entrance to the stage door, however, a doorman sits, checking passes.

"What do you mean, I can't go in?" she shouts at him. "I'm the wife of the conductor. I order you to let us pass."

"I don't care if you are Gorbachev's wife. Without a pass, no one goes in."

The words that B then uses have not yet entered into my Russian vocabulary, but the doorman isn't impressed. He continues to block the entry.

"Come on," B says, grabbing my hand. "Run!"

I expect to hear police sirens coming after us at any moment, but then a brief flare of admiration for B's absolute indifference to the rules of civilized behavior rises up in me. Is this the "freedom" she and A conspiratorially cherish, the Russian wildness that everyone in the West wants but rarely dares to risk? She is obviously on intimate terms with both its dangers and its glories, but maybe that is just because she, like Joplin, has nothing left to lose.

Yesterday, in the kitchen, A regaled us with funny stories about the Kirov on tour. One of them was about an incident in Japan, where the musicians gathered into one of their hotel rooms after a performance and drank vodka into the small hours of the morning. At some point, one of them accidentally set fire to the couch with a cigarette. They managed to put out the fire, but the couch was ruined. Since the musicians were trying to save all of their hard-currency earnings to take back with them to Russia, living on packages of instant soup cooked up on hotplates in the room (also against the hotel rules), their greatest concern was that they might have to pay for the couch. The solution they devised was to dismantle the couch completely, cutting it up into little pieces with a saw provided by members of their tech crew, so that they could discreetly remove it from the room and dispose of it in a hotel Dumpster. The morning after, when asked about the missing couch, they feigned ignorance, saying that the room never had one.

The story was hard to believe, and I later heard that it was apocryphal, but A took delight in telling it. B also laughed, and I feebly joined in, pretending not to be appalled. If I was really going to be her friend, B said, I would have to get rid of my bourgeois moral inhibitions, which could be traced back to the Western reverence for private property, a reverence that didn't exist in Russia, since private property didn't exist, and was forbidden as the root of all evil. The thought of getting rid of my moral inhibitions, whatever their origins and whether or not they were bourgeois, was at once inviting and terrifying. I had the full complement of such inhibitions; it would be interesting to know who and what I would be without them, though this was unlikely ever to happen. Still, I have always been attracted to risk, and this one seemed to offer more than the usual range of opportunities. I would perhaps "escape from myself" in ways hitherto undreamed of, like Babel joining the Cossacks.

Since this transformation has not yet taken place, however, I can't help saying "Excuse me" to the guard at the stage door, and adding, "I'm with her," as if thereby to rid myself of any personal responsibility. I pretend not to notice B's fierce look of contempt as she hauls me down the corridor toward A's office to hang up our coats. "Traitor," says her imperious glance. "Coward."

"He won't forget again who I am," she says, sitting in the leather armchair behind A's massive desk, making a phone call.

"I'm sure he won't," I say, wanting more than anything to be on her side. After all, I tell myself, how much patience is a virtue, how much rage a necessity? Isn't every Russian really a Pugachev in disguise, waiting to seize the moment for rebellion? How many humiliations does it take, drop by bitter drop, for the poison of powerlessness to transform itself into the lust for revenge?

"Without documents you are shit. With documents you are a human being." When émigré aristocrats who fled Russia during the Revolution wound up in Paris and were only able to find jobs as doormen there, they instinctively knew the critical role of hauteur in keeping out the rabble. Russia's benighted masses share this knowledge from a slightly different perspective. Whoever holds the right to grant or deny entrance through a desirable door has more power than most of us can ever dream of possessing. Sometimes there is no way around it except wild improvisation, at which Russians are immensely gifted.

B hangs up the phone and silently examines her nails. Her gray eyes, when she finally looks up, are wintry. "Only the privileged can afford to be polite," she says, and walks out of A's office, closing the door behind her.

A is in the orchestra pit, wearing the tuxedo B finally consented to press for him and the bow tie she straightened for him at the last moment. B is sitting with me in the tenth row, holding my hand tightly. A raises his baton. The year is 1598. We are in Russia's Time of Troubles, at Boris Godunov's coronation. Everyone here knows the score, knows who is who and what is what. They are tight with expectation and the longing for revelation, even though they practically drank in this tale together with their mothers' milk; first Pushkin's version, then Mussorgsky's, and finally Rimsky-Korsakov's variant. The church bells of Moscow are ringing in the ascension to the throne of Tsar Boris, the country's first elected ruler. He is the new hope of the people, the good, suffering Russian people, whose voices fill the stage with their sorrows, their faith, the stirring of their souls in the presence of the murder, intrigue, cruelty, and corruption that surround them. As B says, nothing ever changes in Russia. The audience knows it, the performers know it, A knows it, and so does B. The only one who doesn't know it, who isn't forever entwined in the foreknowledge of fate, is me, the Westerner who believes in change, free will, the active life, who thinks that I am the master of my own destiny and believes that my identity and will, in concert with like-minded identities and wills, can alter the course of history.

There is a conspicuous collective intake of breath during the scene of Varlaam and Missaill's arrival at the border of Lithuania as they are plotting Boris's overthrow. The blood of Vilnius is still fresh on Gorbachev's hands. The Baltics were always at someone's mercy, never an empire, but always under the control of one, whether German, Polish, or Russian, "little brothers" in need of protection. My father was from Vilnius, except he called it Vilna, and I knew it as the Jerusalem of Eastern Europe, the center of Jewish culture that was wiped out by the Nazis. In the tenth grade, one of the questions on the New York State Regents Exam was: Who was Peter the Great? I gave the right answer: A Russian tsar who opened Russia's "window to the West." What window? Where was it? Somewhere around Russia. What difference did it make? Who cared? The critical term wasn't "Russia" anyway. It was "the West." Of course, no one asked me where Vilnius was. Why should they? But guess what? Vilnius turns out to be in Lithuania, and Lithuania turns out to be in the Baltics, those same Baltic States that are now claiming their freedom from Soviet conquest. But wait a second. What's this about Peter's window? Where did you say it was? The Baltics, the Baltics, conquered by Peter the Great in 1721. Of course, the West likes to speak of Peter's good sense in the matter. The only problem is that, for his good sense to make good sense in the West, which supports the Baltics' current drive for independence, they have to leave out the fact that the window was on the Baltic Sea, and independence for the Baltic republics means that window will now be closed. Who knows? Texas might be next, reclaimed by Mexico, to whom it once rightfully belonged.

"Have you forgotten our history?" I heard the investigative journalist Alexander Nevzorov ask on his TV program, *600 Seconds* recently. "It was Peter who gave us the Baltics. Vote to preserve the Union."

During the intermission, I hear whispered conversations in the lobby. The habit of whispering is still strong. One never knows who is listening.

"The Baltics. The miners. The Baltics again."

"Remember the scene in *Ivan the Terrible* when Ivan didn't want to pay Germany for the rights of our Russian traders to go across Baltic land?" (Germany then controlled the Baltics.)

"History is devious, isn't it?"

"Yes, it is. Indeed it is."

Is this just an opera we are watching? Are we in the age of Ivan the Terrible, Boris Godunov, or Gorbachev? And who is waiting in the wings to replace him? The other Boris. And nibbling at the edge of the ancient drama is a fire that is even now approaching from the forests around Kemerovo, in the Kuzbass, just three hundred kilometers from here, where the miners are calling for Gorbachev's overthrow. The audience knows that the climax of *Boris Godunov*, Mussorgsky's revolutionary scene of the people's awakening to consciousness, which takes place in the forest, was banned by Nicholas II during the 1905 Russian Revolution. But isn't history just a deck of cards, shuffled in such a way as to suit the current dealer?

By the end, Boris is dead, having descended into madness, obsessed with visions of having murdered Dmitri, the rightful heir to the throne. But in Russia, every transgression offers the possibility of salvation. From triumph to humiliation to redemption, it's the Russian way. So now a new tsar, a new "Dmitri," falsely claiming the throne in the name of the true heir, is being hailed by the people, believing and deceived four hundred years ago, believing and deceived when Mussorgsky composed the opera in 1872, believing and deceived yet again. Russia is still pursued by its Furies: the "cursed questions" that have echoed down through the centuries as the fate of the tsars ebbed and flowed from assumptions of permanence and inevitability to dreams of revolution. What is reincarnation anyway, if not the reliving of history, the eerie recapitulation of past lives?

Tsvetaeva was right. In Russia, music, poetry, and politics can never be just dessert. The voice of the Holy Fool still wails too loudly in the land.

The decibel level of the conversation around the theater's post-premiere banquet table is rising conspicuously—though, even after four toasts (A, having changed out of his white tie and tails, delivers the first in honor of the entire company), there are still a few bottles with an inch or two of vodka and champagne left on the table. The food, however, has been devoured so quickly that it is almost possible to imagine, except for the crumpled and crumb-strewn tablecloth, that it was never there.

I stand at the edge of the group surrounding B, which includes the Polish princess Marina Mnishek, the Holy Fool, the bell ringer, and the first violinist, A's best friend from Leningrad, who joined the orchestra when A took over.

"He can't get along without you," Marina Mnishek says. "His life is a mess. He's like a child. They all are, but him especially. You shouldn't pay attention to his romances with other women. They don't count. You also have lovers, and everyone knows it isn't serious. The marriage is what counts." She glances at me quickly with eyes that are at once searching and brutally indifferent, sweeping me into and out of the focus of her attention as casually as she would a leftover ice-cream wrapper. I am included and excluded simultaneously. A pane of glass, seen through but not seen.

B now also looks at me with an expression that seems to mimic that of Marina Mnishek, as if she has just realized that I am there and hasn't yet decided how to classify me. Then, suddenly, without changing her expression, she winks at me. The magic circle around her closes again.

"A is a great talent," Marina Mnishek continues, "and he needs you. Be sensible. Forgive him, as everyone else does, and return to normal life. You've had your little experience in America. You've danced the mazurka. Now it's enough. You can see for yourself what his life is like without you. He's lost in another world."

B's face is glowing. She loves the role of the conductor's wife, as long as she doesn't really have to be married to A to fulfill it.

"And by the way," Marina Mnishek asks, "have you been able to do any work in America? How is it going?"

"Oh, they love my work there," B says. "They want me to come back."

Here, at least, I know the terrain. "She's a very talented woman," I say, walking straight into the magic circle. "She could be a big success there. Fine work like hers is unusual."

This is evidently a show stopper. Silence, while everyone turns to look at B and then at me with new regard. The bell ringer pours me a glass of champagne, and someone makes a toast to "peace and friendship." Marina Mnishek's eyes flutter. The violinist wipes his glasses. B reaches out her hand, drawing me into the very center of the circle, and ostentatiously putting her arm through mine as she pulls me close to her side.

"I want you to know that this is my very dearest friend," she says, "who has done more for me than A ever did." She runs her fingers through my hair. "Aren't her curls wonderful? They're completely natural. She was born that way."

I try to smile, feeling my face go lopsided in the process. I'm not a pane of glass anymore. But maybe it was better when I was.

"You're too sensitive," B says, as she walks back to A's office with me. "You have to know how to play their game. They'll be laughing five minutes after we've left the room. Don't take it so seriously. You're a thousand times better than any of them."

"Sure," I say, glad to see A and his Boris coming in for their coats.

B and A and I, all arm in arm, with A in the middle, walk through the snow together with A's Boris, whose real name is Viktor, at B's side. The glare of the snow on the street whitens the night. It is so cold that I can feel the fine hairs in my nostrils prickling with frost, but the rest of me, encased in fur from head to ankles, is warm. My mother's fur coat, as soft as baby's breath, fans out all around me. A flowered red woolen shawl is wrapped twice around my head, topped by an oversized fur hat, a gift from B, which sometimes tips rakishly forward to obscure my vision.

"They hate us in Poland," Victor says. "This was my first performance tour abroad, and I was shocked by their reaction. They even pretend not to speak or understand Russian. Why should they hate us, when we've done so much for them? They practically cheered during the Polish scene in *Boris*. I was so upset that I almost couldn't keep on singing. And the stores there—you wouldn't believe what they have in the stores. Half the time, I had no idea what things were."

B links her arm through his sympathetically. Perhaps she is thinking, as I am, of her first month in America, the questions and the answers:

"No, this isn't a museum, this is a store."

"No, New Yorkers don't pay rent to the government. Most apartments here aren't owned by the city. Communal apartments don't exist. No one here even knows what they are."

"No, it's not that Americans never have any money, they just don't carry cash. They pay with checks or credit cards."

"No, you don't have to show your passport in order to get on the flight to New Orleans."

"No, people don't need a residence permit to live in New York, and I don't have one in Maine either. Propiskas don't exist in America. You can live wherever you want."

It was impossible for B to believe. Even the Korean fruit-and-vegetable stores in New York didn't belong to the government. It seemed that nothing did. And there were different prices in every store.

"That? That's an electric grill. That's a Cuisinart. That's a juicer. That's an espresso maker. This is cappuccino. Those are shoe trees. That's a CD player. That's a child-proof bottle. That's a thermometer—it just looks different from the ones in Russia. That's an electric bread knife. That's fennel. That's spinach. That's asparagus, arugula, radicchio, fettuccine, liquid dish-detergent (they are all the same, really, they just have different names), paper towels, tissues, prosciutto, furniture polish."

"No, people don't steal toilet paper from bathrooms here. Why? Because it's not theirs."

"No, people don't remove their windshield wipers and tires from their cars at night. No, they won't be stolen by morning."

The questions soon subsided. But they continued to clog her mind, unasked, unanswered. How much energy she must have expended on trying to figure things out for herself, concealing from me what she didn't know or what was incomprehensible.

Three feet off the ground in the snow of Siberia, all this seems very far off. But then I suddenly remember the blue stuff you put in the toilet bowl, B's "perfect present," the one with which everyone was entranced. I'm sure that America's advertising strategists have their eye on people just like B, the ones who are just beginning to have cravings. According to them, the problem with Russia is its absence of consumers. People are still thinking only in terms of what they need. It will take a few more years to develop in them a state of limitless, unquenchable desire. Or maybe that's not as far off as it seems.

It is referendum day. The polls closest to the apartment are in the Actors' Palace. A goes to vote early in the morning, before B and I are up. When he comes home, he says that he voted "for Gorbachev," though Gorbachev was not on the ballot. This means that he voted for the preservation of the Soviet Union. B isn't going to vote. She says that she has never voted before and has no intention of starting now. "It's for them to decide," she says. "I do my job and they do theirs. It makes no difference how I vote anyway. They will do what they want no matter what I say. It's the same everywhere. If they can do what is good for themselves, why should they bother to do what is good for me? It's human nature. If you think it's any different in America, you're fooling yourself." Besides, she doesn't live in N——sk and couldn't vote here if she wanted to.

She even refuses to go with me to the polls, so I go alone. Inside the Actors' Palace, a spacious, attractive building belonging to the Actors' Union, are long tables draped with red fabric and bunting, behind which a row of women check off passports against their voting lists. There is only one person registering, so the women behind the tables are relaxing and drinking tea. Some of them are laughing. The atmosphere is festive. I expected it to be dim and threatening, with an undercurrent of implicit danger should one dare to make the wrong choice. So much for stereotypes. The voting booths have curtains just like the ones in America, and all in all, it doesn't seem much different from my local gym on election day.

The women behind the voting tables look up when I enter the room. A foreigner. Their faces are interested, receptive, curious. I scan the group and zero in on the one who looks most welcoming.

"You've come for the performance," she says. "The doors haven't opened yet. They won't for another half an hour. Usually we have a banquet, but this year, because of the situation, we won't. The Party likes to congratulate people who fulfill their duties as citizens, and it's a shame not to have the banquet. I'm sorry if you came early because of that."

I don't know whether to shake my head yes or no, since I haven't the foggiest idea what performance she is talking about and know nothing about a banquet. Maybe this is just the first step in the process, and the actual voting takes place somewhere else, in private places where Papa Lenin keeps a watchful eye on his subjects, cajoling the timid and using stronger methods when necessary.

"Where are you from?" she asks.

"America," I say, instantly aware that, even though I have answered her in what I thought was a low voice, all the women behind the tables have paused in their conversations to listen.

"We are very interested in America," she says. "We've seen some American movies. For example, *One Flew over the Cuckoo's Nest* by Milos Forman, with your great actor Nicholson. Do you like the writing of Mark Twain and Dreiser?"

"Why, yes, I do," I say, startled by the question and unable to think of anything to add.

"And who is your favorite Russian writer?"

I hesitate.

"Are you fond of Pushkin? What about Gogol?"

By now everyone is listening unashamedly. The woman to her right says, "Of course, today, the philosophical questions presented by Bulgakov are of great interest. Have you read *Master and Margarita* or *Heart of a Dog*?"

I stare at her. Where am I? Is this really a polling station? But everyone is waiting for my answer, with expectant faces.

"Actually, right now I'm most absorbed in Dostoevsky. My favorite poet is Akhmatova. I haven't read Bulgakov yet. But of course I intend to, as soon as I have the time."

I see that my answer hasn't been quite adequate, though I can't tell why. I feel trapped, and have a sudden impulse to rush out of the room.

"Would you like some tea?" a woman sitting at the far end of the table says, already starting to fill a cup with water from the nearby samovar.

"Thank you, yes," I say, grateful for the interruption.

But they're not going to let me off the hook so quickly.

"If you wish to understand our life, you must read *Heart of a Dog*," my literary interlocutor persists. "It is very close to us in its examination of Soviet realities. We have only recently been able to read some of the works of Bulgakov, since many things were forbidden before, but now that we are free, we can read everything, and we see how perfectly he perceived the reality of existence, and the depth of his philosophical understanding."

"Actually, I have *Heart of a Dog* at home," I say. "I've been meaning to read it, but . . ."

"You have it, but you haven't read it," she says, as astonished as if I had refused bread and tea after a long journey without food.

"I have many books, but unfortunately I don't always get around to . . ."

This time it is the woman to whom I first spoke who rescues me.

"Our performance is about to begin," she says, coming around from behind the table and linking her arm through mine as she guides me toward the far end of the room, where a line of people are waiting in front of a set of double doors.

The doors open, and suddenly I find myself in a theater, being introduced as "our honored American guest" to the house manager, who is standing right inside the door.

"We're delighted that you've come to our performance," he says, shepherding me to a seat in the front row on the aisle. "We hope you'll enjoy it."

The theater is filling up rapidly, and it is already impossible to say that I didn't come for a performance but to watch the voting. The curtain goes up on a French bedroom farce, which lasts an hour, with no intermission. There is a triangle, of course, with who knows who going into which bed and being caught, or not caught, in the act. The actors are aiming for worldly French sophistication, though sex is not permitted onstage. Evidently, the people in N—sk have sufficient imagination, and the actors are skilled enough, that it's not necessary to supply all of the details. The audience laughs in some of the right places and some of the wrong places, but it doesn't matter, because the room is full of pride and pleasure at the Frenchness of it all.

When it is over, I anticipate a quick escape, but the house manager is at my side before I have gotten out of my seat. "We have a theater critic from Moscow visiting," he says. "We are meeting with him now to hear his comments and suggestions. We told him that there is an American in our audience, and he is quite interested to meet you."

Once again, I am captured and led into the lobby, where the cast and crew gather around to hear the Moscow critic's evaluation of their work. They sit in respectful, expectant silence, obviously eager to know his opinions, which he delivers not as an outside observer, whose purpose is to pursue an independent line of thought that will lead to a scathing review, or any review at all, but as a collaborator in the mutual task of enlarging and improving their capabilities. They are all, apparently, on the same side of the fence. The side of art.

The discussion over, I am introduced to the critic, who wants to know my favorite Russian playwrights. I take a stab in the dark. "Chekhov," I say.

"Yes, of course," he says, nodding wisely. "Dear Anton Pavlovich is rightly beloved by all. Have you been to the Taganka in Moscow to see Lyubimov's production of *Three Sisters*?"

"Who?" I say.

"Lyubimov," he says. "Our great director. He lives in America now."

"I'm sorry," I say, "but I'm afraid I haven't heard of him. I've only been to Moscow once."

"I see," he says, letting me know that the critic in him is not altogether inactive.

I look at my wrist, at the watch that isn't there. "Oh my god," I say. "I had no idea what time it was. I really do have to run."

And before anyone has a chance to stop me, I have fled out the door, grateful that waiting for me in the apartment are A and B, who will finally tell me where I have been and what has really happened.

Something has gone wrong, but I don't know exactly what. It starts with the arrival of A's brother and sister-in-law from Russia's Far East, and within three days, our odd little family is in tatters, with B shouting at A, and A shouting at B, and A's brother threatening murder and mayhem. All I know is that B is at fault, that this time, for some reason, she has gone too far. Apparently, A's brother and his wife are not in complete agreement with B's theories, especially after experiencing them in practice at close range. I have seen B go too far before, but seemingly never far enough. An "outside observer" has at last defined the limits. Maybe B and A have come to terms with the idea that anything short of murder is kindness, but A's brother hasn't, and anyway, he knows whose side he's on.

Any fool could have seen it coming. But there's something hypnotic about those habits in the life of the couple that have evolved so gradually that no matter what horrors they express, they somehow seem like mere accommodations to the fault lines in each other's characters.

In the end, B's belongings (those she has not succeeded in packing into muslin bags at the post office and mailing back to Leningrad), along with B and me, are all outside the door of the apartment, and one of her suitcases is skittering down the stairs. I am a little bit shocked, though not completely surprised, to find us standing on the landing with the door closing behind us. I look at B. Her eyes are deadly cold. I see in them the absolute certainty that she is in the right. The spell is suddenly broken. I stop loving her.

The door opens. A joins us on the landing, and we all go out for a walk together. By the time we come back to the apartment, A and B have come to an agreement. B gathers up their dog while I pack up my own things and then, as if nothing at all unusual has happened, shake hands with A's brother and sister-in-law, who wish me a pleasant journey back to Leningrad. Miraculously, within minutes of everything's being ready for departure, a taxi appears at the door, and A, pelted with protests from his sister-in-law, nonetheless decides to go with us to the station, where our baggage turns up on the platform just in time for the arrival of our reserved train for Moscow. A watches us mournfully as the train pulls out of the station and waves good-bye to the dog, whom B holds up to the window for him to see. It is difficult to say whether A is suffering over B's departure or the dog's, but in any case, just before he disappears from sight, we see him making the sign of the cross and then wiping his eyes with the back of his hand.

I have no desire to talk with B, and she apparently feels the same way. We pass several hours in complete silence.

"I hope you never treat me the way you treated him," I finally say, an hour after the train has pulled out of Omsk.

"You!" she says. "How could I? Never. There's no comparison between you. None."

I don't answer, but am aware now that I know something that I adamantly refuse to know, and in the next long silence that follows, I apply all of my energies to undoing that knowledge. B, for her part, is smart enough to leave me to my own devices, certain that, without any direct interference from her, I will find my way out of this particular morass back into the light of her newly radiant smile, which she little by little begins to dispense like balm to an invalid soul.

"You poor dear," she says as we pass through Tyumen, with its dismal oil-speckled snow, its chiaroscuro landscape of dark bodies and smudged unidentifiable humps posed against a white sky. "You poor, poor dear. You didn't understand anything, did you? Absolutely nothing at all."

"I'm sure I didn't," I say, keeping my flushed face turned to the wall of our compartment. "Nothing. Absolutely nothing at all." It passes through my mind that when I have unintentionally witnessed someone doing something shameful, I always feel ashamed for them, as if I have seen them naked when I wasn't supposed to, and am myself responsible for the error.

"You look cold," I finally say, taking my fur coat off the hanger near the door. "Here, cover yourself with my coat."

She smiles at me. "What an angel you are," she says. "You've always been my guardian angel."

f i v e

■

B stands in front of the mirror near the refrigerator, her fingertips tapping out small circles around her eyes, descending to her cheeks, chin, and throat, then back to her eyes and forehead. Her sister's homemade cream, made of spermacete, lanolin, vitamin E, olive oil—leaves a barely visible luster on her face, and when she finishes, her skin is even more luminous than when she started.

"Minimum half-hour every day," she says, practicing her English. "Must be automatic part life."

"I've never had the luxury of spending half an hour every day on my face."

"It not luxury, it necessity," she says, wrapping a towel around my head. "You pretend neglect self is virtue, but not so. What more close to you than you? Massage in *banya* once in week, facial regular, and many sleep minimum for woman if you want mans to look on you after forty. That and no sleep with man in first date."

She is trying to restore herself in my eyes, and speaking English with me is one form of concession. She hasn't yet realized that the road back to perfection doesn't exist.

"In America, only rich people usually have facials and massages," I say. "It's very expensive. I don't even know those kinds of women."

"Here not expensive. Everybody do this. Also, you need new coat. This was okay when your mother wore, but forty years long time. This fall in pieces, and make you like balloon. You need stop hide self; nothing bad in be beautiful."

She puts two spots of cream on my cheekbones. I tip my face up toward her as her fingers drum rapid circles around my eyes, patting and smoothing. A faint pulse beneath my right eye beats against the fleeting glissando of her fingertips, which by then have already wandered from my eyes back to my cheeks, fluttering there like hummingbirds in suspended flight. When she has finished smoothing the final traces of cream into my skin and I have settled into an almost primordial calm, she kisses me swiftly on the mouth; for a second, I could almost swear that her tongue has flicked against my lips. "Appetite grows in the presence of food," says the Russian proverb, but B seems indifferent or oblivious to this and anything else as her fingers continue their ritual conquest of my face. In the background, the radio is announcing the results of the referendum: 70 percent of the population has voted in favor of preserving the Soviet Union and in favor of Russia's having an independent presidency. No one seems to care that these two ideas are mutually exclusive, and bound, sooner or later, to collide. I have scrutinized Yeltsin's face, and I don't like it: a shrewd face, cold in the eyes. Is he what Russia really needs?

The phone rings. B answers it. When she comes back into the kitchen, she says, "I found you job."

"What kind of job?"

"How I know? People no speak about this on telephone. She come tomorrow. You know when she here."

She pours tea and puts a dish of raspberry jam beside my cup.

"When my daughter was twelve," I say, "she had to memorize a poem for school. I helped her choose one of Akhmatova's." And I recite:

He did love three things in this world:
Choir chants at vespers, albino peacocks
And worn, weathered maps of America
And he did not love children crying
Or tea served with raspberries
Or woman's hysteria
. . . And I was his wife

I eat a spoonful of jam and sip my tea. "Let's go to the Akhmatova Museum tomorrow."

"We go to Philharmonics," she says, putting a pile of newspapers on the table and spreading them around her.

"That's at night. We could go to the museum during the day."

"You want too much," she says. "You run one thing to other. Then you no remember where was you or what see. Americans do this—they look quickly—interesting, this was rich man or great artist—and enough. Then out from this place to another. And already they forgot. For me, to go to Philharmonics is holiday. I need day to think about this, to prepare my soul. But if I start think on Akhmatova life, and all what happened, and how she said and did, this will finish me concert. I not enjoy this concert. Akhmatova is serious exhibition. Maybe you can look and forget, but I no can."

I turn on the television. It occurs to me that, as soon as B forgot about restoring herself in my eyes, it happened by itself. The news is on. Gorbachev is talking. Looking weary, he announces that, as a result of the referendum, he now sees it as his task to fulfill the will of the people and preserve the Union. He makes no mention of Yeltsin, who is making faces behind his back, dreaming of revenge.

B doesn't look at the TV. She has spread out almost twenty newspapers and magazines on the table and is absorbed in deciphering them. *Pravda, Komsomolskaya Pravda, Chas Pik, Sovietskaya Kultura, Smena, Nevsky Prospekt, Izvestia, Ogonyok, Nyedeli, Sovietskaya Rossiya, Vyecherny Leningrad*—representing everything from the Communist Party to radical free-market enthusiasts, each with its own views on culture, politics, and everyday life—a groaning table of ideas at which you can gorge yourself to the point of illness. Her immediate goal is to have an opinion. But which opinion? Although the taste of freedom is on everyone's tongue, the dulling habit of it isn't. What is one to do with this freedom, which demands answers from you as soon as you open your eyes in the morning? It's a game of Beat the Clock, a time bomb ticking on Russia's future.

B finds an article in *Pravda* about A's production of *Boris*, which praises it for its contemporaneity. Now we also have our false Dmitri, *Pravda* says, so popular with the people, who is leading them away from the truth. It doesn't take much reading between the lines to know that Yeltsin is the false Dmitri. B cuts out the article. She is again weighing the advantages of being the wife of the conductor.

She returns to the newspapers, reads, looks up.

"What is this 'privatization'?" she asks. The article she has been reading is about foreign capital, and she can't understand a thing. "I have to find every word in dictionary, but our dictionaries have no such words," she says. "This privatization—is it clothes or food or what? Who gives it you? What you can do with it? Such business words no exist in Russian. If you no know English words, no possible understand."

All I know about privatization is that it means taking property out of the hands of the government and putting it into the hands of private citizens. But which private citizens and how they get it is as much of a mystery to me as it is to her. I tell her so. Her reaction is to sweep the newspapers onto the floor with a single grand gesture and leave them lying there. She goes into the living room and comes back with a book of Repin's paintings. She opens it and sits staring at a single plate for a long time without saying a word.

"What are you looking at?" I ask.

"*Those Who Waited*," she says. "In Russian Museum. You saw. Is about father come back from Siberia."

She seems to feel that this is sufficient information for me, and doesn't offer to show me the book. When I come over to her side of the table to see it, she covers the page with her arm.

"Why are you hiding it from me?" I ask.

"I not hide," she says. "Private property. No trespassing. I saw these signs in America. Not your business. I privatize."

She returns to the painting, while I try to remember exactly what it looks like. When B was eleven, her father also returned from Siberia. Her mother had remarried. He came too late.

After midnight, I come back to the kitchen. The book is still open on the kitchen table. I look: An open door through which a young man with burning eyes has just entered the room. Inside the room, a woman and two children. The father's eyes are fierce, the kind of eyes you can't forget. I go into the bathroom. The newspapers B was reading are now torn into neat strips, resting in a pile next to the toilet. The price of toilet paper has soared. B says, "In America, people talked about recycling as if they had just discovered it. Here, we've been doing it for a hundred years."

When I wake up at three in the morning, the light in the

kitchen is still on, and B is looking at the Repin book again. "Sit," she says. I sit. This time she shows me the plate and speaks in English.

"Father returned from Siberia after maybe nine years," she says. "He activist-populist—bring new ideas in freedom to muzhiks. Son look at father with big eyes—he remember, but no remember this man. Big excitement and afraid. Daughter maybe eight. She no remember father. Maybe he no see child. Mother tired. They no hear from this father so long. They not know he alive or no alive. And then he walk in door unexpected. She not know what to think, to feel. Maybe she loves another; maybe she with new husband."

"I see," I say. "Is there anything else you want to privatize?"

"That's my secret," she says in Russian, and closes the book.

Nadezhda Sergeevna wants to know what I want, but I don't know myself.

I want to know what she wants, but she won't tell me.

She is wearing a white lace hand-embroidered collar over a green velvet dress with cap sleeves. We are eating the last of the joint-venture salmon B's brother-in-law gave us. "Would you like to meet some deputies from our Leningrad Soviet, or journalists from *Smena*?" Nadezhda Sergeevna asks. "How about the Association of Small-Business People? Whatever you want, I can arrange it. Who else would you like to meet?"

"The job," I say. "I'd like to know about the job."

She glances swiftly at B. "We can talk about the job later," she says. "I would like you to meet interesting people. You haven't been here long, and you need to meet interesting people."

"Actually, all I want is a job."

She looks disappointed. It occurs to me that maybe B made a mistake. Maybe there is no job.

"You are a native English-speaker," she says. "Anything you say to them could be valuable."

"Who are 'they'?"

"They come to us from different professions. Engineers, scientists, geologists, economists, psychologists. Educated people."

"But what do they come for?"

"The market," she says. "The market is coming, and they need to be ready for it."

"I'm not an economist. I don't know anything about markets."

"You do," she says. "You're American. You've lived with them. You have experience. We don't. We don't even know what the market is. We just know that we have to be prepared for it when it comes, and we aren't. You know about different prices, for example. We don't. Our prices have been the same for the last thirty years. But now suddenly prices are different everywhere and change every day. We understand nothing about this. We are told that there will be stimulation, but what does that mean? Yeltsin is our St. George, suffering for his people. He is leading us toward the market, but exactly when it will be here, we don't know. That's why we need people like you, so that we can know what it is and recognize it when it comes. Tell me, please, what will be the theme of your first class?"

"Quite frankly, I haven't thought about it yet."

"But I need to know it immediately."

"I teach literature, not markets. I wanted to teach a course in success and failure in American life as seen through American literature. I thought we would read fiction and poetry. I brought books with me."

Her eyelids droop. "My dear," she says, "the problem right now is that we don't need poetry, we need practice. That would be a wonderful course . . . but only for a small group of specialists, not for normal people. And we are teaching normal people. So please don't say anything about poetry or literature. I have to put an ad in the paper right away. If I put literature in my ad, only three or four people will come, and I need students. How about just . . . 'Success and Failure in American life'?"

Is it possible that I am hearing this in Leningrad, on literature's holy ground? "I'm a writer," I say. "Telling me not to talk about literature is like asking Akhmatova to avoid the subject of poetry. Russia has always needed poetry. That's what makes it Russia, not America."

Nadezhda Sergeevna sees that she has made a mistake. A writer! And of course, like all writers, hypersensitive.

"You're right," she says. "I'm terribly sorry. The problem is that it's not doing us any good being Russia. Look at America. We have poetry, and they have everything else. Besides, these students aren't so sophisticated."

"It's not a question of sophistication," I persist. "It's a question of soul."

The word "soul" acts on her like a cattle prod. It is to a Russian what the word "freedom" is to an American.

"Yes, yes," she says, straining now to close the gap that has opened between us and is threatening her beloved project. "Soul is everything. And as I said, this course which you propose would be a wonderful course. It's just not something I could organize in a few days. If we could perhaps do this a little bit later, it would give me great pleasure. Really such pleasure."

I can see that she is on the verge of exhaustion, but also exhilarated and a little frightened. Our encounter has developed beyond anything she anticipated. But she has a practical job to do, and she needs to do it now.

"Would you mind coming just once?" she says. "You can talk with them about anything you want. I'm sure they would love to meet you. Some have already signed up for the course. We paid a cooperative for the names of Americans who could come to teach or wanted to learn Russian. But they cheated us. No one came. Maybe it was because of the war in Iraq, and they were afraid to travel. I had already arranged everything for them: an apartment, meals at the Kavkaz restaurant, the use of a car, just in exchange for having conversations about American life with our students. Now I have a program without teachers. Maybe I could introduce you to our mayor. He is a very cultivated man. He loves culture, and poetry."

I am beginning to understand.

"All right," I say. "I'll come once, and after that, we'll decide. Where should I come? And when?"

"I'll pick you up," she says. "We don't have a permanent location. We're not officially registered yet, so we meet at Miloserdiye."

"What is Miloserdiye?"

"People trying to help other people. Mothers with many children, for example. If you'd like to meet an organization of mothers with many children, I could arrange that too."

"Thank you," I say. "Not right now." I'm not going to ask her about salary. There probably isn't one, and that's why she's offering me all these introductions. Well, it's a start anyway. Maybe one of her students can help deliver my boxes of humanitarian aid, which have surprisingly turned up at the airport after B, in desperation, said that I was a writer with a direct line to the president of the United States. Despite what Nadezhda Sergeevna says, being a writer still stirs a Pavlovian response in many quarters, especially those quarters that are threatened with exposure to higher powers.

At least until the market gets here, the written word is valuable currency.

But it still helps to have connections. I wonder if any of her students knows someone in customs.

I finally consent to the theme of the first class: "Who are you? Who am I?" The door to literature is left open.

What are Boy Scouts?

What is the Salvation Army?

What is health insurance?

What do I think of Graham Greene?

Have I read Tyutchev? Gogol? Berdyayev?

What about Bulgakov? (Here we are, back to Bulgakov. But this time I'm prepared, having read *Heart of a Dog* as soon as B and I returned from N—sk.)

In the end, they're still Russian. What else could they be? They are preparing for the market, but literature is still their meat and potatoes.

After the first class, Nadezhda Sergeevna presses fifty roubles into my hand. It doesn't amount to much, but I'm pretty sure that for her it's a lot. I protest. "It's not official," she says. "Just don't say anything about it."

After the third class, we decide to read Raymond Carver's short story "Cathedral." I tell the students not to worry. If we take care of our souls, the market can't bother us. I know and they know that this isn't true. I don't tell them that one of the reasons I have come to Russia is to escape from the market, from its omnipresence.

Nadezhda Sergeevna still wants me to meet interesting people. I agree. I agree to get together with the mothers with many children, with journalists from *Smena*. With deputies. With anyone she wants. Olga Sergeevna is satisfied. Her school has just been launched.

■

B is in mourning for her life. She, who said that nothing ever changes in Russia, and for whom this fact was a source of often unpleasant but necessary security, is now being buffeted by the transformation of her world. What was illegal and immoral yesterday is right and necessary today, and everyone is expected to fall in line with the "new thinking," which amounts to nothing more or less than throwing away everything associated with the past seventy years of Russian history. No one here says anymore, "What is your work?" but only "What is your business?" or "I hope we can do business together," or "our businessmen." And surrounding the concept is a veritable fever of expectation. Who can help us? Who can sponsor us? Who will form a "joint venture" with us? (This "joint venture" is currently the most fashionable phrase, but B says that, no matter how hard she tries, she can never remember it, sometimes calling it a "joint invention" or "joint adventure," thus inscribing it in her "privatized" English lexicon, which in-

cludes such constructions as "electric city" instead of "electricity," and "bubbles" instead of "bulbs.")

Nadezhda Sergeevna represents just the tip of the iceberg,
and B knows it. For Nadezhda Sergeevna's primary aim is to understand the market and meet it halfway. She sees that knowledge has its price, as it always has, but that under capitalism this
price is understood differently from in Russia, and that, somehow or other, she has to arrive at a comprehension of its deeper
meaning. She, like B, has embarked on a tortuous mental journey.
Who knows— certainly not I—where it may lead.

One thing is clear enough, however: before ordinary Russians can be in a position to buy any of the tarted-up wonders
that are constantly being paraded in front of their eyes, they
have to find the means to sell something. With the collapse of
the barter trade with Eastern Europe, no one is bringing anything at all into the country, and life often seems to disintegrate,
quite literally, right in front of your eyes, like a particularly delicate mushroom in a state of deliquescence. For absolutely
everything, some necessary ingredient is missing—spare parts,
medicine, asphalt. And surrounding this is a kind of generalized
panic and desperation, which, for the moment at least, takes the
form of a peculiarly optimistic and naïvely crude salesmanship,
amounting at times to a willingness to sell the entire country for
the sake of some immediate cash.

Fortunately for B (fortunately for both of us, she insists), she
has found us a mentor, an economist who deals with the export
of oil and lumber on behalf of the state. Dmitri Ivanovich is
seated between B and me at Easter dinner at the home of one of
my students, a single-mother geologist whose dreams for the
market consist of having enough money to expand a three-foot-
wide storage corridor in the two-room apartment she and her
child share with her mother into a room of her own, four and a
half by six feet, by hacking out, with the tools of the geologist's

trade, a section six feet by a foot and a half of solid brick exterior wall. By the end of the meal Dmitri Ivanovich has succeeded in implanting the germ of an idea in B's mind. He himself has recently decided to become a businessman, and he urges B to do the same. In fact, he thinks that B and I should become partners in a joint venture, and he is eager to help us to do so.

My protests that I am a writer, not a businessman, cut no ice with him. After all, I am an American, and therefore by definition a *biznismen*. The word "businessman," like the word "privatization," is an American word with no corresponding meaning in Russian. In Russian, people who buy or sell for personal profit are called *zhuliki*, or perhaps *farzofshiki*, both of which refer to the kind of people who steal caviar from state stores and sell it on the street to foreigners, or change money on the black market, or conduct any one of a seemingly infinite number of possible illegal transactions. A businessman, however, is something else, though precisely what, no one wants to say for sure, not even Dmitri Ivanovich. For now it is sufficient just to pronounce the word with great pride, as children do when they have made a discovery.

As a result of their dinner-table conversation, Dmitri Ivanovich has recognized the survivor in B as well as the woman in mourning, on the edge of a divorce, and with no place to live as soon as the divorce is consummated. With his eye for the golden opportunity, he sees in her distress all kinds of possibilities for transformation, and he is therefore encouraging her to leap into the future with all of the strength and courage at her disposal, to forget about the satisfactions of making one-of-a-kind performance clothes for people who really need them, people who are prepared to go to enormous lengths in order to scavenge the necessary fabric and buttons and ribbons, people who are eternally grateful to her for her singular ability to rescue them from fashion oblivion onstage or at their weddings, and to substitute for these pleasures the more concrete and sober pleasures of making money and being a success.

B, as always, is interested but skeptical. She hasn't figured out yet what's in it for Dmitri Ivanovich, but recognizes as correct his assertion that, as far as joint ventures are concerned, she, unlike everyone else wandering the streets of Leningrad in a state of hyperactivity and desperation, doesn't have to find a foreign partner. She has one available right in her own apartment (or, rather, A's apartment).

The only question that remains is what the joint venture should do. A joint venture, Dmitri Ivanovich says, needs a product. Once you have found the right product, everything else is possible.

B agrees to give the question some thought, and within a few days, she has come up with an idea. She has decided that I should become her manager. My speech about the quality of her work at the banquet in N—sk made a substantial impression on her, and she has come to the conclusion that the only thing separating her from the brave new world in which she is about to be launched is a sponsor. Every artist needs a sponsor, she says, and I am the right sponsor for her. It hasn't occurred to her that, as a writer, I would probably also enjoy having a sponsor; she just assumes that if I need something I know how to get it, and that if I don't have it that's probably because I don't need it. I don't want to injure her pride by saying that my speech in N—sk was just that, a speech intended to rescue both of us from a humiliating situation, and that the demand for hand-made clothing in America could, as Dmitri Ivanovich has suggested, prove to be limited. Besides, my speech has not only transformed her in her own eyes from a visitor in America to an essential element of its international prestige, it has also transformed me into a highly desirable object, more desirable than anything she had heretofore imagined. She sees now that it is my patriotic duty as a true American to help her realize her goals.

The fact that I have always had to work for a living in one way or another makes no impression whatsoever on her. She thinks that I must have my reasons for taking on odd jobs, reasons that are obscure to her only because she isn't American, or else that I'm not really a writer at all but something else entirely, something I don't want to talk about. If I were a real writer, I would behave differently. I would have respect and prestige and awards from the government. The fact that I seem to have no connections at all with the government (despite her lies in service to humanitarian aid) can mean only two things: that I am hiding them, or that I am insignificant. She suspects that the former might be the case, that I am secretly rich from unknown sources. In any case, my being American excludes the possibility of my being insignificant. There is no such thing as an insignificant American, a fact Dmitri Ivanovich has taken great pains to emphasize to her.

Dmitri Ivanovich now calls us every day. She has floated the idea to him of me as her manager, but he has so far failed to see the value of the product and is encouraging her to go in another direction—for instance, selling souvenirs to the West. As an artist, she would know how to select the right souvenirs for the American market, which would guarantee her success. I, of course, would put up the money for the purchase of the souvenirs. Neither he nor B has asked me whether I have the money to fulfill this expectation. It is simply assumed that, as an American, I must, and that if I don't I have enough connections to know how to get it. In Russia, everything is a matter of connections. This must obviously be true of America as well.

B has decided that Dmitri Ivanovich is KGB. Why else would he be paying so much attention to us?

Only yesterday, he called wanting to know about my plans to go to the mines in the Kuzbass, three hundred kilometers from N—sk, to talk with the miners. The miners are the key to what is happening in Russia right now, and I've decided to write about them after one of them shared our compartment on the train coming back from N—sk. He told us about how the miners have become politicized, and how some of them had even gone to America to visit the coal miners there. "The mines in America are so clean that you can go into them with white shoes, and when you come out they are still white." The coal miners' union in America gave them presents, including things like fax machines and video cameras. The miners in America thought that such items would help them in their struggle. So far they had helped greatly: the delegation members who went to America had been selling the gifts quickly and pocketing the money. Our companion in the compartment understood clearly enough that this wasn't the intention of the miners' union in America, but he didn't object; that was just the way things were in Russia, the way they always had been. On a trip to Paris, the great eighteenth-century Russian historian Nikolai Karamzin, when asked what was happening in Russia, said, "Stealing." Sergei Dovlatov, in his 1986 novel, *The Suitcase*, commented that people no longer stole parts from bulldozers, they just drove through the security gates with the whole bulldozer, cheerfully waving goodbye to the security guard.

B was very interested in her conversation with the miner from Kemerovo, and the more involved she got in the conversation, the more she stopped translating to me what he was saying, first of all because she isn't a translator, and second of all because she thinks I can understand everything myself. Sometimes I do, sometimes I don't. This time I didn't. I kept interrupting her and saying, "What did he say?" until eventually they ignored me altogether and kept right on talking to each other. It was like listening to my parents speak Russian with each other. As soon as I realized that I wasn't supposed to understand, I stopped understanding. So that was the extent of my interview with a Siberian miner, and since they stopped talking about politics and instead talked about "real life" as soon as my participation in the conversation ended, I had very little to say, though I tried to explain to B that, if I was going to write something for, say, *The New Yorker*, a smattering of inaccurately perceived or casually translated conversation would hardly inspire their confidence in me.

Dmitri Ivanovich asks who is organizing my trip. He says it was such a delight meeting us over Easter dinner that now he can't stop thinking about us. B is suspicious. Why, she asks, can't he stop thinking about us? Why does he care about my plans to go to the mines in the first place? Is it just because the miners are usually off limits to foreigners? Whereas I used to suspect B of paranoia, I now think she may be realistic. But I have questions of my own. For instance, if B really thinks that Dmitri Ivanovich is KGB, why did she tell him anything at all about my interest in the mines?

I notice that B's tone of voice when she talks with Dmitri Ivanovich on the telephone is slightly flirtatious, a reflex she sees as an inevitable consequence of the fact that she is a woman and he is a man. In any case, if he really is KGB, she thinks that we ought to keep him on our side. After all, we need all the help we can get.

"If you want to know her plans," B says, "why don't you come over to our house and talk about them?"

He is evidently startled by the suggestion and immediately accepts.

"Wonderful," I say. "Aren't we special. Our very own private KGB man. No group deal for us. Maybe he can even help you get an apartment."

"That's not funny," she snaps.

"What's not funny?" I say, noting how the word "apart-ment" has the capacity to galvanize her attention as nothing else can. "About the apartment or about the KGB? Besides, you're the one who told me that joint ventures have the right to buy apartments, that if we formed a joint adventure we could buy one. Isn't that what you said?"

She looks at me warily. She never knows what information I am going to absorb. She thinks it's going to be one thing, and it turns out to be something completely different.

"You should never joke about apartments," she said. "There is nothing more serious in Russia than apartments. Propiskas and apartments. Apartments and propiskas. You can spend your whole life trying to get one or the other or both. Besides, the apartments that the government is offering to joint ventures cost two thousand dollars. And that's just the official price. How many people do you have to bribe in order to get one of those apartments?"

"It can't be that many," I say. "And two thousand dollars isn't so much to pay for an apartment, even if the law on joint ven-tures changes and invalidates the purchase. If you have a joint venture, you'd probably be willing to risk two thousand dollars."

"But we don't have a joint venture," she says. "Since when do we have a joint venture? And since when do you have two thousand dollars? That's fifty thousand roubles. Only speculators have that much money. They're the ones who are making these joint ventures."

I am silent. How can I confess to her that Dmitri Ivanovich's assessment of me as a rich American has just become correct, that I am neither a speculator nor a businessman, but that if it was a matter of getting two thousand dollars for an apartment I could surely find a way to do it, even if it meant borrowing the money.

"We could figure it out," I say lamely. "Somehow or other, we could figure it out."

This is not a good enough answer as far as she is concerned. This is just pissing in the wind. She is not yet prepared to contemplate the fact that I may actually have, or be able to get, two thousand dollars, which makes the price of buying souvenirs to sell in the West look like peanuts. And I am not prepared to tell her that if I had two thousand dollars I would never spend it on souvenirs, but would spend it on an apartment, simply as a matter of value. If I were to introduce the theme of "value," however, I would immediately and irrevocably be branded as an American businessman, and this is what I am determined to avoid. So I don't say anything at all, and just listen as B explains to me that, even if we did become a joint venture and did buy an apartment, we would constantly have to pay protection money to the Mafia. On the scale of things, we are lucky to have our own KGB man. We would not be lucky to have our own Mafia man.

"They could wipe each other out," I suggest.

But she doesn't think this is funny either.

In fact, she doesn't seem to think anything is funny anymore. This is all because of the apartment question, which dwarfs all other questions entirely, including whether it is a good or a bad thing that Dmitri Ivanovich is KGB. It is more important than my writing about miners in the Kuzbass for *The New Yorker*, more important than a job or the changing price of bread or even than the divorce, except to the extent that the divorce is involved with the apartment. She has explained all of this to me before at great length, and now I understand that a propiska is a residence permit, which gives you legal permission to live in Leningrad or Moscow or any other location for which you have a propiska. The propiska gives you rights: the right to have an apartment in Leningrad, the right to work in Leningrad, the right to receive free medical care, a free education, and the entire gamut of free social services linked to residency. A Leningrad propiska is gold. Without one, you officially don't exist here. And it is precisely this propiska which she doesn't have.

I have asked her how it is possible that she has been living in Leningrad all of these years and married to A but still doesn't have a propiska. The explanation is long and extremely complicated, but as I understand it (perhaps wrongly), the gist of the issue is that she is still registered in her parents' apartment in the town of Z—sk, fifty kilometers outside the city limits, where she officially possesses her own twelve square feet of legally allotted space, the amount of space that the Soviet government has deemed necessary for the well-being of every Soviet individual. She and her mother and her father each have the right to one-third of their two-room apartment, though neither she nor her father now lives in the apartment. For many years now, A has been urging B to give up her rights to the apartment in Z—sk and exchange them for the right to a larger apartment together with him in Leningrad, but she has always declined, even though it would give her a Leningrad propiska. Why? The answer is simple. She trusts her mother more than she trusts A, even though she is not so sure that she trusts her mother either. In fact, she is not sure that she trusts anyone, excluding of course me.

The apartment question is becoming more and more pressing. It is difficult to say which is more painful for her, the loss of A, the potential loss of the apartment, or the breakdown of the world order with which she has lived all of her life. Maybe we can afford to pay fifty kopecks for bread that cost fourteen kopecks a week ago; maybe we can shop in the farmers' market instead of standing in long lines for state stores; but that isn't the point. The point is that she remembers the time when the stores were filled with Salamanders and clothing from Finland, Germany, and Italy, when a cutting board cost one rouble. The point is that you could count on the price of bread. It was always the same, almost all her life it was the same. And the same was true of meat or sugar or potatoes. But now life has been inundated with all the horrors that come from the West—the messiness and uncertainty and unpredictability of everything. How can people live this way, when their pensions are worthless, their savings worthless, their plans to buy a wall unit or travel to America rendered futile? (The rouble price of tickets to America has just tripled, and is equal to two years' pay. Only fifteen seats on each flight are reserved for rouble payments, and there is a waiting list of two thousand people. For dollars, of course—$550—you can get a ticket immediately. But Soviet citizens are still not allowed to possess dollars.)

As for the apartment, probably no one who lives anywhere but in Russia can possibly understand the grip it has on her imagination. How many Soviet marriages are undertaken for the sake of an apartment? How many divorces postponed indefinitely for the sake of an apartment? How many divorces executed in theory but never realized in practice, since neither of the two divorcées has the possibility of moving to another apartment? How many love affairs aborted by the absence of an available apartment? How many mothers-in-law and daughters-in-law and sons-in-law at one another's throats because of the lack of an apartment?

Only the day before yesterday, the apartment question brought us to the brink of disaster. B had been planning for months to speak with her mother about the possibility of her mother exchanging her apartment in Z—sk for two smaller apartments, one of which would be B's. Under Soviet law, no one has the right to be officially registered in more than one apartment, so if B moves out of the apartment with A she has only two options: move in with her mother, or persuade her mother to sell the apartment so that she can exchange her own twelve square meters of official space for a one-room apartment of her own, or twelve meters of space in a communal apartment. B's plan, while seemingly complex, was no more elaborate (and possibly less elaborate) then the plans of most people who spend a multitude of sleepless nights trying to figure out the logistics of apartments. What she finally figured out was that she would pay extra money in order to get a larger apartment for herself and her mother, and then would do another exchange of the larger apartment for two smaller ones—one for herself and one for her mother. This process of exchanging is the only legal method of acquiring another apartment.

With the goal of convincing her mother to agree to this strategy, B and I took the train out to Z—sk, though B had already warned me that, since her mother is eighty years old and regards it as a triumph that the government gave her this apartment in the first place after she had spent ten years chopping down trees in the Gulag for crimes that had never been established, and another ten years living in a house alongside the railroad tracks built by B's father, where B as a child carried buckets of water from a communal well and shared her bed in winter with a baby goat, apartment negotiations could turn out to be tricky.

As soon as we got to Z—sk, however, it turned out that B's mother had news of her own. B's older sister, Lyudmila, an economist who works in the Far North and is approaching retirement, had decided to return to Leningrad and, instead of living in her own studio apartment in one of the new districts, wanted to live with her mother, who was getting too old to live alone. They had together decided on B's behalf that B should move into her sister's apartment. The only problem with this arrangement (aside from the fact that no one had asked B her opinion in the matter) was that her sister's apartment was a rental, whereas B's mother's apartment was cooperative. Why should B give up her rights to a cooperative in exchange for the rights to a rental when she had determinedly held on to those rights throughout the twelve years of her marriage? She could have had a Leningrad propiska years ago if she had been willing to give up her share of the apartment. This only went to show that she was wrong to trust her mother in the first place. Both the quantity and the sumptuousness of their exchange escalated quickly, and then deteriorated just as quickly, until B finally exploded with rage and all became chaos. At one point she called her mother an "old idiot." I seemed to be the only one who was shocked by this, and I started to cry as B stormed out the door.

Anastasia Mikhailovna, however, was firm. People live together not because they want to, but because they must. B already had a place to live, an apartment in town with her husband, and that's where she should stay, even without a propiska. No sane person leaves a marriage if it means losing an apartment. If B continued to persist in her folly, then she would simply have to accept her older sister's offer. Why B couldn't understand this was entirely beyond Anastasia Mikhailovna's comprehension. *"Sumaschedshaya,"* she said repeatedly of B, pointing to her forehead and making little circles with her finger. "She's crazy." Standing by the window, she looked out at the forest to which B had fled, shaking her head and sighing.

It is Saturday morning. B and I have been discussing the apartment question, and I have been trying to convince her that we should try to get an apartment together. After all, I am considering the possibility of continuing to live here and need a place to stay, while she needs a design studio. In any case, I would have to pay for an apartment. The only question is how to go about it. But B insists that, no matter what I think, there is really only one way, the right way. If I imagine that it is just a matter of finding an apartment and putting down some money to pay for it, I am suffering from delusions of grandeur. Where do I think I am, in the West? There are only two realistic alternatives. One is to find someone with a good apartment and marry him in order to acquire a legal stake in the apartment, and the other is to find a Jewish family who are planning to leave the country and want to sell their apartment for cash, which they can receive in Israel or America. The notices posted on the sides of lampposts or bulletin boards advertising apartments for sale are only ruses. Yes, there are people who will gladly sell an apartment to you, but since it is illegal for them to do so, you will have no protection if they change their mind and take off with the cash. And if your belongings are stolen out of the apartment, no one from the militia will help you, because you got the apartment illegally in the first place and it isn't registered in your name and you are not even a legal resident of the city. Furthermore, it is virtually guaranteed that your things will be stolen out of the apartment, since everyone knows that you acquired it illegally, and spite is one of the most universally recognized traits of the Russian character. One night you will come home, and—boff—the next day they will find your body. Is it worth it? Are you sure?

B suggests that maybe I should try to speak to someone at the synagogue, after Shabbat services. After all, it is close by, and I am Jewish and American, so they won't be afraid to speak to me. On the other hand, the minute they know that I am American, the price will skyrocket. Be careful if you do this, she says. Choose the right person. But you are a better judge of character than I am, I say. I am always misjudging people. Why don't you come with me? No. Absolutely not. The minute they see a real Russian, not Jewish, they won't trust her; they will think she is KGB. I have to go alone. And do what? I ask. Stand in the courtyard of the synagogue waiting for "the right person" to come out of the services? And then whisper in someone's ear that I am looking for an apartment in Leningrad? For whom is this apartment? For myself? For my Russian friend? We rehearse. "I am looking for an apartment to buy in Leningrad. Two rooms. City center or Vasilevsky Island. Together with my friend. Not too expensive. Do you know anyone who might have such an apartment?" "Hello. I am from the United States. I'm looking for an apartment in Leningrad. I'm Jewish." "Excuse me, hello, do you mind if I speak with you for a moment? Do you by any chance know of anyone who is emigrating and has an . . ." No. Impossible. Don't say anything about emigrating. They will be sure that you are KGB. Maybe just stand there and listen to what people are saying. Maybe someone will speak about an apartment, and then show that you are interested. But not too interested. How often does she think that I will have to do this? Who knows? Maybe once a week for six months. Maybe only one month. The important thing is to find the right person. That's most important.

So I am finally going to synagogue in Russia on Shabbat. I never thought it would happen. You have to be practical, B says. It's the only way. Maybe you'll find someone you like there, someone to marry. That would solve the question of the apartment. That would be the best solution of all. Then we could all live together in peace and harmony.

Shabbat services are in progress at the synagogue. I still haven't decided whether actually to attend the services or to remain outside. I repeat to myself the lines I have memorized, but as I enter the synagogue courtyard and approach the rear of the building, where Saturday-morning prayers are ordinarily conducted, the Russian words suddenly get mixed with the Hebrew prayers in my mind, and I can't distinguish the musical cadences of Adon Olam from the deliberately bright phrases B has constructed for me. *"Izvinitie, pozhalusta, mojno pogovorit s'vami? Ya ishchoo kvartiru, v centre goroda. . . ."* ("Excuse me, please, may I speak with you? I am looking for an apartment in the center city. . . .")

My heart is beating wildly, drumming the word "blasphemy" against my chest. On Shabbat, it is forbidden to carry money. It is forbidden to think about business, about deals of any kind. It is the day to contemplate the radiance of the Sabbath bride, to rejoice in the world of the spirit. . . . Hello, I am looking for an apartment, how much?

I enter the synagogue. The women are separated from the men. I hide myself among the women. I can feel my face flushing. I start to read the prayers in Hebrew. I chant. Forgive me my sins. I am an impostor. I did not come here to pray. People are looking at me. I am a stranger. I look like a foreigner. Who is she? From what country?

The services are almost over. When they finish, people pour into the courtyard. Someone speaks to me in Yiddish, but I don't understand Yiddish. I look at him blankly. He looks at me suspiciously. If I don't understand Yiddish, I am automatically suspect. "I speak English," I say in Russian. "I am from America."

The man has a full Old Testament beard. "No Yiddish?" he says in Russian. "What about Hebrew?"

"Little," I say. "I used to speak Hebrew, but I haven't spoken it for a long time."

"Typical American," he says with irritation. "What kind of Jews are these Americans anyway? They speak only English."

"But I don't speak only English," I say. "I speak Russian. Maybe not so well, but . . ."

"Russian!" he says. "Who needs Russian? A real Jew speaks Yiddish."

I can't figure out why I am being put on the defensive. Maybe he thinks that I am a spy. Maybe he's testing me. But I'm so nervous now that I can't remember what I was supposed to say about the apartment, and anyway, it's clear that I could never say it to this man, who is already accusing me of committing a mortal sin for not speaking Yiddish. Little does he know what evil lurks in my heart.

I escape from him as quickly as I can. This project will have to wait a week. I can't do it now. But if not on Shabbat, then when? Shabbat is when people come to the synagogue, and I can't find someone who wants to sell an apartment if no one is there.

I start walking toward the gate. People are milling around in the courtyard, talking with each other. I see that some of them are looking at me. There is a young woman standing alone. I go over to her.

"Excuse me," I say. "I am looking for an apartment."

Her face, which for a moment had seemed warm and receptive, slams shut.

"I don't know anything about apartments," she says coldly.

I turn away from her and flee.

s e v e n

■

Nothing has been solved, and it is already June. A has invited his Dutch girlfriend to live in the apartment this summer. Where B will live is her problem. Maybe she'd like to come to Maine again, I say. Maine is beautiful in the summer. My visa is going to expire soon, so I have to go back to America anyway. I've been offered a "real teaching job" here next year, for the second semester. By then we could figure things out. But B says that if she comes to America for the summer she will never again see any of her belongings. The splendid rosewood armoire standing in the living room of A's apartment (it is now clearly defined as A's), with its ornately carved crest, filled with the fabrics she has accumulated over a lifetime of sewing, will be lost to her forever. So will the rosewood buffet, the hand-woven Daghestani carpet hanging on the wall, the dusky burnt-orange silk drapes she made for the living room, and all of the other fragments of her shared domestic life with A. The time to take everything she owns out of there is now, before the divorce is finalized. Now means NOW!—this week—as soon as she can find a truck to transport everything she owns to her mother's apartment.

I look out the living-room window at the yard, where a three-foot-wide trench running parallel to the front of the building has divided us from the outside world for the past month, with only a shaky wooden plank providing access to the yard and the street beyond.

"Now?" I say. "Couldn't you at least wait until they've finished excavating? How are you going to get your things across that trench?"

"A trench in front of the door is exactly the reason why we should do it now. A knows about the trench. I have to move when he thinks I wouldn't. Anyway, what makes you think that the trench won't be here for a year? This is Russia, not America, with its holes in the ground that open and close before you even have time to get used to them. A is pushing for the divorce now, so it would be easy for his "Holland woman" to move in while we're in America. Then all of the cards will be in his hands. They'll change the locks, and I'll never be able to walk in the door again."

"What makes you think that he knows about the trench? He's in Siberia. How would he know about it?"

"He has his ways. He always knows what it suits him to know."

"Why can't you work out an arrangement to rent the apartment from him? That way we would have someplace to live when we come back here. We still need a place to live."

"Are you crazy? Pay him good money to live here when I've been his slave for the past twelve years?"

"Not exactly slave," I say. "I've never noticed you to be anyone's slave."

"That's just because I'm smarter than he is. If I wasn't, believe me, I would be his slave. Anyway, what makes you think that if I gave him money my things would be safe? It's your Western naïveté again. No Russian woman in her right mind would trust her belongings to her ex-husband."

I try to envision her mother's two-room apartment, the future home of all B's possessions, but all I can remember is that it is already filled with furniture. Where are all of these things going to fit? I should have been going to synagogue all winter, making inquiries about apartments for sale, instead of allowing myself to fall in love with this apartment and this neighborhood, assuming that we could continue to stay here if we wanted to. I like my desk in front of the window here, even though it now looks out on planks and a trench and B has recently confessed that it is, in fact, A's desk. I want to keep on writing about the coal mines at Kemerovo in the Kuzbass, where I went down into the mine shaft to talk with the miners about their lives, slogging through knee-deep water for what seemed like a mile, while the ceiling of the shaft, held up with wooden posts and crosshatchings of dubious strength, and so low that it was impossible to stand upright, creaked and groaned above my head. I want to write about the miners' belief that under capitalism everyone would own his or her own car and own house, and about my awareness that in any Western country the mine in which they worked, which produced low-quality brown coal buried deep underground, would have been shut down long ago. I want to write about how we all sat huddled together on planks in a corner of a shaft, with me the only person wearing the required helmet and safety goggles ("What good could they do if the mine collapsed? You'd be dead and buried anyway"), talking of the future, about my trying to explain to them that in Western countries, no matter what they think, miners don't work six months of the year and spend the other six resting at a pension on the sea at government expense, because mining is a

hazardous profession and miners deserve the government's protection. "But it is a hazardous profession," says Volodya, who
earlier in the day made the whispered confession that he hoped
for the monarchy's restoration in Russia.

"I know it is. We all know that. But in the West there are
other questions. What concerns these investors you're dreaming
about is that mines can't make money if the mine itself isn't
profitable. Do you understand what I'm trying to say? Investors
won't invest if there's nothing to invest in."

"But it's for the good of Russia."

The ceiling of the mine creaked. The miners waited for me
to give them the keys to their salvation. How much money do
you earn in a month? How much money do you have in the
bank? Do you own your house? What kind of car do you have?

We came up out of the mine. And for two weeks, all I could
remember about my trip to the mine was the sound of the
mine-shaft ceiling, creaking. The pages set aside in my journal
for writing about my trip remained blank. A week after that, I
saw an article in *The New Yorker* about Kemerovo which was
more thoroughly researched than anything I could possibly have
written. The only thing it didn't mention was the creaking.

"Do you think A would mind if we kept the desk?" I ask.

"What difference does it make if he minds?" B says. "If you
want it, we'll take it."

Since I really did want the desk, in the end we took it. It was
one of the last things we unloaded at her mother's apartment,
where her mother resolutely ignored the unloading and sat in
her room, hemmed in by her furniture, watching the news on
TV. It was almost midnight, and still light outside. The apple
trees were covered with blossoms, which, in the pale light, were
barely distinguishable from a continuous drift of clouds shaping
the indistinct edges of the sky. The smell of lilacs rose up from
the yard. The TV announcer was broadcasting the results of the

elections for president of the Russian Republic. Yeltsin had just become president. Anatoly Sobchak was the new mayor of Leningrad, which would shed its name and become once again St. Petersburg. The French, of course, would be delighted. "Ah, Saint-Pétersbourg!" So would the Germans. And everyone could dream again of becoming civilized, just like the rest of Europe. As for me, it seemed I was losing the ability to tell the difference between good news and bad news, though, one way or the other, it looked like we had come to the end.

B didn't watch the news at all. She was too busy figuring out how to fit everything she owned, including "that damned desk," into one room and still be able to close the door.

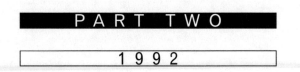

PART TWO

1992

■

e i g h t

■

The Soviet flag has just been lowered from the Kremlin. The Soviet Union has ceased to exist. B's marriage has also ceased to exist. This is obviously a coincidence, but, judging from the public reaction to the first event, it might just as well have been the second. Why isn't everyone wailing hysterically, or even protesting? Why does it seem as if the entire country is smothered in cotton wool from which not a single sound emanates? I keep feeling that I should be reminding people, lest they forget, that their country has vanished, or, rather, that it has lost what amounts to its arms and legs. How is it possible that Kiev, the birthplace of ancient Rus, the "mother of Russian cities," is now in a foreign country called Ukraine? According to the old Russian proverb, Moscow is the heart of Russia, St. Petersburg its head, and Kiev its mother. What will Russia do without its mother? Will the earth weep in its sleep? Wait patiently for her return? Scour the planet for a replacement? Or just suffer in silence?

My mother's birthplace, Odessa, was physically on Ukrainian soil, but always remained Russia's child, even though it sheltered under its wings more than a hundred different nationalities. What the devil has happened to gay, cosmopolitan Odessa, gone gray overnight? Why is it suddenly not just "in the Ukraine," the way Bangor is in Maine, but part of a nation with a border dividing it from Russia, as if Maine had become part of Canada? Mama! Mama! Don't let go of my hand! Don't let the river sweep me away.

Picture Tsvetaeva's ghost, wandering freely through time, unexpectedly able to land, fifty years after her death, at the home of her dear friend Max Voloshin, at Koktebel, the Crimea, in 1991.

During the early 1960s, Khrushchev, in an expansive mood, gave the Crimea to the Ukraine. After all, the Soviet Union was a union, and the Ukraine, just part of the whole. As a result, Tsvetaeva wakes up on New Year's morn 1992, after the collapse of the Soviet Union, in a Crimea which has become part of the Ukraine, a foreign country requiring all of the documents that foreign countries require, no longer joined to Russia. For her, this is nothing new. During the civil war in 1920, people woke up every morning not knowing whether their country was in the hands of the Reds or the Whites. Now they wake up realizing that by some accident of fate, they are in a country that is no longer their own.

Is it possible that in addition to war, famine, emigration, forced relocation, and extermination, there will now be something like internal exile, when you have gone nowhere, haven't even moved down the block, around the corner, or out of your bed, yet exile has still quietly come to claim you? You are where you are, but you're not.

In 1939, Tsvetaeva returned to Russia from the West, and in 1941, wearied by too many losses and too many changes of heart, hanged herself. This time around, Russia is too tired for revolution. For a hundred years she has been waiting for the apocalypse. Some say that it is not so far away now.

"That was horrible," I said, when it was all still news and we were still in America. "I'll never forget the way Yeltsin shook his finger in Gorbachev's face for the whole world to see, as if Gorbachev, held captive at his government dacha in Foros, had been truant from school, and then fallen into the hands of the school bully for punishment. Have you ever noticed that Yeltsin has fingers like sausages?"

"My sister Veronika needs money," B said. "After the coup, when she decided to visit us in America instead of our going back to Russia right away, you said you would lend her five hundred dollars and she could give it back to you in Russia. Where is the five hundred dollars?"

"I don't have it right now," I said. "I can't just reach into my pocket and pull out five hundred dollars. I'll see what I can do. There's an obituary in the *New York Times* for the Gorbachev era. When I read it, I cried. I can't believe that the Soviet Union is gone. Just like that. Gone. What a way to celebrate New Year's."

"My sister needs the money now. She has to buy things before she goes back to Russia. You said after we worked at that fair for Cultural Survival, and sold the shawls and the hats and gloves Veronika knitted, that you didn't want any of the money we made. So where's the money? You said that a thousand dollars was for me. You said I could have it."

"I just told you that I don't have it right now. You said that you wanted me to put that money in the bank and get interest on it for the apartment. Cultural Survival takes forty percent of the profits. In a few weeks, they'll send us a check for the rest. I had to pay for our expenses ahead of time, and I still don't know what will be left after that. Whatever it is, it's yours. There's nothing more I can do about it right now. Besides, with so much going on, I have a few other things on my mind."

"What mind?" B said. "You don't have a mind. Fuck the Soviet Union. Fuck America. And fuck you too, with your banks and your interesting. I don't care about your interesting. I need that money now."

She knew by then that there was a dark intent behind all of my mumbo jumbo about checks and banks and expenses, that it was all nothing but a sham to conceal my plan to steal her money. "Thief," she shouted at me at two in the morning. "You're nothing but a capitalist thief."

Of course I gave her the money. As soon as the bank opened in the morning, I went in and wiped out my savings account. When I handed the money over to her, she looked at me with disgust and said, "That's what you should have done in the first place." Then she and Veronika went shopping.

Their first excursion was to the supermarket, where they studied twenty different brands of toothpaste and laundry soap and came out in a state of spiritual exhaustion, having bought nothing. After that they decided to change tactics. For the next week, they picked up bargains of all kinds at thrift shops, loading up two enormous duffel bags they'd bought on Canal Street, and two oversized suitcases. They did not buy a TV or a VCR, and I knew that Veronika thought I should have made even more money at the fair. After all, why had she paid to come to America if she was going back no richer than when she arrived? And I couldn't believe that on her first trip to America, first trip to New York, she was spending all her time shopping for secondhand clothes. I told B that the luggage was oversized and overweight, and they would never be allowed on the plane with so much. She didn't listen to me. I said to myself, How do you think you would feel if your country had just vanished? Wouldn't you too be in a rage?

When she calmed down a little, I asked her what all the clothing was for. "It's none of your business," she said, and I didn't probe any further. It was a long time before I realized that Veronika couldn't think about all of the cultural and touristic pleasures of New York because she was too busy buying clothes to resell in Russia, and was ashamed to tell me. That led me to the reluctant conclusion that maybe B was right, that when it came right down to the truth of things, I really didn't have much of a mind.

Of course, it would have been worse than useless to say I told you so. At the airport, Aeroflot demanded eight hundred dollars in overweight charges. B, in a frenzy, started to scream at them. What was this anyway, a plot against her and her innocent sister for having come to America? Was everyone at Aeroflot KGB? The agents were a bunch of whores. She vilified them and me (standing at a strategic distance and feeling some relief that at least now I wasn't America's only possible source of evil) for half an hour, and when I pleaded with her, saying, "Give me two of your bags, I'll bring them with me when I come back to Russia in two weeks. It's insane to pay eight hundred dollars for a pile of used clothing," she ignored me. I was tempted to remind her that all she had was one thousand dollars, and that eight hundred was almost half the price of the apartment in Leningrad, but I knew it wouldn't do any good. Reason never had carried much weight with B, and there were no grounds to expect it would now. So I wasn't really surprised when, two minutes before the flight closed for boarding, she shelled out the eight hundred dollars and ran for the plane with Veronika. Of course she didn't say goodbye to me, and in the end, I couldn't say for sure which was worse, the dissolution of the Soviet Union or what was beginning to look like the dissolution of my friendship with B.

When the flight was already in the air, somewhere over Newfoundland, I started looking at things another way. After all, how much difference was there really between the woman who, a year ago, had given her best earrings to an American man who had admired them and thought they would be a wonderful present for his wife, the woman who impulsively gave me the only pair of French stockings she would ever be likely to own, and the woman who had paid eight hundred dollars for overweight charges on used clothing. It was only a matter of degree. Isn't that what she meant about being free? But then I saw Dostoevsky's great-great-granddaughter standing in front of me, demanding money and looking offended when I gave her too little. I had come to Russia in search of the Russian soul, expecting to find Prince Myshkin and Sonia Marmeladova. But what was to say that she might not turn out to be Grushenka or Nastasya Fillipovna?

As any Russian can tell you, hope dies last.

There is only one single bed in B's friend's apartment, and B and I sleep in it like soldiers at attention, on our backs, with our arms at our sides or folded across our breasts as they would be in coffins. There is also a collapsible cot in the apartment, but neither of us is willing to sleep on it. The apartment consists of one room and a kitchen, far from the city center. There is an electric stove in the kitchen, but I have never been able to cook on electric stoves, and besides, I can find only one small pot and one small skillet. This is obviously an apartment meant for one person who doesn't spend much time in it, and doesn't want to leave any cherished belongings for strangers who might rent it from time to time.

My relationship with B is predictably deteriorating. I decide that it is time to start looking for an apartment of our own again, ignoring all of the available evidence that it is absolutely not the right time to do so. If we stay much longer in her friend's apartment, we will start to hate each other. "I don't know about you," she says, "but I already do." She is so eager to get rid of me that once, when we take an unfamiliar route back to the apartment through courtyards and underpasses, she suddenly vanishes, and I find myself standing alone under a railroad trestle with no one in sight and no idea where I am or where to go. After that, I start thinking again about how B treated A and about her saying she would never treat me that way. When I mention this to her, she says, "You depend too much on me. It makes me feel like I can't breathe."

I present the lame argument that this is Russia, and that I'm no different from any other foreigner who depends on Russians to figure out solutions to life's ordinary complications, which in Russia are never ordinary. Wasn't she dependent on me in America the same way?

"Yes," she says. "That's why I hated it there."

I see her sister's handwriting in the remark. Only two weeks after Veronika's arrival in America, she had already persuaded B that her life in Maine was going nowhere. For what reason had she come to America anyway, Veronika said, if not to find herself an American husband, the way every other normal woman in Russia was trying to do? Living in Maine, out in the wilderness (as Veronika perceived it), how could she possibly find a husband?

"B doesn't need another husband," I said. "She needs an apartment."

Shortly after this, B abruptly stopped holding my hand on the streets of New York or walking with her arm linked through mine.

"All over Europe, women walk arm in arm or hold hands," I said to Veronika when I learned that she was the source of B's change of heart. "It's only in America that people think it's strange. My father used to kiss his friends the way Russians always do, and people here thought that was strange too."

"If you knew that," Veronika said, "why did you let B make a fool of herself in public? This isn't Russia. This is America."

That night, I asked B whether or not she thought we should be able to say everything to each other, just the way Americans say everything to their soul doctors.

"Of course not," she snapped. "No one should ever say everything to anyone."

America! It was supposed to be the source of B's salvation. Instead (at least in retrospect), it was like being buried alive. Now, back in Russia, her face grows paler every day, her irrationality erupting fast and furious. She sees a dark and malevolent intent behind everything I say. Who knows? Maybe even I am CIA!

B's eyes are the eyes of a trapped animal. She is home, but home doesn't exist anymore. It has vanished, along with everything else belonging to a recognizable past. The Chicago Boys, economic guns blazing, have ridden into Moscow. The grand experiment in shock therapy has begun, but for now at least, it is all shock and no therapy. All is well in the realm of macroeconomic theory, but what about the realm of meat and milk and potatoes? The rouble is plunging into darkness, dragging the entire nation down with it. In comparison with this, the breakup of the Soviet Union is merely conceptual. Most people are too tired of looking at the price of cabbage and having to tell their children "no" to chocolate and ice cream, even to think about it.

There is nothing made of silver or gold to be found anywhere. Every silver spoon or tray in town has already been snatched up. Overnight, currency has become worthless. A lifetime of savings is reduced to fistfuls of paper. Veronika says that in America a tin of beluga caviar costs six hundred dollars. In Russia now, the price is exactly the same. And anyone lucky enough to have six hundred dollars is buying it. Why? Because there is nothing else to buy. So why not eat caviar instead of cabbage?

"Did you get some?" I ask.

"Of course not," she says. "I don't have six hundred dollars."

So what is to be done? And who is to blame?

I turn around for a peek at who's behind me, but no one is there. So of course it must be me. Me. The American. America.

"You bought me," B says. "And now you've got me on a short leash."

"That's not true," I say. "You were happy while you were in America."

"I was never happy," she says. "You just thought I was, because it was what you wanted to think. It had nothing to do with me. All along, I just wanted to come home."

"I don't know what to do about B," I say to Veronika. "She sleeps all of the time and wakes up in a fury. I think she's going to pieces. The empire collapsed, and she's going down along with it."

"You and your empires," she says. "The trouble is that you don't understand Russian women. We're not like you, experimenting with our lives. We're very domestic. Home for us is the only place that's safe from the outside world. For two years now, she's been without a real home. Her dog is still at my mother's apartment. She can't have a dog with her, or even a cat. She can't have plants. Nothing grows when you don't have a home. Why do you think Russians can't emigrate? Just because of visas? No. It's because, for better or for worse—and now is worse—Russia is home. Jews can emigrate. It's in their blood. But not real Russians. Our roots are too strong."

I don't argue with her. There would be too much to say. About my mother sleeping for weeks after the emigration from Russia, waking up only long enough to be fed. About my father's family, dying in the concentration camps, unable to get out of Poland/Lithuania, the Russian/Soviet Empire, whatever the hell it was. So what am I doing here if, as she says, "it's in their blood"?

"I'm going to start looking for an apartment," I say. "One way or the other, we're going to get an apartment."

Veronika looks at me skeptically. These days B doesn't look at me at all. I'll show both of them, I think. In the end, they'll see.

n i n e

■

Band I have something in the works. In Russia, this can mean anything at all, covering the entire spectrum, from having an idea soaked in vodka to developing a realistic plan that could conceivably come to fruition sometime during the third millennium. For the most part, however, it assumes the marriage of brains and talent to bureaucracy, a marriage inevitably doomed to failure. Nonetheless, we have decided to plunge decisively into the new realities, to join the hordes streaming toward the brave new world of the joint venture. Dmitri Ivanovich is as happy as if he had fathered a child, for it is he who introduced B to Ildar and encouraged her to get involved with Orenburg shawls, which were, after all, "right up her alley." What are Orenburg shawls? I ask. She shows me. At first, all I can see are downy gray or white lace woolen shawls. Nothing to grab the attention of your average "we've already seen it all" American. Is this all Russia has to offer the West? But when I look closer I see that each shawl is unique—snowflakes, diamonds, stars, and miniature animals, knitted into patterns so delicate that they almost escape the attention of the casual eye, a glass menagerie in lace. How many months does it take someone to knit one of these? Are they, like Russia, outside of time altogether? What are they made of? Why are they so light and airy, like cobwebs shimmering after rain? Silk and cashmere, B says. "*Pookh*. The down of goats." She pulls one through a ring. "That's how you prove they're authentic."

So we go to Orenburg, a formerly closed military district near the border of Kazakhstan, set in the middle of the vast Russian steppes. In Orenburg I meet Ildar. He is Tartar, a former member of the militia, kolkhoz lawyer, and now one of Orenburg's first businessmen. His entire family is involved in shawl-making, and he is ready to start our joint venture with him as the third partner right away. I'm not. So, instead of starting a joint venture, we trade fourteen shawls for a used fax machine, and wait to hear from Ildar about how much each shawl should cost. In March, still having no news from Ildar, we decide to go back to Orenburg on our own. We spend an entire day driving through the steppes in a near blizzard in search of prize-winning shawl-makers from distant villages. The snow is so deep that nothing but the road itself is visible, between walls of snow, and the sky. I am hooked. This is the real Russia, the Russia of remote villages and vast extended families of Russians, Tartars, Kazakhs, Uzbeks, and Bashkirs, all mixed together, who have been combing and spinning and knitting the down of goats into shawls for generations. This isn't business. This is poetry.

Pushkin's story "The Captain's Daughter" takes place in Orenburg, part of it in a military fortress and part of it in a blizzard.

The driver set the horses at a gallop, but still kept glancing eastward. The horses went well. Meanwhile, the wind grew stronger and stronger every hour. The little cloud grew bigger and rose heavily, gradually enveloping the sky. Soon snow began to fall, and then suddenly came down on us in big flakes. The wind howled. The snowstorm burst upon us. In a single moment, the dark sky melted into the sea of snow. Everything was lost to sight.

"It's a bad lookout, sir," the driver shouted. "Snowstorm!" I peeped out of the chaise: darkness and whirlwind were around us. The wind howled with such ferocious expressiveness that it seemed alive: Savelyich and I were covered with snow; the horses walked on slowly and soon stopped altogether.

I can feel the wind howling in the steppes, the blinding whiteness of it all. And suddenly, out of nowhere, comes the rebel Cossack Pugachev himself, stirring up the spirit of rebellion among the peasants, disguised as a wanderer and only later appearing on his white horse to declare himself a peasant tsar and conquer the besieged Belogorsky fort twenty-five miles outside of Orenburg, where Piotr, rescued from the blizzard by Pugachev, has fallen in love with the Captain's daughter. Right here in Orenburg, in these very steppes. The Pugachev Rebellion! And the blizzard! In this very region, in these very snowstorms, among these very Bashkirs, Tartars, Kazakhs, Cossacks, and Russians.

I spend the entire night in the bliss of Pushkin's arms, and by morning I am ready for anything.

"Anything" turns out to be a thousand dollars' worth of investment in the Russian economy, representing thirty shawls of the finest cashmere hand-knit lace, making us, according to the standards set by the Russian government, substantial owners of private property. To B and to Ildar, the thousand dollars is just the beginning, outlining a vista of unlimited plenty, a future cornucopia. To me, it is the end, indicating an empty bank account. Naturally, we will have to find a way to sell the shawls. Naturally, everybody who can appreciate what they are will want them. But who are these everybodies? And where can they be found? In France, we decide. Naturally, there will be a profit. Ildar, at least, is sure of it. For that reason, he charges us exactly what he thinks we would be able to get, thereby avoiding the possibility of there being any profit at all, since he knows, just as we do, that in Russia there is no more serious crime than making a profit, that the true goal of business is to help Russia.

Thus we are launched, on our way to becoming an authentic joint venture. In Leningrad, Dmitri Ivanovich invites B and me to Dom Architektorov, the House of Architects, for Russian champagne, vodka, and caviar in splendid mahogany surroundings. Once, in what now seems the faraway and long ago, A and B and I came here for *zakuski*, a vast assortment of Russian appetizers, including caviar, smoked salmon, and sturgeon. It was like a club then, with people going from one table to another and talking with their friends. I have never been to a restaurant with B. Women don't go to restaurants without men in Russia. And in general, the habit of getting together for dinner at a restaurant hardly exists here. Why go to a restaurant when it is so much more comfortable, so much more intimate at home, where no one at the next table is inscrutably listening to your conversation or stumbling drunkenly into you? Dmitri Ivanovich is a man of importance, but he lives in a small room in a communal apartment together with his ex-wife. How can he possibly invite an American there, even if the American protests that she has nothing against communal apartments and is already used to the Russian way of life?

At Dom Architektorov, we make many toasts to peace and

friendship but none, of course, to profit. Somewhere in the back of my mind is the nagging thought that, for the second time, I am looking at a thousand dollars that could pay for half an apartment. I say nothing about this to B. There are some risks that even I am not prepared to take.

The next step is to find a lawyer, someone we can trust to dedicate himself to the gargantuan task of officially forming and registering our joint venture. Why form it officially in the first place? I ask. Because in Russia everything that isn't official is illegal. So you want to participate in a fair in Paris, to acquaint the French public with our shawls? Just walk through customs into France and engage in some form of spontaneous experimentation? But you don't have an official stamp allowing you to do this? Of course you can't. Why not? What kind of question is that? Such questions are unworthy of a responsible Soviet citizen. By the way, where is your job passport, which shows your entire life's job history? In Orenburg? What is it doing in Orenburg? Don't you know that you are always supposed to have it in your possession?

There is no point in trying to explain that B's job passport is in Orenburg because B needs to deceive the Russian government (only temporarily, of course) about being unemployed. Unemployment does not exist in Russia, and now that B is divorced, she is required by law to have an official job. Since our joint venture doesn't exist yet, she can't yet be its general manager, so, instead, as a convenience, rather than having Ildar become a partner in our joint venture, B has become the foreign manager of Ildar's company. This too is only temporary, of course, but the problem right now with this convenience is its inconvenience. Ildar has recently begun contemplating his Muslim Tartar roots, and as a result he has just gone on a hajj, a pilgrimage to Mecca. He won't be back for another month. As Russian law requires, the company director must retain your job passport as long as you're working for the company. Only he has the official company seal. And without official permission, confirmed by the company seal of your general director, you can't go anywhere or do anything, even if you are the company's foreign manager.

This is where the lawyer comes in. Because, with a lawyer and the right documents, you can do absolutely anything. You can create an officially registered joint venture, you can be your own general director and your own president and sign your own documents. You can give yourself permission to go to France. You can put your company seal on any document that strikes your fancy. (This I find particularly appealing.) And, above all, as soon as you are an officially registered joint venture, you have the official right to buy an official apartment. Partners! With all the rights and privileges and opportunities previously denied to you in this lifetime. Unless, of course, the laws change between now and the time when your joint-venture agreement is consummated. How long does this process take? Six months, the lawyer says. Six months to a year.

B says that it can be done a lot faster than that, it's just a question of money. She looks at me expectantly, but I am silent. "It won't cost much," she says. "Let me talk with him."

I quickly decide that, by the time we have to pay the lawyer, we'll have figured out a way to do it. The most obvious thing to do is sell the shawls, but we can't do that until we have an official joint venture (that would be speculation, not business—and certainly not poetry), and we can't have the joint venture if we don't pay the lawyer. One of the problems is that our lawyer keeps disappearing. He doesn't have a telephone where he can be reached, and his office migrates from one location to another. He vanishes, and then unexpectedly resurfaces in a room in one of the new districts where renovation is always in progress, and the future offices of RSV&P are always about to be opened. Other lawyers, I have heard, have bodyguards posted in front of the doors to their offices, and peepholes and secret code words for entry. No one has yet told me why.

Ivan Ilyich agrees to register our joint venture by the middle of April, time enough for us to be able to participate in the Paris Fair, which starts at the end of April and lasts for ten days. But now we can't even find him in order to get the process started.

"If he promises to have it ready by the middle of April, we'll have to wait until at least June," I say.

"Don't worry," B says. "People in the West are always worrying about nonsense. It doesn't help anything to worry."

So I try my best not to worry. Except I know things B doesn't know—that I've had to borrow money, for instance, in order to sustain the illusion that I'm not some cheap capitalist bastard, that I really do care about Russia's future and can be as generous as the Russians are. My father was generous. Even when my mother was scrimping on food money, when times were tough, he was always the first to offer to pay for everyone's drinks. If we went out to a restaurant, he told me not to pay attention to the right side of the menu. My mother, who didn't want to go to a restaurant anyway because they were too expensive, said to me, "Be reasonable." I had to choose between them. Since I loved my father, I was extravagant in my choice; since I understood my mother, I went to the bathroom in the middle of the meal and threw up. I want to be like my father. I just don't want to suffer the consequences.

It is the beginning of April when Ivan Ilyich finally calls. He is in a hurry and invites us to meet him at noon at a faraway location. Of course we go. As soon as we sit down, he says, "There are only two of you, so this should be quite simple. First of all, what percentage of the joint venture would you like to have?"

The question is directed at me. It is a question I have never thought about. B's impassive face offers no enlightenment. Ivan Ilyich, apparently surprised at my hesitation, is looking intently at me.

"Fifty percent," I finally say. "Shouldn't it be fifty-fifty?"

His eyes shift over to B and then back to me. "Are you sure you're satisfied with fifty percent? Foreigners usually want a controlling interest. Fifty-one percent minimum."

I'm waiting for B to say something, but she doesn't. You could start a fire, though, with what's hovering in the air.

"I'm not doing this for myself," I say. "It's mostly to help B. So fifty percent seems only fair."

Until now, Ivan Ilyich's face has expressed fundamental detachment about the proceedings, but now his pale eyes seem to emerge from their slumber, awakening with a jolt. Anyone who claims to be doing something in order to help someone else is probably lying. I must have something up my sleeve. The only question is what.

I contemplate the options. Obviously I can't tell him that I'm sure we're never going to make anything on this joint venture anyway, so it doesn't matter what percentage I get. Fifty-one percent of nothing is still nothing. The apartment is the issue, I'm tempted to say. And getting over the collapse of the Soviet Union. And B's having the chance to go to France. In America, they say that you should always tell your lawyer the truth, no matter how terrible it is. But this truth isn't terrible, it's just absurd. Maybe I should just say 60 or 70 percent.

He sucks at the tip of his thin beard thoughtfully. Then he smiles. "All right," he says. "Fifty-fifty it is. Now, what about your initial investment? Twenty-five thousand roubles is the minimum requirement for a rouble bank account, which has to be opened in the company's name."

"We don't have twenty-five thousand roubles," I say.

"What do you have?"

"Nothing. We have shawls."

"Shawls!" he says. "Just shawls!"

"Thirty shawls," I say. "Of the best possible quality. An excellent investment. We could show them to you if you'd like."

He stands up. "All right, then. In that case, we'll have to figure out something else. I'll be in touch with you shortly."

"Do you have a card?" I ask.

"Not at the moment," he says. "But I should have one soon. As soon as we get settled in our new location."

"I see," I say.

"Would you like to give me yours?" he says.

"I don't have one either," I say. "I never have. You see, I'm really a writer. I wouldn't know what to say about myself in a card."

He is already escorting us to the door. "You'll need a card for your joint venture," he says. "You can't be a joint venture without a card. Think about a name for yourselves. You'll need it in order to register your company. You'll also need a company stamp."

"We've already decided on a name," I say. "It's going to be Skaska."

"Skaska," he says. "That's a fine name. Everyone loves a fairy tale."

"Yes," I say. "Especially the ones that come true."

What makes life in Russia so interesting is its unpredictability.

What makes life in Russia so impossible is its unpredictability.

Nothing ever changes in Russia.

Everything is arbitrary.

If Russia was America, all of this would be a contradiction in terms. But since this is Russia, there is no such thing as a contradiction in terms.

Ildar is back from Mecca. He says that the solution to all of our problems is for us to have a sponsor, and that he knows someone in Orenburg who would be interested in sponsoring us. His friend has a holding company, and the money we need in order to participate in the Paris Fair (two thousand dollars, payable in advance) would be nothing for him. He is an orphan from Kazakhstan, a former Komsomolets who grew up in the Party, knows the rules inside out, and knows exactly how to get around them. With his support, all of the obstacles standing in the way of our participation in the Paris Fair will simply vanish. I am by nature suspicious of situations in which obstacles simply vanish, preferring to overcome them on my own steam. But what if these obstacles keep multiplying at a rate far beyond the possibilities for overcoming them?

We have grown accustomed to the etceteras of Russian bureaucracy; we are now being introduced to the etceteras of French bureaucracy. But when the French say *"Je suis désolé, mais malheureusement je ne peux pas vous aider,"* they really mean no. When Russians say no in the most emphatic terms, it just means that you have to figure out the right way to get around them. It is commonly assumed that this means a bribe. But that is not always the case. Tears, or other distressing evidence that you are at the end of your rope (if you really are—false emotion doesn't wash in Russia), can be just as effective if the person in charge remembers being at the end of his or her rope and therefore recognizes in you a fellow sufferer.

The Paris Fair has sent us an application for participation in the fair by regular mail. As could be expected, we haven't received it, and B has been told by the French consulate that in order to get a visa to France she needs to have a receipt from the fair showing that we have made the required down payment on a booth. This can be accomplished if we transfer the funds from our bank to theirs, a transaction they consider simple. They don't seem to know that in Russia bank transfers don't exist, even if we did have the money to transfer, which we don't, because roubles are nontransferable and hard currency theoretically doesn't exist, at least not in the hot little hands of people like ourselves. And even if we could make the down payment, what if it turned out that B didn't get her visa?

So we go back to Orenburg again. We stay at a hotel for the military, which Ildar and his friend arrange. His friend reclines on a couch, like an Oriental pasha dressed in an Armani suit. Unfortunately, he says, right now he will be unable to sponsor us, because the Central Bank has frozen his hard-currency bank account. In fact, they have frozen everyone's hard-currency bank account. It is impossible to get any money right now at all. Soon this will all be resolved, but obviously not in time for the Paris Fair. Since this is Russia, such things are to be expected, though of course neither he nor anyone else expected it. He invites us to lunch at a little restaurant owned by a Tartar family, who are lavishly hospitable and insist on our eating there every day until we leave. We do. The proprietess's grandchildren climb into our laps and show us their toys, which are brand-new and Western. They show us their apartment, which is spacious and newly renovated. We admire everything, though it seems to me that there are too many toys for normal children. They embrace us often, and insist that we must come back to Orenburg. They are a lovely family. After our last meal, Luisa, the proprietess, takes me aside for a private little talk. Would I be interested in buying some mercury? she asks in a warmly generous voice.

"Mercury!" I say, astonished and ashamed to confess that I don't know exactly what mercury is, except that it's in thermometers, but I have a feeling that transporting it, for whatever reasons, is either dangerous or illegal.

"It's only a small quantity," she says. "Just a kilo. You can have it for very little money."

"Thank you," I say. "But I think I'll have to pass on this one."

She squeezes my arm. "That's all right," she says. "But let's just keep it between us." She smiles, showing many gold teeth. "Now, promise us you'll come back to Orenburg. You must always think of our home as your home."

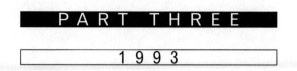

PART THREE

1993

■

t e n

■

I t is one-thirty in the morning. Sonia Morozova's thirty-eighth-birthday party is ending. The cloth-covered table, which has been extended to its full length, fills up the entire living room–bedroom–dining room, so that guests had to squeeze their way around it in order to sit down. The teenagers all left hours ago, and there is almost nothing on the table now except for two birthday cakes, a dozen half-empty bowls of *zakuski*— all kinds of salads, sausage, and pickled mushrooms—empty dishes of caviar with a few grains still clinging to the edge of the dish, platters of tongue, and quantities of vodka, champagne, and American cherry and coffee liqueurs, the latest rage in Leningrad, selling at Yeliseyev's for the price of a normal month's salary. Still, a birthday is a birthday, no matter what it costs. Though the street kiosks—full of exotic Western drinks, Marlboros, Snickers, a new brand of Russian cigarettes called Real (which come in a pack draped with an American flag), and Russian vodka and champagne—are cheaper, it's not safe to buy alcohol in the kiosks. God only knows what they might put in the bottles.

Maxim, Sonia's sixth husband, younger than she by seven years, heats water for tea in the samovar. Tamara, who keeps asking, "Where am I going to sleep tonight?" and has made several futile attempts to leave the party before Leningrad's metro stopped running, finally falls asleep in a chair, her head cushioned by a pillow Maxim puts under it. Valery Nakhamkin picks up a small bronze statue of an angel from the shiny wall unit behind his chair and begins to examine it. Sonia turns up the hi-fi again, and dances alone in the tiny space between the table and chair in which Tamara is sleeping. Then she goes into the bathroom with Polina to help her try to remove a stain from the silk blouse Sonia brought back from her last trip to China. If it was polyester, Sonia says, you could forget about getting it clean. With silk, real silk, you just have to use soap and water and rub the area until it's dry. Afterward, you won't even notice the difference.

Valery turns the angel upside down and reads what is written on the bottom: "1892, Victor Feodorovich Kuzmin." Svetlana, sitting beside him, is picking at the birthday cake. He strokes her back with his free hand, and she pushes him away. Now that he is unemployed, he touches her every minute and almost never leaves the house, following her around like a dog. It drives her crazy.

"This is an antique," he says.

Svetlana reaches for it to see for herself. "It says 1892," she says, confirming Vasya's opinion.

"It can't be," Polina says. "It's a mistake. They didn't make angels like that then."

"The bronze isn't really heavy enough," Valery says. "Feel it."

"What's wrong with the bronze?" Natasha says. "It feels heavy enough to me. And the inscription is real. Sonia could sell it to the Americans and buy a Mercedes-Benz with the money. The Americans will buy anything. They're crazy for antiques."

"Why should I sell it?" Sonia says. "It belonged to my grand-mother. It's a remembrance of her."

"Anyway," Marina says, "they have a lot of antiques in America. The stores are full of them. I thought that they came here for ours because they didn't have any of their own, that we were the only country that had kept our antiques. I thought that everything in America was new. But it's not true. They probably have a lot of bronze angels. I didn't see any there, but I'm sure they have them."

"Not like ours," Svetlana says. "What's ours is ours. I think the Americans just want to have them, that's all, not for any rea-son, just because they're ours, not theirs."

"It's more expensive to buy one of those angels here than it would be in New York," Marina says. "The same with porcelain dogs. I can't find anything here now for less than thirty thousand roubles. There, you can find them for a dollar sometimes at flea markets. Really, they have a lot. You should see how big our col-lection is now."

Valery says that if the angel were his he would sell it to pay for repairing his car, which will cost half a million roubles to fix, af-ter he turned it over on a sharp curve while hunting last week in Karelia. He tells how the accident happened, but not where the money will come from for the repairs. Everyone knows bet-ter than to ask. Then the others tell how their accidents hap-pened, who stupidly pulled out in front of them, who took a left-hand turn without signaling, which old man wasn't looking where he was going and smashed into a brand-new Volvo, de-stroying his own Zhiguli totally. The one accident no one talks about is Sasha Poliakov's. It is too fresh in their minds. Besides, what's the use of talking about it when he's dead, the first one in their group to die.

Maxim used to work as a driver at Kirovsky Zavod, Leningrad's biggest defense factory, where they also made tractors. But the times changed all that. Now he works as a chauffeur for a new cooperative, which deals in "acquired" construction materials, building houses for new millionaires. Marina's husband, Anatoly, also recently added driving to his usual job, though he isn't a professional like Maxim. Anatoly makes extra money picking up food for the Pribaltiskaya hotel where he has been a chef ever since it opened about ten years ago, and now works a "new shift," one week on, one week off. He and Marina always had plenty of good food, especially meat, the pick of the hotel's stock. They still do; only now they have to pay for it.

They all agree that there are no professional drivers on the road anymore; even the taxi drivers aren't professionals, they are only professional when it comes to forcing the bus that used to stop at the International Building at Pulkovo II Airport not to pick up any passengers. The bus drivers don't dare to go there anymore. The taxi drivers are having a field day, charging fifty thousand roubles to come into the center city, and no driver who brings a passenger to the airport is willing to wait there more than five minutes and have his windshield smashed. The control is complete now.

Cars. Driving. Who is a better driver, a woman or a man? Why is Tolya such a nervous driver? When should studded tires come off the car? Does anyone have a connection for a new windshield?

Valery swallows more vodka, and kisses Svetlana's shoulder. It is after 2 a.m. Tamara wakes up. Everyone talks about leaving, but no one does. Tamara says that now she will have to hitch a ride with an off-duty tram that is on its way home. Fifty roubles, and the driver will take you anywhere that his tram can go. It's like hijacking.

Tamara goes for her coat in the bedroom, where Sonia's parents are asleep in the bed with the two boys. Everyone gets dressed and goes out on the street. Snow has started to fall heavily. That holy stillness of fresh snow falling on the birch grove in the middle of the housing complex of new-old apartments in the new district at the end of the metro line, the end of the tramway line, the end of the world, where the city abruptly turns into the country. Everyone clusters around the car, ungloved hands brushing off the snow. Marina says that she will walk home; it's only fifteen minutes down Prospekt Engelsa and another five or so down Lunacharskovo. "Don't be crazy. Get in the car. I'll drive," Valery says.

"You can't. They'll arrest you. You've been drinking."

"I'm a professional driver," Valery says. "There are very few professional drivers, but I'm one of them. If I have a job or I don't have a job, I'm still a professional driver."

Marina doesn't care if he's professional or not. Six years ago, she lost her unborn baby in a car accident. She was in Kiev during the explosion at Chernobyl, and afterward the ultrasound showed that the baby already had a full head of hair inside the womb, and looked more like a six-month-old child than an unborn infant. It was fate, *sudba*, that that baby wasn't born. It wasn't meant to come into this world. Still, she isn't ever taking any chances again, no matter how professional Valery is.

But it isn't safe to walk the streets anymore, Svetlana protests. It's not like it used to be, when you could walk anywhere anytime. The past is past and all that. Marina capitulates. They all pile into the car, sitting on each other's laps. Valery starts it up, driving along the inner-courtyard road with the smoothness, speed, and grace of a vicuña. Out on the street, he skates with it, knowing just when to brake and glide and slide. The streets of the city are almost deserted. He isn't driving, he's performing. He never in all his life imagined that at the age of forty he would be unemployed in Russia, where no one had ever been unemployed in the last seventy years. They all went to high school together, and then to technical colleges. They had good training. They were educated. They waited on the right lists for their cars, for their cooperative apartments, for the lottery that gave them a choice of three. Now their numbers were supposed to be coming up. Just now. He was part of the wave that was ready to crest, to make its mark on the country, defining its place in history. Everyone knew it. Sasha had been his best friend, a metro driver. The metro workers' vacation sanitarium in Z—sk had always been one of the best. The metro workers were the best. To be a metro worker was to be on top of the world (in a manner of speaking). He remembered when everyone was proud to be a driver in the "workers' paradise." Some paradise. That was what it had all come to, building socialism. It had come finally to nothing.

Marina leans her head back against the upholstery. "A year ago," she says, "I would have told you that nothing in the world could ever make me leave Russia. Nothing. Now I'm ready to go tomorrow. America, Poland, I don't care where. Anything to get out of here. Can you believe that you heard me say that? I can't. There will be no end to it, though. Things will just keep on getting worse. What kind of future will Katya have? I don't want my daughter to live like this. I don't want anyone to live like this.

"'Is your mother working?' people ask Katya. How is she supposed to answer? We never talk about it. Of course, it's obvious when I come home after being away for three days that I must have been somewhere. But we all pretend that it hasn't happened, or that there was some normal reason, that there's nothing odd about it. But I'm getting ill from traveling under those conditions, and my nerves are ruined, from fear, I suppose, and disgust. I could never imagine myself feeling terrified to pass a border guard in the Baltics—three borders, in fact—all of them small and insignificant, and their border guards so scornful of us for being Russian instead of Latvian or Estonian or Lithuanian. They don't care what you bring into or out of Russia; they just want their cut. They walk up and down through the cars of the train with their palms outstretched, not looking at anyone, just waiting for the money to be put in their hands. The trains are packed with people, ants, trudging back and forth from one bazaar to another, buying and selling. Twenty-four hours to get there, twenty-four hours back. Half a day in a cold waiting room. Conditions there are worse than they are here. No meat, no hot water, no gas. And then I spend a few hours in the bazaar with horrible people. You feel like you're selling your body, not just buying and selling clothes to put on it.

"The most terrible thing in life is to be ashamed of your work. I don't want people to know what I'm doing. To me, it's dirty. I do it, but I'm not proud of it.

"In America, they aren't ashamed. They talk about it openly. There's only one important question for them: did you make a profit? If you did, that's good. If you didn't, it's bad. Even artists aren't ashamed to be businessmen. Physicists drive taxis. If I make a profit, I feel that maybe it explains or excuses a little bit what I did, that people have to understand that it wasn't what I wanted to do, but what I had to do. All our lives, we called that speculation. And to me, it still is. I can't change that. And I can't believe that I'm the one who is doing it, that all around me there's this terrible heavy feeling, because we're all living completely against our principles. What kind of life can we build that way?

"Sometimes I think about what it was like to do facials and massages for clients who came to the apartment—for people like us, normal people—when I still made all of my own creams from herbs and spermatozoa and lanolin and vitamins. The Japanese are buying all of the spermacete now. I couldn't touch it.

And who can afford facials and massages? The ones who can, I wouldn't trust to have them come into my house; they're too dangerous. The other day Tatiana Grigorievna was telling me that some friends were listening to an old Brezhnev speech on TV. They were laughing at him, but then, all of a sudden, she started to cry, and others did too. I don't want to go back. But what are we going forward to? Look at us now, at what we've become. Last week, Dmitri brought home a gun. Don't anyone tell him I told you. He wants to teach me to use it. He says I need it for protection. From whom? For what? Is this our future?"

Valery says nothing. He knows the whole story already. Svetlana goes on the trips with Marina too, buying and selling the same way she does, making money, like *farzofshiki*, people whom, in the past, they didn't want to know in public. But there's nothing to be done about it. Life is life. People have to live.

He drives into the courtyard of Marina's apartment complex, looking out at the grove of birch trees at the center of the complex. Suddenly he gets an urge, and starts zigzagging through the grove, and around the day-care center in the middle of the complex's park, driving off the pavement altogether. Everyone in the car is quiet, their attention instantly refocused on him. He spins the car forward, then spins it back, finally gliding neatly into the space in front of Marina's apartment as if he has just concluded a pirouette. Now, that was professional. They all sit in the car, applauding him silently for rescuing the moment, as if they were at the ballet, watching Odette undulate her dying-swan wings for the very last time.

e l e v e n

■

am standing in front of the Kirov Theater, looking at the opera-and-ballet repertory for the month of June and planning my strategy for acquiring tickets to the performance given every June by the graduating classes of the Vaganov Ballet School, the Kirov's grooming ground for its future dancers, when a mousy-looking young man comes up to me and says, "I've seen you before, haven't I? This isn't the first time you've come to the theater, is it?"

"No, it isn't," I say, thinking that this skinny man with his long head that seems to extend straight up from his shoulders like a weasel's does seem vaguely familiar. "I've been here before." I've learned from experience here that it is best to say as little as possible in such situations, so I don't add that the husband of a friend of mine used to play in the orchestra, and that I came here with her, or else with B.

He snaps his fingers. "I do remember you," he says. "Weren't you in the lobby once, buying tickets? Let's see, it must have been a month or so ago if I remember correctly."

The key phrase in this is "in the lobby . . . buying tickets." Of course, the box office is in the lobby, and it should normally be assumed that this is where one would buy tickets, but since this is Russia, what should normally be assumed should never be assumed.

"Yes," I say.

"Do you want tickets for tonight?" he asks amiably. "No," I say, and then make the mistake of adding, "I want tickets for the Vaganov Ballet School performance on June fifteenth. Today is May twenty-fourth. So they should go on sale tomorrow, shouldn't they?"

The amiability dims. He looks at me impassively and doesn't answer. "I mean the ones that are sold twenty days in advance," I add, leaping rashly into the void. "I guess I should be here at about ten in the morning, is that right?"

His expression doesn't change. Only his muscles tighten ever so slightly. "You don't need to come in the morning," he says. "No reason to stand in line, is there? I can get tickets for you. How many do you need?"

Now I recall exactly who he is, this Mafia lackey, and I remember his boss, too. It was about a month ago, as he says. I was trying to figure out how to buy a ticket without B and her connections, watching the little old ladies on pensions stand in line to buy tickets and then resell them immediately to a tall young man with a mustache who was standing on the sidelines. They clustered around him like flocks of birds, turning over their prized purchases, and collecting their payments from him, a dollar or two on every transaction. You're only allowed to buy two tickets at a time, so it took a lot of little old ladies to buy up the orchestra and the *bel étage* and the *baignoire*.

He was a good-looking guy, this Mafia Don. Not only that,

but he seemed friendly and solicitous of his flock, an almost heroic figure, the kind who might appear in a Socialist Realist painting of a good Soviet worker. For a moment, I imagined him as Robin Hood, helping pensioners to make an extra dollar and then offering the tickets to tourists just before the performance for what they would pay in the West anyway.

But I, on my teacher's salary in roubles, couldn't afford his hard-currency prices—almost one hundred times the official prices. So I was willing to stand in line for an hour or two in order to get tickets twenty days ahead of time and keep them. But the line never seemed to move, or kept expanding inexplicably in front of me, until I realized that I was never going to succeed in buying any tickets. I said as much to the little old lady in front of me. There was fear in her eyes as they darted in his direction, and from the furtive way she offered to get a ticket for me, and insisted on meeting me outside in an hour, I knew he wasn't Robin Hood. "Don't look at me now," she whispered, her voice trembling ever so slightly. In the end, I didn't buy her tickets anyway; she was offering them at a price not much lower than his, which was still more than I could afford, so I left without any tickets at all. By then, I was a marked woman, a sitting duck. Yet some perverse instinct made me push my luck even further, so I went right up to the Don and said, "Can I talk to you for a minute?"

"I have tickets," he answered. "Which performance are you looking for?"

"I'm not looking for tickets," I said. "I can't afford your prices. I'm just interested in you. You're a speculator, but you seem to be helping all of these old ladies, so you can't be that bad."

"I'm a businessman," he said.

"What does it mean to you, being a businessman?"

"Buying cheap and selling expensive. That's what businessmen do."

"Not exactly. Most businessmen try to build something, or at least many of them do."

"That's just fancy language. In the end, it's all the same. Buy cheap. Sell expensive. So how can I help you?"

"I told you I can't afford your prices. I'm a writer."

"What nationality are you?"

"American."

"I don't sell inexpensive tickets to Americans. If you were Russian, maybe. But not Americans."

"I can't argue with that. You're probably right. It just happens that I don't have a lot of money. I teach at the university here, and my salary is very small. I get paid in roubles."

"Do you have money in America?"

"Yes, but not a lot."

"So don't talk to me about small salaries. Why are you working here for a small salary?"

"Because I like the work. I like my students. And I feel that I'm doing something that makes a difference."

"Do you like it here in Russia?"

"Yes," I said. "My parents are Russian. Life is difficult here, sure, but . . ."

"Don't worry," he said. "Things are going to get much worse, and then you'll like it even more. So what do you want? Are you married?"

"No."

"It's not so nice sleeping alone, is it? You're a good-looking woman."

"I'm not looking for someone to sleep with."

"Why not? You should be."

"Never mind. I was just interested in talking with you."

He looked at me contemptuously. "I hope you continue to enjoy working for a lousy salary," he said. "But I have to get back to work. And I'll never sell you any tickets. Even if you had the money, I wouldn't sell you a ticket. Because I don't want to. Do you understand? Your type . . ." He didn't finish his sentence, but it was clear that he would just as soon spit in my face. "Is the interview over?"

"Well, I enjoyed talking with you," I said brightly, though inwardly I was trembling.

But here I am, a month later, back at the theater, and this time the Don's mousy little helper remembers me and has latched on to me. Even though that is starting to make me nervous, I'm not ready to give up.

"I need four tickets," I say in answer to his question, not adding that three of them are gifts for friends. "But I can come here tomorrow morning and buy them myself. I have time tomorrow morning."

"No reason to stand in line," he repeats. "I'll get them for you." And then, "You can get them from me whenever you have time. I'm here every day until one o'clock. That way you can relax and be sure you'll have them."

I feign naïveté. "It's really nice of you to offer. If I'm not able to get here in time tomorrow, I'd be happy to have you get them for me. Will they be expensive?"

"Not very," he says. "Middle-price. Don't worry about it. I'll take care of you. I'm glad to help out."

"Thanks," I say.

"I just do it for a little bit of extra money," he says in a well-oiled tone. "I used to be a musician myself. Not professional or anything. Just play the violin. But these days everyone has to do something extra, if you know what I mean. It's a bad situation now. I'm sure you understand." He looks at me pointedly. "You're a teacher," he says. "Maybe you can help me. My daughter needs some help with English, history, literature. She wants to go to the university, if you understand what I'm saying. You teach at the university. You might be able to help her. Of course, you know people at the university. She's just about ready to enter, if you understand. . . ."

"I can ask if anyone is available to do tutoring," I say, pretending not to understand him—pretending to be just your average naïve American who thinks that words mean what they're supposed to mean. "I'd be glad to ask."

"Stop by whenever you get a chance tomorrow or the next day," he says. "I'll save the tickets for you. You don't ever have to worry about getting tickets."

"Thanks again," I say. "I really appreciate it." I walk away, heading for home, but after I've gone a block, change my mind and instead of taking my usual route, go back an entirely different way.

The next morning, I am at the theater at nine-thirty. Only a few people are milling around in front, but among them I recognize some familiar faces—the same people who were standing in line the last time I came. The doors don't open until ten, and there doesn't seem to be any formal line. Casually, I position myself as close as possible to the big wooden front doors, assuming that a real line will form later inside the theater.

A tiny old lady, who looks to be in her late eighties, is standing directly in front of the double doors, and just as one of them opens, she suddenly clutches the handles and sinks to the ground, her arms outstretched, straining, seemingly to keep them from closing, even though it is too early for them to be open. I am astonished at her desperation. She looks like a 1960s demonstrator trying to force her way into the Pentagon, passively resisting the policeman threatening to drag her away from her appointed post. Her face is pale, distorted, feeble. The others cluster behind her, watching in silence. The doorman is watching her also, impassively. She remains in this position for several minutes, sinking farther down toward the ground, and gradually the awareness seems to grow in the crowd that she may be ill, rather than trying to force her way into the theater. In fact, she may have collapsed. The doorman is pushed aside. The crowd throngs in.

"She needs a doctor," someone shouts, "get a doctor!" But then the mob sweeps past her into the lobby, almost trampling her underfoot. The crowd is intent upon its task, and I, swept in with them, become a part of them, walking as fast as I can toward the box-office window.

As the line starts to form, I am third, and triumphant. But little by little, I find myself being squeezed against the lobby wall, my position being usurped. "Dyadya Petya," one old lady without teeth chirps, pushing her way past me and joining an old man with thick glasses who is standing in front of me, wearing a baggy, threadbare gray coat. "We're together," she says to me, as a group of old people rushes toward me, some of them hobbling, some of them toothless, all eager to join this "Dyadya Petya," with his thin, wispy hair flying wildly around his head, at his place in line. Now, instead of being third in line, I am tenth, and the box office hasn't even opened yet. Gradually, the entire crowd of people who were standing in front of the theater, now supplemented by additional small groupings of old people, has gathered around me, pushing me into a corner. Finally, I grow impatient. "Wait a minute," I say. "I was third in line."

One woman pushes me. "You're not supposed to be in this line anyway," she says. "Get in line where you belong. Find your place."

"What do you mean?" I say. "I'm in my place."

"This line is only for handicapped and *blokadniks*," she says. *Blokadniks* are survivors of the Leningrad blockade during World War II. "These are ten-day tickets. You're no invalid. When this line finishes buying our tickets, then you can buy your tickets twenty days in advance, together with other normal people."

I look around, and don't see any normal people. She's lying, I'm sure of it. I decide to stand my ground, even though they've boxed me into a corner, and people are still managing to squeeze in front of me. If only I could get up to the window, I could tell the woman selling tickets that one of the tickets is for a woman who lost her leg in childhood and another really is for a *blokadnik*. I don't have proof, but it's true. Still, why should she believe me? It's worth asking anyway, though. So I wait, with a growing sense of futility, as the line forms and re-forms, going around once, twice, with the same people buying two tickets and going back to the end of the line. I can see that they do have something special with them. Red and green cards, supplied by the government for invalids and survivors, and the woman in the box office is registering each of them as they buy the tickets. I still haven't moved, though. It's like being in a dream—I'm unable to move, but feel as if I should be able, I must be, how is it possible that I'm not?

I look behind me, toward the lobby. The little old lady who was clutching the doors is sitting on a velvet bench, being attended to by a doctor, and not far away from her, my pal the weasel is standing there, staring at me.

I start to feel nervous. The line is becoming more and more aggressive, more and more hostile.

"Who is she anyway?" one woman asks.

"A foreigner," says another woman.

"So let her buy tickets for dollars. What is she doing in this line anyway?"

"We've been here since eleven o'clock last night," another woman shouts at me. "We've been waiting all night, and you think that just because you got in line first you can buy tickets. Look at us. We're invalids. This line is only for invalids."

"There is no line," I say. "I can see what kind of line it is. I see what's going on here."

"Which performance are you looking for? Tonight's?"

"No, the fifteenth."

"They're not even selling the fifteenth now, they're selling the fifth."

This time I really shove my way forward. "Is it true?" I yell at the woman in the box office. "Is it true that these tickets are for invalids and that they're for the fifth?"

"Yes," she says. "When this line is finished, we'll do the fifteenth."

"But one of the tickets I'm buying is for a woman who has an artificial leg. The other is a *blokadnik*. Can I buy tickets for them?"

She looks at me as if I am completely out of my mind.

"No," she says. "They have to come to the theater with their card ten days before the performance."

"What if I bring their cards?"

"No, they have to come in person."

"This is a wonderful regulation. Helping invalids and *blokadniks*. But how many invalids and *blokadniks* can fight their way through lines like this?"

Her face is a little bit sorrowful, a little bit disbelieving, a little bit mistrustful. What fool hasn't learned this yet? What fool believes that anything good is for anyone who deserves it?

"Just wait a little while. Believe me," she says. "Believe me, you'll get a ticket. But after I finish with the ten-day tickets. Let me finish with these tickets. When this line is finished, we'll do the twenty-day tickets. Stay right here. Don't move."

"But this line will never finish," I say. "There is no other line."

She shrugs and looks away from me.

"You have to reserve a place in the other line," one woman says. "Find out who's in front of you. Here, I'll help find her for you."

I don't trust her. In fact, I don't trust anyone anymore. But it's clear I'm not going to get a ticket this way, so what choice do I have?

She moves out of the line into the lobby, wandering among the people standing quietly there. "You're behind her," she finally says, showing me a slender young woman standing alone in the middle of the lobby.

This woman really does look like a normal person, the only one who does. "Are you really in line?" I ask. "Will you be able to get tickets?"

"Maybe," she says, and laughs. "It depends. I come once a month or so. Sometimes I do. Sometimes I don't. I'm a student at the conservatory. But you're right behind me in line. So you do have a place anyway."

I look around me, and see Robin Hood lounging near the doorway, collecting tickets. He eyes me coldly. His pal the weasel is standing near the wall, watching the line intently. I follow his eyes, and then look back at him. He smiles at me, but the smile has teeth to it, like a skeleton's. I walk over to him. "Thanks for offering to help me," I say. "But I was able to come here myself."

"You didn't need to come," he says emphatically. "I told you that you didn't need to come."

"It's a complicated system, that's for sure," I say, acting as if the form of it still eludes me, "but I guess I'm in line now. Someone found my place for me, but I still don't know how they knew where I was supposed to be."

"Roentgen," he says. "X rays. Everything here is done by Roentgen."

"Pardon me?" I say.

"I said Roentgen," he repeats, his smile turning into a grimace. He speaks very slowly now, very emphatically. "Do you understand me? Do you understand what I'm saying? There was no need for you to come. As I told you. Now do you understand?" He is emphasizing each word separately, spitting them out as if they were bullets.

I start to shake. People are killed here every day of the week for doing less than this. So what makes me so special? It occurs to me that I have never registered with the American consulate here. If something happened to me, no one would know who I was. I'm not even carrying my passport.

"I'm starting to understand," I say slowly. "Or at least I think I am. I guess I'll just wait my turn."

Then I walk away from him, toward the student from the conservatory. "Is it always like this?" I ask in a trembling voice.

"Yes," she says. "It used to be children who did the job. But now it's pensioners and invalids. Pensions are so small now that they don't have enough to live on. Before, people had no money, but they had everything. Now we talk in millions, but we have nothing. This is a way to get extra money. It's a job."

I tell her about the weasel. "Maybe I should leave," I say. "I don't want to have my arm broken."

She looks back at him and winks, then looks at me and laughs. I start to wonder whether she is his wife or his girlfriend or his sister, or maybe his accomplice. Won't I ever learn to keep my mouth shut?

"They won't do anything to you as long as you're just trying to get a ticket for yourself. If you were organizing something, getting in on their game, then you'd be in trouble. But not for this. They just want to scare you."

"Well, they succeeded."

"What did the woman in the box office say?"

"She said that I should stay where I was, that she'd get me tickets as soon as she was finished with the ten-day tickets."

"Maybe you should," she says.

I look at the sea of humanity surrounding the box office. I have to go back into that? For what? The crowd swells in my mind, edging its way into becoming an angry mob as I approach it. I've gotten this far. I can't quit now, even though I'm starting to feel a little bit hysterical. These tickets are presents, and you can't quit when it's a matter of presents. People in the West don't understand about presents, how far people will go here to get the right present for the right person. Presents are a burning issue. And these tickets are the right presents. Nothing else will do. There's something else, though, as well. Somehow this business of standing in lines has started to affect me the way it affects Russians. Lines have a life and a logic of their own. It is inconceivable to abandon a line, even if there is nothing at the end of it. To abandon a line is to abandon hope, and what would life, especially Russian life, be without hope? No. Once you start in a line, you're committed to it until the bitter end, no matter how bitter that end might be. Lines, in all of their infinite permutations, are Russia's collective obsession, her destiny. As long as there is a line, there is a future.

But now I have something else to conquer, not just a line I shouldn't be in in the first place, a line that represents private property's most sophisticated permutation, its ideal Platonic form, its ultimate aspiration. I have to conquer my fear of the weasel and his Roentgen eyes. If I can't do that, I'll never be able to survive in this land of commonplace terrors. It's too late to turn back, though my taste for the ballet, my love for this theater, for the Vaganov School, for Russia itself, all seems to be receding along with my dreams of acquiring these tickets, these glorious gifts to share with my friends, who will never know that I didn't just shell out a pile of dollars to pay for them. On the other hand, when they open the newspaper and see my dead body spread out all over the place, maybe they will know. Who can tell? I might even end up on *600 Seconds*.

I battle my way back into the place where I was before, wedged once again into a corner. "She told me to stand right here," I say to the astonished crowd. "She told me not to move."

"Fucking foreigner," someone screams. "Get her out of

here." Elbows start to jab me, crutches poke at me, an old man leers in my face, a blonde with red lips laughs raucously at me, throwing her crinolines in the air and showing off heart-shaped black panties. I am going down, sinking into the mob, suffocating. Maybe I really will die.

I start to cry. "All I want is to buy a ticket," I sob. "All I want is to watch children dance."

"What children?" the blonde says.

"The Vaganov School," I say in a trembling voice.

She looks at me disgustedly, as if I have made a poor choice.

Her crinolines deflate into a knee-length skirt, and the color of her lipstick subsides into ordinary red. Her expression is saying that I am a feeble specimen, hardly up to the Darwinian struggle for survival. You would lose, her eyes say contemptuously. You would go out with the dinosaurs.

"She told me to stay right here," I repeat. "She told me not to move."

The weasel is standing at the edge of the crowd. He has a fistful of money. He reaches over the tops of people's heads and passes it to the woman in the box office. Her hand reaches out. She takes it. "I told you," he says, looking at me compassionately. "Now do you understand what I meant by Roentgen?"

I glare at him with all the fierceness and rage I can muster. I will not give in to him.

"Let her get a ticket," the blonde says.

"Why? What for?" her neighbor says.

"Can't you see she's hysterical? Foreigners get hysterical."

"For what?" the neighbor repeats, looking at me as if I am a creature from outer space.

And, in fact, I am. This is what it means to be from the West, to have the luxury of crying over a ticket. They are invalids, they are handicapped, they are survivors of the Leningrad blockade, survivors of the demise of their country, the disappearance of the rouble, the disappearance of pensions and medicine, sur-vivors of forced relocations and communal flats, survivors of a million broken promises, a million broken dreams, survivors of the illusion that socialism, being kindhearted, could give them tickets to the Kirov. They are veterans in the war for survival. And I am just a woman from the West, who expects to get what I want.

In the end, I buy two tickets, the two I am permitted to buy, and they even let me get in line again to buy a second two. No one pushes me out of the line. I have been reduced to small change.

I leave the theater with four tickets in my hand. The woman who collapsed at the theater door is still sitting on the bench, looking wretched. I know about compassion, or at least I used to. In my life I have been a compassionate person, but all that is behind me now. I clutch the tickets in my hand. One for a *blokadnik,* one for a woman with no leg, one for my friend, and one for me. The hell with it, I think. These tickets are mine.

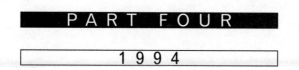

PART FOUR

1994

■

t w e l v e

■

B is leaving Leningrad for Orenburg. Caroline, our American journalist friend who has come to Russia to write about Orenburg shawls, is going with her. Their bags are already at the door of our newly purchased apartment. The taxi will be here in half an hour to take them to the airport. While Caroline and B are in Orenburg, B will show her everything, just as she did in the beginning with me. She will take her to the homes of all the shawl-makers in the villages. She will introduce her to the director of the museum and show her eighty-year-old shawls. They will stay in Tartar homes and drink extraordinary amounts of vodka and eat huge meals at every household whose threshold they cross. By the time Caroline leaves, she will know everything that it is possible to know about Orenburg shawls. Maybe she will mention B's name in the article. Maybe she will say that B is the general director of a joint Russian-American venture, and that I am its president. B carries with her our official registered seal from the city of St. Petersburg, which we still call Leningrad. Our initial listed investment capital is one fax machine, one answering machine, an Olivetti manual typewriter, and a Singer sewing machine from the seventies. No bank account, and no cash. I am B's best friend. Who else could be her partner?

Right now, however, my reputation in the villages is hanging by a thread. I never did produce an article that would prove to them that an authentic American writer had been in their midst. I also failed to buy every shawl in the region for an astronomical price, selling them for an even greater fortune to the Americans, "who will buy everything." I have tried to explain to B that anything I could possibly write about Orenburg would destroy the image of themselves people there wish to create, and that I don't know enough about knitting and stitches and the down of kashmiri goats to write something suitable for a crafts magazine. I am a different kind of writer. B knows this. Why else has she spied on my journal, and torn pages out of it that she considered dangerous, telling me that I'm not in America and can't write whatever I please? "But, B," I said, "this is 1994, not 1984." For her, it doesn't make any difference. After that, I locked everything I wrote in a bookcase in the study and held the shoulder bag with my notebooks in it close to my body whenever I got on the bus or the metro. After that, B and I ceased to trust each other.

B says, and of course she is right, that I am not serious about being a businesswoman, that devoting my energies to teaching at the Pedagogical Institute (recently rechristened as a university), for which I receive the same miserable salary as all of the other, Russian professors, having to grovel to get even that much, is a sign of my being "an *idealistka*" instead of concentrating on business that could make us some money. I prefer not to mention the Mafia Don at the Kirov, or how she used to tell me that Americans always thought about money and Russians didn't, couldn't, and never would—it was simply not in the

Russian character. When I said then that Americans thought about money because they had to, she thought it a poor excuse. The rest, of course, is history, a history that is unfolding right before my eyes in her own particular person. She has forgotten that we only started this joint venture so she would have an official job, a requirement of Soviet life, and by having an official job, be granted the right to travel, and the right to own an apartment. That too is history. You're not making enough money, her eyes now say accusingly. You're not a rich American. In response, I can't help lowering my eyes. I am ashamed, though I'm not sure for whom.

She is sitting at the table, drinking tea. I know that in the morning I cannot count on her to answer any questions. Still, I have to say something before she leaves. I am trying to figure out how to raise the question that is on my mind, and can't. I finally ask her where she will be staying in Orenburg, and she says that she doesn't know. Of course she knows, but she has decided not to tell me. B loves secrets, even when there is absolutely nothing to hide. They give a certain piquancy to otherwise ordinary information. Keeping secrets is a habit formed as a result of Soviet life. Who knew what could be used against you? Best to say nothing, especially in front of writers who don't know the difference between safety and danger. But this time I really need to know.

"Will you stay at the home of the museum director?" I ask. She shrugs and doesn't answer.

"I'm only asking in case I need to reach you," I say. "What if I have to go to the hospital?"

"What hospital? Why should you have to go to the hospital?"

I am embarrassed. "Because there is blood in my shit," I say. "I just saw it now."

"You're being hysterical because you don't want me to go," she says.

"That's not true," I say, thinking that maybe she is right. "There really is blood in my shit. I didn't flush the toilet yet. You can see for yourself."

She looks disgusted. Clearly I have transgressed all of the normal boundaries of propriety, like Lyndon Johnson showing the American public his scar. "Flush the toilet," she says. "I don't want to look at your shit. Show it to a doctor if you want to."

"Which doctor? I don't know any doctors here. Do you have a regular doctor?"

"No, I take whoever is available. Call the American consulate. That's what they're there for."

"I don't think they would agree. The American consulate basically considers that your life is your problem unless it relates to American interests. Besides, it's impossible to get through on the phone. The line is always busy."

"You're a grownup," she says. "You've been coming to Russia every year for seven years. You've been living here for three years. You speak Russian. You're not helpless. You can deal with this problem yourself. You're just trying to keep me from leaving."

"I'm not," I say. Of course I could figure out some way to take care of this by myself. But why should I have to? Just to prove that I don't need anyone? I don't need anyone. But if I don't need anyone, why does it feel so terrible not to have anyone? Why do I feel that she is abandoning me? Because she is abandoning me. Because I have a right to expect . . . This is hopeless. It will never get me anywhere.

Caroline comes into the kitchen. "It's amazing how big Russia is," she says. "When you first told me that Orenburg was three hours away from St. Petersburg, I thought you meant three hours by car or train, not by plane. I just looked at the map. By train it's really far."

I go into the bathroom, look in the toilet, and flush down the evidence, then come back into the kitchen. "The trip takes almost sixty hours from Leningrad to Orenburg. It is far," I say. "The first time we went, in 1991, we were coming from N—sk, and we had to sleep in a dormitory car on one train with a bunch of soldiers and prostitutes all the way from Chelyabinsk to Orenburg, because no compartments were available. They went up and down the aisles all night long. We were the only women in the car aside from the prostitutes."

I look B straight in the eye. See? my expression says. I can do a performance too. I can be master of myself.

"Why do you still call St. Petersburg Leningrad?" Caroline asks.

"St. Petersburg is a fantasy of the past. Leningrad is the reality of the present. Calling it St. Petersburg is like saying you still believe in Santa Claus. If they changed New York back to New Amsterdam, would you go along with it? Everyone from here still calls it Leningrad. I still call it Leningrad. And you'll see at the airport that the International Arrivals terminal has 'St. Petersburg' emblazoned at the entrance, but the national terminal still says 'Leningrad.' I think that accurately reflects the local ambivalence."

I don't know why this subject always gets me going. Russia is constantly denying its history by rejecting the most recent past. There is a Stalingrad Boulevard in Paris, but the city where the battle took place doesn't exist anymore. Poof, history instantly remade. It's impossible to figure out which street is which these days. You wander around in a city that has completely lost its identity. Dzerzhinsky was head of the KGB, so I can understand changing Dzerzhinsky Street back to its old name of Gorokhovaya. But Herzen, or Pushkin? For what? And street signs sponsored by Coca-Cola, complete with logo?

I turn back to B. "So who should I call if I need a doctor? Irina Maximovna? Or Andrei?"

"Call Andrei," she says. "He's your friend. You see, I told

you, you didn't need me to figure it out. You always think you do, but then you're fine on your own."

"Who's picking you up at the airport? Rumiya?"

"Yes."

"That means you'll stay at her house."

"I told you I don't know where I'll stay."

"I have Rumiya's number. I can call you there."

B doesn't look at me. But I see that her face is stony.

I go to the door with them when the taxi comes. B says to me, "Don't worry. Caroline isn't more important to me than you are. No one is."

"I wasn't thinking that," I say.

"Yes, you were," she says, and hugs me.

They sit for a minute, which Russians always do before going on a trip, and which I do too. And then they are gone.

She's right, I think, after I close the door. I was thinking that.

I call my friend Andrei from the dean's office. I describe my symptoms and ask about a doctor. Maybe I should have some lab tests. I keep repeating that I don't think it's anything serious. "Wait right there," Andrei says. "I'll call you back in five minutes." Ten minutes later, he is telling me to get into a taxi right away and go to Botkin Hospital. He has a friend there, a specialist, who will see me immediately. There is a dangerous form of dysentery going around the city, and it is essential to be seen quickly. "Don't worry," I say. "There's nothing to worry about. I'll come, but I don't need a taxi. I can take the metro. Tell me where I should go."

I walk from our apartment to the metro at Sennaya Ploschad, and get off at the recently opened metro stop Dostoevsky en route to meeting Andrei at Alexander Nevsky. The platform is lined on both sides with lights shaped like old-fashioned gas lamps, and benches set into niches against wrought-iron back-drops in the form of gates, the word DOSTOEVSKY in wrought-iron Cyrillic set into gilt frames above them. I sit on one of the benches near the exit. There is something I am still trying to fig-ure out. This metro station, so long delayed in its realization as the final grandiose public works project of the now-deceased Soviet Union, has just come into existence, yet it seems to blend seamlessly with Dostoevsky's universe, a universe into which I have blindly stumbled and from which I can no longer extricate myself. I watch several trains go by at three-minute intervals, in my direction and in the opposite direction. I am tempted to go back home and forget about the blood in the toilet, which has already begun to seem melodramatic. I could call Andrei and tell him that it was probably just from beets that I did or didn't eat yesterday. I walk back and forth from one side of the platform to the other, and finally board the train for Alexander Nevsky.

Five minutes later I get off and find Andrei standing at the top of the escalator. He kisses me as if I am made of glass, with a look of surprise that I appear to be normal, but the worried expression doesn't fade from his face as we walk to the hospital through a maze of buildings surrounded by broken slabs of con-crete and twisted metal, the usual Russian debris. His specialist friend asks me a lot of questions, takes my temperature—it seems that I have a low-grade fever—and tells me to register.

"It's nothing serious," I say. "I'm sure it's nothing serious."

"We just want to check," she says. "We want to be sure."

Andrei and I go outside again, and it takes us a long time to find the right place. Eventually, I am in a shabby office where a pinched-looking receptionist with one blue eye takes down my information. I have no documents with me, not even my pass-port, which is being held by the university administration. She keeps asking where my propiska is. I keep saying that I don't have one, which she insists is impossible, only giving in reluctantly after repeated questions and elaborate, though apparently unconvincing explanations on Andrei's part that I am a foreigner, that I don't have a propiska, and that there are no propiskas in America. "How can you get help from the government in the proper district if there are no propiskas?" she asks craftily. "What kind of society can it be without propiskas? Who is responsible for people?" The more Andrei explains, the more skeptical she becomes, disdaining as an incomprehensible lie the idea that people are responsible for themselves. She finally capitulates to the extent of writing "CMA," the Russian for "USA," in big red letters at the top of my file, and then she releases me, instructing us to go to what look like a series of outdoor sheds but are actually individual examining rooms, isolated from each other, I am told, as an anti-infection precaution. It seems that I am in the city's hospital for infectious diseases, popularly and contemptuously referred to as the "Botkinsky Barracks." I later learn that this hospital has one of the city's only AIDS units, and that one of the first blood tests I am given, as would be true at any hospital here, is a test for HIV.

The examining room is cold. A woman wearing a heavy coat and fur hat comes in. Her face has the same slightly worried expression as Andrei's. Would I mind staying at the hospital for two or three days? she asks. Actually, it would probably be five days, which is the minimum. They are concerned about my staying alone in B's and my new apartment, which has no telephone. I have been trying not to think about B, trying to summon up my Western education in self-sufficiency. But now they are telling me that I don't have to, and what's more, that I should not, that being ill and alone without a phone in a foreign country is abnormal. Something childish and long forgotten, the genesis of a wail, stirs in me. I capitulate instantly, with a minimal display of reluctance, choosing to interpret their decision as confirmation that there is probably nothing wrong with me that a telephone and B's presence in the apartment wouldn't cure. They plan to put me in a new wing set up especially for foreigners in anticipation of the Goodwill Games, scheduled here this summer. I will have a private room with a television. This seems excessive to me, and I say so. "No, no, it's fine," the woman in the fur hat says. "Don't worry about it." But would I mind being examined by some other doctors? "No, of course not," I say, and stretch out on the examining-room bench to wait after she leaves. Covered with my fur coat, I quickly fall asleep, and wake to the hello of a woman gynecologist who examines me thoughtfully, gently, thoroughly. I tell her about my fibroid tumor, which I know is large but not dangerous. She touches my arm sympathetically and says that she sees I am an optimist and hopes I will keep my optimism. But would I mind having a surgeon look at me? "We have very good doctors here," she adds. When she leaves the room she squeezes my hand and says, *"S'Bogom"*—"God be with you."

Soon four other doctors are in the room, and one who says, "I am a surgeon," is bending over me, pressing and tapping and listening, inching his way across my belly with infinite care. His face is intent. He touches the same places repeatedly, checking to see precisely where it hurts, seeming to listen to some wavelength well beyond the powers of his stethoscope. I can't remember ever having been examined in quite this way before, with hands that seem to possess an almost preternatural sensitivity. There is a gravity and focused attention in his face that gives me a calm security I have never before experienced with a doctor. He is obviously in no rush. The meter isn't ticking. I remember what friends have told me about Russian doctors making up for an absence of technology with their golden hands. So now I am in the care of those hands, those golden hands. For perhaps the first time in my life, I feel spiritually safe.

"I understand that you speak Russian very well," he says. "So I can speak with you in Russian."

"Not bad," I say. "Could be better."

"Well, the fibroid is a fibroid. It has been there and will be there, though it is very large. That's not what concerns me. The place where you are feeling pain is not there. It's a dangerous place on your intestine."

He confers with his colleagues, and one of them, a woman, says, "There are some nuances. We would like to do tests." It would be best to put me in a surgical ward, where there is no television, unfortunately. I would probably share a room with one other woman, if I don't mind. "No, I don't mind," I say serenely, thinking that there is something lulling about this constantly repeated inquiry, as if all the choices in the world were truly mine to make. I know already that, whatever the problem is—and I feel no inclination to ask anything more specific, nor does the surgeon, Felix Emilianovich, seem to have any inclination to tell me—I have put myself in his hands. My serenity is accompanied by a sense of *sudba*—fate again—and an uncharacteristic lack of interest in asking Western analytical questions, a state that I later decide reflects my having begun to take on the colorations of my surroundings. "Don't worry, there is no charge for any of this," the woman doctor says. "We are a free hospital." I blink. "Thank you. Thank you very much." I know that patients in Russia traditionally give their doctors cognac or chocolates rather than money. Is that all? Isn't there someone I am expected to bribe? If so, whom? And when? How, in a country so gripped by corruption, lies, and everyday cruelty and indifference, is it possible to find such pockets of intense, everyday, extraordinary decency and, yes . . . well . . . goodness? I am starting to realize that this may not turn out to be an altogether ordinary hospital stay, and that I may have to wait to understand anything at all. I have only five thousand roubles with me, about three dollars. There is little point in thinking about where it will have to go.

I am tired. I need rest. I will learn patience.

There are X rays first, and then I am taken upstairs to the surgical ward. The corridor leading to my room has yellow walls and a multitude of potted plants that look as if they have been carefully cultivated for many years. There is a hand-painted mural of a birch grove at sunset with light slanting through the branches of the trees on one wall; at the end of another corridor is a blue wall with a mural of cranes flying into the sunset. Through a half-open door I glimpse a pile of soiled, rolled-up mattresses stacked on the floor near a similar stack of pillows. The room itself has old-fashioned glass doors with what looks like a glass-enclosed display case on one side and glass panels on the other, leading to an entry with a sink in it and another set of glass doors, which open into a room where two women are lying on chipped and rusted iron bedsteads. The floor is clean in the way that Russian floors, endlessly mopped with not quite clean water, often are, but the room seems comfortable enough in a homey 1950s way, and the windows look out on a balcony and beyond to Alexander Nevsky Monastery, with its gilded domes glittering in a gray sky.

I hadn't really expected to stay. I have brought no slippers with me, no nightgown, no towel. Although coats and outdoor shoes are supposed to be exchanged for slippers at the entrance, I have somehow managed to get this far without doing so. The *sestra khoziaistva* (housekeeping sister) takes them, along with my fur hat, saying that I will get them back when I leave. In exchange, she gives me sheets and a rolled-up mattress, brand-new. I cannot help wondering whether it is the only new one they have, and where they managed to find it for me. This gesture of Russian hospitality, offered without fuss or comment, moves me, though a moment later, as the housekeeping sister disappears into the corridor with my fur coat, fur hat, and boots, I am already thinking that I may never see them again. In a few moments the *sestra* is back. "Is this natural fur?" she asks. "Yes," I say, not adding that it is fifty years old, was worn by my mother when she emigrated to America, and has an intense but purely symbolic value. "Maybe I'd better take it with me in that case," she says, and walks out the door. What if she isn't on duty tomorrow? What if my coat winds up being sold on the street? Is this the bribe I didn't have to pay? How will I survive the rest of the winter without it? If I mention this to my roommates, they will think I am paranoid and ungrateful. Better not to say anything at all. Better to worry about it alone, remembering the time when I put my luggage on a porter's cart at the train station seven years ago and all of it vanished. B spent weeks trying to locate it. How diligent she was on my behalf in those days.

A "medical sister"—a nurse—comes in and takes blood from my finger. (Russian words that involve even chance encounters emphasize collective family relationships—old women are all "grandmothers" or babushki, neighbors and family friends are referred to by children as "auntie," and female hospital workers of all kinds are "sisters.") Another takes blood from my arm, and a third gives me a shot in the rear. I have my first moment of real fear: the hell with my coat, what if these aren't disposable syringes? It wouldn't be the first time I heard of such things happening in Russia. My mind is suddenly filled with images of dirty needles, and remembrances of scathing articles about the appalling conditions found everywhere in Russian hospitals, horror stories that impel, at a minimum, a certain degree of skepticism— an attitude that a patient lying in a hospital in weakened condition is not in the best position to entertain.

How deceptive can appearances be, though? Here are young, attractive, evidently competent nurses drawing blood from my body. Here is a doctor with golden hands, and a multitude of people who have demonstrated sufficient compassion and concern that the condescension implied by my doubts would be a slap in the face. Dreading the insulted reaction, I ask about the needle anyway. The nurse looks at me coolly, neutrally. She is blonde, young, with luminous skin and eyes that convey nothing at all. She doesn't say, "What do you think we are, savages?" She just says, "Of course they are used only once," and leaves me to battle with my perceptions.

"What's your name?" asks Irina, a thin, jaundiced young woman with big dark circles under her eyes and henna-dyed hair. She and my other roommate, Sonia, a woman in her early twenties who is recovering from peritonitis, offer me tea, which they make in a glass, using a small submersible electric water-heater and *liagushki* ("frogs," the Russian slang for "teabags"). We are roommates, their faces say. We will need each other. We will need to know each other. It is best to begin properly.

Irina has been in and out of the hospital for six months. They still don't know what is wrong with her, she says. She has pain in her intestine and kidneys. That is all she knows. The circles under her eyes are clear signs of kidney problems, but doctors in Russia often don't tell patients what is wrong with them: they tell the relatives, and leave it to the relatives to decide whether or not to pass on the information. Maybe that's what's happened with Irina. But why, then, is she on the surgical ward? Sonia is going home in a day or two. She has been here for two weeks already. Both of them have a lot of food on the night-stands next to their beds—juices, fruits, home-cooked chickens and soup—brought by their families. Who will bring me food? Irina offers me some homemade jam to go with my tea. I am embarrassed to take it. I have nothing of my own to offer. The tea with jam is sweet and soothing. I will have to reconnoiter some supplies. I will have to depend on the kindness of strangers, friends, and almost-friends. I am not used to being without B. This too I will have to learn.

Food, when it comes, is passed into the room through the glass display case that opens out to the corridor. The plates are picked up from the same display case. I'm not supposed to eat anything, but I can look. Consommé. Gray meat. Rice. Nothing I would want anyway. Relatives bring real food. After dinner, I am hooked up to intravenous glucose, vitamins, and minerals. Irina doesn't say anything, but from her bed she keeps an eye on the fluid level in my IV bottle and checks that it is dripping properly. Periodically she comes over to adjust it. When she sees that it is almost empty, she goes out into the hall to look for the nurse, who is already on her way. I don't have to ask for Irina's help. She assumes the naturalness of giving it.

My surgeon, Felix Emilianovich, appears again, to listen and press, listen and press.

"Tomorrow morning we will do an ultrasound," he says. "How do you feel?"

"Not bad," I say.

"We have some concerns," he says. "We don't know yet exactly what the problem is, but we have ideas. Tomorrow I will also do an internal exam with a light, to try to see more of what is going on."

I don't ask him to tell me anything more about this procedure, but I am scared. Does this mean a colonoscopy, a sigmoidoscopy, all of the words I remember, without attaching any specific meaning to them, from my father's illness and subsequent death?

"My father died of colon cancer," I say. Felix Emilianovich winces and makes a face. "What does that have to do with it?" he says, in a way that makes the possibility seem outrageous. But I am still scared. I am sure the procedure will be painful. What are they doing to me? What do I have? I know that they haven't just dumped me here to forget about me, that they seem to be paying a lot of attention to me. Maybe it is just because I am a foreigner, or maybe they think it's cancer and I am going to die.

I think about dying and start to cry. The woman who mops the bathroom floors, limping, half toothless, looks at me and asks why I am crying. My first instinct is to lie. "I don't know," I say. Then truth asserts itself. "The doctor has said that there's some problem with my intestine, and all I can think about is my father's death."

"No tears," she says. "Here only laughter is permitted."

I try to smile but don't succeed. I finally fall asleep, thinking that everything I always considered unfinished business isn't really. I am astounded that fear, instead of coming closer, seems to be receding, replaced by a sense of reconciliation and peace. Nonetheless, during the night I feel the wings of what I recognize as the angel of death brush against my face and pass on.

In the morning, a chirping, energetic nurse in her fifties, less than five feet tall, with frizzy red hair, comes prancing into the room. "Don't be afraid, my dear little bird," she says, "don't be afraid, my darling," as she delicately administers a series of shots. One shot hurts. "The bird sipped some nectar and flew away," she says, patting me kindly on the behind, singing as she dances out the door. She is followed shortly afterward by Felix Emilianovich, who asks for a nurse to accompany me down to the ultrasound room. In a low voice he says to her, *"Bez ocheredi, pozhalusta."* This means that he doesn't want me to stand in line for the examination. But I am embarrassed at being privileged, and tell him that I don't mind waiting. Though he is startled, my refusal only intensifies his gallantry. When I come downstairs carrying the obligatory square of sheeting that I have been told is for me to lie down on, and is to accompany me to every examination, he is hovering around the door of the ultrasound room, trying to ease my passage through the system. He wants me to have no bad experiences, having decided that, as an American, I am accustomed to the best. And I can see in his eyes that he thinks that his hospital isn't good enough for me, that I must be appalled by it. People in Russia watch TV. They pay attention when someone on the TV broadcasts of *Santa Barbara* is taken to the hospital. They see what American hospitals are "really" like. What can I say to this surgeon that he will believe? No one believed me when I told them Russian chickens were good. No one believes me when I say that I like Russian sausage and jam and homemade face cream and *banya*s and babushki and trains. (I could see in their skeptical eyes that they thought I meant the special compartments for foreigners, not the trains on which they themselves travel.) How can anyone from the West like anything about Russia—backward, miserable Russia— which is never in a thousand years going to catch up with the West?

Felix Emilianovich cannot comprehend how grateful I am to him, or to the woman in the fur coat who insists on my staying, or to the gynecologist with the sympathetic eyes. Why should I be grateful for ordinary human compassion? For time that unfolds naturally, without constraints? For being able, for the time being at least, to forget about money? For being released from fear and worry? None of this is extraordinary to him. He is instead worried about my having to wait in line.

Of course the waiting room is full. An old woman sits beside me. How can I barge into line ahead of her, or ahead of the skeletal man with the huge belly? I wait with them for half an hour—with the nurse sitting next to me, apparently expecting me to take the first step—and finally move to the bench near the door, still ahead of my turn.

As soon as the doctor opens the door and sees me, he plucks me from my seat. On my way into the examining room, I try to signal my apologies to all of the others, who are still patiently waiting their turn, but it seems to me that they are hardly paying attention to me, that such privileges happen all of the time and are, of necessity, ignored. A warning light goes on in my mind: One way or another, you will pay for their humiliation. Remember Dostoevsky. It cannot be otherwise.

Inside the ultrasound room, the lights are dim. A secretary sits at a desk in a corner. The examination begins, the radiologist describing what he sees to the secretary, who transcribes by hand everything he says onto lined sheets of paper. It seems that the actual ultrasound image is not being preserved. My "file" and its interpretation are being created simultaneously. I later learn that the hospital doesn't have the necessary equipment for transposing ultrasound images onto permanent surfaces that can then be stored. All the documentation of my condition is to be transmitted verbally.

Within moments, however, I am distracted by another realization, which is that the doctor is not imaging my fibroid or my intestine or my uterus. He is instead checking all of my internal organs one by one, and describing their condition one by one. I am overcome by relief, by the dissolution of a fear I never knew I felt, the fear of doctors never really finding out what is wrong with me because they would be looking at the wrong organ, examining my liver when the problem is really with my bladder, or vice versa. My mind flashes back to previous ultrasounds I have had, all of which were "targeted." Did I have the same fear then too? Memories cluster around the question. Yes, I'm sure I did. I never trusted them to know the whole truth. But here is a radiologist painstakingly recording the state of my whole body, treating it as a whole, as a single unit susceptible in myriad unanticipated ways to invasion by unknown forces. There is no insurance company to say that the fee for the procedure is unacceptably high, or that there is no demonstrable reason for examining all of my insides. It simply seems the appropriate thing to do, or else Felix Emilianovich has asked him to do it. Is this once again a privilege? Or is it standard procedure? I brush aside the question. I am not, after all, here as an investigative reporter. I'm not observing the hospital. I'm *in* the hospital, and, rightly or wrongly, something odd is happening to me: I am beginning to feel that I have been transported to some kind of paradise beyond technology, to a universe in which I don't have to ask for what I want, but can expect my needs, even the ones I don't recognize or can't acknowledge, to be taken care of. For now, I am not just a patient with an ailment, but a person whose soul is hanging out like raw ganglia.

I am ill. They are taking care of me. What more does anyone have the right to expect?

This hospital is not a Potemkin Village. These days Americans on the loose in Russia, wandering around without KGB protection, can easily end up in the wrong places. There are a lot of right places, but the Botkinsky Barracks isn't one of them. Do doctors like Felix Emilianovich really exist in Russia, or is he only a product of my feverish imagination? I like it here. I feel secure. I am adrift somewhere in the universe, awaiting my destiny, and of the thousand and one places where I could possibly be, this one feels the safest.

In Russia, since the time of Catherine the Great, whose beloved Potemkin prepared towns and villages for her in advance, whole cities are still spruced up in anticipation of the arrival of a foreign dignitary. Why shouldn't the same be true of this hospital, or of any other door through which I accidentally wander, transforming by that simple action the nature of the experience itself, and turning it into a potential Potemkin?

On the other hand, consider this: In 1992, the great poet-bard Bulat Okudzhava—who, along with people like Vysodsky and Sakharov, had been a revered voice of conscience in the Soviet Union—required emergency heart surgery while he was visiting America. The care he received in a Santa Monica hospital was excellent. The surgeon donated his services. But then Okudzhava received a bill from the hospital for over twenty thousand dollars, a bill that, of course, he couldn't pay. When asked about this breach of American hospitality toward a famous foreigner, the hospital director calmly told reporters that a hospital was a business like any other, and that it was his job to make sure they were paid by their "customers."

The hospital in America was everything that any Russian might imagine a hospital could be: efficient, immaculate, technologically advanced. The worm in the apple was invisible. Did that make the hospital a Potemkin Village?

Not long ago, a Byelorussian architect came to America with his young daughter, and was quickly caught up in New York's social-services bureaucracy. He spoke no English and wound up in a homeless shelter. One day he jumped out the window, dragging his daughter, who tried to stop him, down with him. The daughter survived, but remained in critical condition, in a coma, for a long time. It turned out that the child had been abducted from her mother in one of the usual family wrangles over custody. The mother and grandmother rushed to the child's bedside in New York, and all were reconciled. Contributions for the child's medical care poured in. Mother and grandmother were charitably installed in New York's Regency Hotel, one of the city's finest. The child received the best possible treatment and recovered. Did their experience take place in a Potemkin Village?

Anything is possible, here or there. It doesn't matter where you are, someone is always trying to sell you an illusion.

t h i r t e e n

■

have one very special privilege. There is a telephone in the
doctors' lounge, where they also write up their reports, and
I am permitted to use it. No other telephone is available on
our floor. On my second day at the hospital, my anxiety about
my students and the fact that no one, with the exception of Andrei, knows where I am, begins to escalate. The conviction that
I have abandoned my students mushrooms in my mind. There
they are—one group in the middle of reading *The House of
Mirth,* learning that Gus Trenor has lost all of Lily Bart's money
in the stock market; another caught up in the extravagance of a
Gatsby party, with Gatsby, ever alone, ever lonely, standing and
watching his guests from the steps of his mansion; a third watching a brutal Nathanael West cockfight staged by a dwarf and a
Mexican in an arroyo on the outskirts of Hollywood; and a
fourth witnessing the murder of a window washer who, cut
loose from his scaffolding, plummets down into Times Square
while Billy Bathgate, still in his apprenticeship to Dutch Schultz,

watches it all from a Mafia escape car driving around and around the block. I have yet to explain to them that Thomas E. Dewey was a real person, as was Walter Winchell, what exactly the stock market is, or what checks are, or about bootlegging. The phrase "fixing the World Series" will be an absolute conundrum to them. As will be Lily Bart's killing herself, apparently over her inability to afford "to keep up with the Joneses." Why were appearances so important to her? Or, on the other hand, why couldn't any of Lily Bart's friends lend her the money she needed to maintain appearances and then forget about it, the way friends in Russia would? I have left five groups of students stranded on the rim of the capitalist crater, waiting for me to guide them through or around it, and from there to the imagining of paradise. How could I leave them there, without a compass and with no fixed moral center?

Felix Emilianovich says to me, "I know your type. Your job comes first no matter what. Use the telephone in the lounge. Call from there." My first call is to Svetlana Semyonovna, who also teaches at the institute and was in the dean's office when I first called Andrei. She had offered to call an acquaintance who works at the Military Hospital. She had been expecting me to call her that evening. "Where are you?" she asks. "What happened?" I can hear the astonishment in her voice when I tell her. "At the Botkinsky Barracks!" she says. "But why there? I could have gotten you into a good hospital. The Military Hospital is the best in the city. The Botkinsky Barracks is . . ." She doesn't finish her sentence. "I'm fine," I say. "Really I am. They are treating me very well." "But it's a hospital for . . ." Again the sentence is unfinished. Does she mean that it is a hospital for poor people, or that it's for AIDS patients? I protest that I don't need a Potemkin Village, that she doesn't know what this place is really like. She insists that she does. I change the subject, and ask her to let the university know that I am in the hospital and will have to cancel my classes. I ask her to give my students written assignments that I will be able to correct while I am in the hospital, if she wouldn't mind bringing them to me. She quickly answers that she is going to be very busy all week. "Anyway," she says, "you should concentrate on your health. Forget about teaching for now. I'll find out about getting you out of there."

My second call is to B's sister Veronika. I ask her if she can bring me a few things from the apartment: a nightgown, toothbrush, cup, towel. "You shouldn't bring anything into that hospital, especially clothes," she says. "You'll have to throw away everything you use there. You'll need to burn your books."

"Veronika," I say, "that's ridiculous. This is a normal hospital. It isn't a leper colony."

She is silent.

My third call is to Vera Leontievna, who helped me get my teaching job at the institute, and whom I consider a friend. The anxiety in her voice when she hears where I am is even more acute than Veronika's or Vera's. "Who did this to you?" she asks angrily. "How did you end up there?"

"A friend brought me," I say. "Because at first it seemed as if I had some kind of dysentery."

"Which friend?" she says sternly. "Who is he? Give me his telephone number."

I protest. "There is nothing wrong with this hospital," I say.

"No visitors are allowed there. Is that true?"

"It isn't true. Many people come. I am in the surgical wing."

"I see," she says, though obviously she doesn't. "You won't be able to come back to the university," she says.

"Why not?" I say, a chill coming over me.

"It's not healthy," she says. "Not for anyone."

I am horrified. Suddenly it dawns on me that I *am* in a leper colony. The word of my incarceration is going to spread like wildfire among students and faculty. Even if the university doesn't forbid me to return, my students' mothers will forbid them to come to my classes. Then I remember that when I went for X rays I wasn't wearing any underpants, because I had just washed the only pair I had. I could catch anything that way. I see my teaching job vanishing before my eyes. My friendships too. No one will come anywhere near me. Even B.

But AIDS is not an airborne disease. And this is not a contagious-disease unit. Still, it doesn't matter. Fear is contagious. That's what matters. The collective fear starts to grip me as well. I should get out of here as quickly as possible. Andrei should never have brought me. How could he have done it?

I am trembling, trapped in a tightening web of panic. This, after all, is a society that lives and breathes the poisonous air of gossip, intrigue, denunciation, a poison more dangerous than any of the infections within the walls of this hospital. Now I too have been contaminated. I walk out of the doctors' lounge in a daze, like someone newly condemned to hell. No one can save me now. Everything is lost.

Two hours later, my fear has dissolved as quickly as it crystallized. The hospital is a world unto itself, a microuniverse in which the single common denominator is suffering and its elusion. The realities of intravenous feedings, injections, diagnoses, examinations are far more powerful than who thinks what on the outside. I am sent downstairs for a barium enema and more X rays. There the X-ray technician complains to me about her miserable salary and the declining standards at the hospital, not like "before," when they had all the supplies they needed, when people were dedicated in their jobs for a lifetime, when everything was clean. Her lovely young assistant also apologizes for the conditions in the hospital, as if she herself were responsible for them. "I know that in America everything is much better," she says. When I say, "Not always," it is clear she doesn't believe me. After the examination, the X-ray technician accompanies me back upstairs in the elevator, where she recounts an additional litany of woes. "Life is so difficult now," she says, "impossible for normal people to live. On my salary, I can buy only a kilo of butter a month. Who can survive that way?" The way she says this makes me feel that she expects me to give her something, but I have on only my hospital gown and no money. I ask her where she lives. "On Nevsky Prospekt," she says. "In a communal apartment?" I ask, knowing that many apartments on Nevsky are communal. "No, independent," she says. "We privatized it. And we have a car." She starts to speak of her situation with pride, but suddenly remembers that she has just been telling me about how bad it is. She quickly backtracks. "We bought it all just in time," she says. "Before prices went up." But it is too late. She sees in my eyes that the image of herself as a downtrodden hospital worker has been ruined. Her face closes. Her eyes become narrow and spiteful. She doesn't say another word to me.

When I return to the room from X ray, Sonia's bed is empty. She has been released from the hospital, and they are wheeling in someone new, fresh from surgery and only half conscious. They roll her from the stretcher onto the bed. The surgeon arrives. I ask him if they know yet what is wrong with me. "Maybe some infection," he says vaguely. "Possibly salmonella. Or possibly . . . We really don't know for sure."

In any case, since it is Friday, my test results won't be known until Monday. There is nothing to do but wait. It is going to be a long weekend.

My new roommate, Yelena, recuperating from an appendectomy, is beautiful in the way that Russian country girls are often beautiful, a round, vigorous twenty-three-year-old with skin like fresh cream. She comes from Pushkin, on the outskirts of Leningrad, where she has lived all of her life. Her mouth is full of gold teeth, and she smiles often, struggling at every moment to get back on her feet, turning resolutely from one side to the other, trying to stand up as quickly as she can despite the pain, determined to return to normal life with a minimum of fuss. She never complains, and it is obvious that she has always relied on her own resources, that she is as strong as a horse. By the evening, I know that she works as a bookkeeper at Svetlana, formerly one of the giants of Soviet industry, which produced mostly electrical equipment for both military and civilian use, as well as a wide range of consumer products. At the factory now, there is no money to pay any of the workers. They are being given sets of factory-made dishes instead of money. It is their choice whether to go out and try to sell the dishes, a choice that everyone who doesn't need ten sets of dishes will have no difficulty making. But Lena has not been so successful at selling her supply of dishes. She doesn't want to get involved in paying off the Mafia to allow her to stand on a street corner near the train station in Pushkin, or in town, near the metro, so now she has a lot of dishes and no idea what to do with them, or even where to keep them. With or without pay, she continues to go to work, though there is almost no heat now at the factory. The indoor temperature recently registered eight degrees centigrade (forty-six degrees Fahrenheit). She couldn't keep her hands or feet warm enough to concentrate on doing any work at all. Her fingers thickened. She was unable to write or calculate figures.

"If I am pregnant," she says suddenly, "do you think they will do an abortion because of the effects on the baby of all the drugs they gave me for the operation?"

"Why?" I ask. "Do you think you're pregnant?"

"Yes. But not even two months."

Then she changes the subject. "In high school, my favorite subjects were math and physics. I applied to the institute where you teach, but my school didn't send in my grades on time, and I wasn't accepted. I have always loved physics. In my class, I always received a 'piatiorka'"—the equivalent of an A, she says. "But I guess it wasn't my destiny to be a physicist.

"Tell me something," she continues. "It is often said here that America is a country without culture. I wonder if this is true. I think every country has a culture. Maybe it is only that America's is more pragmatic. I want to know about education in America, about your daughter's education. Tell me something interesting."

I tell her everything I can think of, elaborating on details. My daughter is adopted. She was an abandoned child. I started a fish business in Maine in order to help pay for her university education. Her natural father couldn't read or write. Yes, there are people like that in America. Sometimes, when they have trouble getting a job because they can't read signs, they start taking lessons in secret, learning to read. Sometimes they start when they are fifty, or when their children are in school, or when they are grandparents, when life teaches its usual lessons. You can find such people everywhere. In Maine they can get away with it for a long time. Fishermen especially. There are no signs on the ocean.

When I am finished, Lena tells me about the house where she lives, a big old wooden house, which from her description looks like a nineteenth-century New England summer cottage on the outside, but is different on the inside. First of all, eleven families live in it. One family per room. No hot water. Their room, seven square meters, is too small for a family of three. Furniture is crammed into every available inch of space, though they don't have much: convertible bed, table, dresser. There is barely enough room for their refrigerator or television. She and her husband and son have to walk around each other carefully, in order not to bump into anything. Her parents live in the room next door. She has complained about the size of her space to Raispolcom, the former District Party Headquarters, but without result. Anyway, she says, she is well off compared with others.

Then she tells me about a picnic she and her friends had during the summer, about their mishaps along the way, their closeness, the fact that they all grew up together, what they laughed at, where they walked to, how long it took them, everything that happened. She wants to know if we go on picnics in America too, and demands to hear stories about things that happened on one of them. I tell her about a picnic to one of the islands, before I knew about Maine tides, about putting the food and the canoe on the beach and going for a walk around the island. "When we came back, the food was gone and so was the canoe. At low tide, we picked mussels and dug a pit in the sand and filled it with rocks covered with driftwood. Then we built a fire, and when it burned down, we piled seaweed on top of it and put the mussels and some lobsters, which we'd kept in an insulated box in the woods, on top of the seaweed and covered it with more seaweed and a tarp. Then we waited for the mussels and lobsters to cook and we ate them on the beach."

"What happened to the canoe?" she asks.

"Someone found it. Someone else found the paddles. We waved our hands around for a long time, and eventually a fisherman found us too. That was our picnic."

She likes this story. The gilded domes of Alexander Nevsky Monastery glow in the evening light. I have forgotten all about contagion, forgotten about fear, and we lie there all day, until two o'clock in the morning, telling stories. I know now why Russian literature is what it is. People are always telling stories in Russian novels, talking about their lives, weaving together chains of events, historical sagas, elaborated on and embellished with the kinds of details that illuminate an entire life. Russians always remember details. It's never just, "We saw the Colosseum," but, "When we were there, a man was standing outside wearing a red shirt and he was shouting something about air destroying everything, more than wars even, and . . ." That's how a Russian story goes.

Sunday is a big day for visitors. Liuba, one of the housekeepers, scrubs the floor three times in the course of the morning. My surgeon is off duty, so Lena's surgeon examines me. He speaks in English.

"We were worried that we might have to operate immediately," he says. "But now we think that it is possible to wait. Your condition is better."

"Why did you think that you would have to operate immediately?"

"Because the problem can be caused by a tumor. Here we don't tell patients this, but I know that in the West doctors feel that patients have a right to know. That is why I am telling you."

"Thank you," I say, too shocked to add anything more. I remember the comments of the first gynecologist who examined me, her encouragement of my optimism. Did she know already? What does this doctor mean when he says that they were worried before—that they aren't worried now, or that they are still worried but want to wait to be sure and then decide what to do? Do I have a tumor or not?

Visitors start to arrive. Two of my students come, bringing flowers, bananas, apples, and oranges, luxuries that cost a fortune. All of this food, which I am allowed to eat for the first time today, seems like a triumph of discovery, a feast. The students—a third-year couple who spend all of their time studying together, at the library, at his house, at her house—seem to be utterly unaffected by any fear of contagion. They are cheerful and concerned. They ask me questions about what is wrong with me, direct, uninhibited questions that I avoid answering. They tell me that my students are worried about me, that I have to think only about myself now, about my health. They offer to go to my apartment and bring me whatever I need. Do I want some books? They will tell the students what to do in my absence. They will arrange everything among themselves. They promise to return . . . if possible, every day.

Then Andrei comes, bringing an egg, an orange, a fresh cucumber, even some matzoh. It is the first day of Passover, and I was supposed to come to his family's house for a seder. He talks about the possibility of my being released from the hospital for a few hours in order to come. I am surprised. Do they do that kind of thing here? I am no longer hooked up to the IVs and I feel much better. Andrei says that people often leave the hospital for the weekend, returning on Sunday night. Anyway, this is only for a few hours. He asks the doctor, and the doctor says no, I can't go anywhere. Andrei thinks I should go anyway. No one will know that I am gone. There will be only a skeleton crew of doctors on duty. His family is eager to see me, to have me celebrate the holiday with them. His father is starting to learn Hebrew. They don't know the rituals so well, but they are trying. I could teach them many things.

"I'm sorry. I can't do it. Not if the doctor says no." Then he pulls a present out of his knapsack for me. It is an erotic novel. In the hospital, of all places! And what am I supposed to do if it has its desired effect?

Maybe he thinks that it will give me energy and renewed enthusiasm for life. I read it after he leaves, or at least I read "the good parts," many of which are laughable in their exaggeration of possibility, their attempts to extend fantasy beyond its natural frontiers. When I finish reading it, I start to feel depressed. If they operate on me, who knows what they will remove from my body? Maybe I will never have any erotic experiences again. I put the book away, feeling annoyed at Andrei.

Lena's husband is here, sitting near her bed, holding her hand. He is fifteen years older than she is, and looks at her with love in his eyes. They have been married for six years. She is his first wife. Although he works for the city sewer system, laying pipe, he has the bony, intelligent face of a teacher. He hovers over her, covering her nightstand and filling her drawers with the food he has brought for her. My other new roommate has company too. Her sister and brother and nephew sit beside her bed on little stools, talking in soft voices and opening up packages of food. Liuba mops the floor again, twice.

In the afternoon, I have another visitor. It is the woman gynecologist who first examined me. Today is her day off, and she has come just to visit, to see how I am feeling. She sits on my bed, clasping my hands, and says that she has a surprise for me. Her daughter is one of my students at the university. She has heard about my teaching, that the students love my classes. She tells me that as soon as I am well she wants to invite me to their home. They have many guests from abroad, and I am always welcome. She stays with me for half an hour, and before she leaves, writes down her name, address, and telephone number, and offers to bring me anything I need the next time she comes.

As soon as she is gone, I start to cry. So I am not a leper after all. And everything isn't over, finished, destroyed. I eat the first orange, savoring the sweetness of the juice. Life is beautiful. I am not going to die.

Veronika arrives late in the afternoon. She has brought chicken soup and news. She has finally reached B, who will be leaving

Orenburg for Moscow tomorrow and then coming back by train as soon as she can, sometime next week. At first she didn't believe that I was really in the hospital. She thought that it was all a ruse intended to make her come back to Leningrad. She was certain that I would never agree to stay in a Russian hospital, that I would fly back to America if it was anything serious. I might be a fool, an *"idealistka,"* but I'm not a complete moron. Veronika says, "She didn't come back when A was ill, she didn't come back when Father had his stroke, she didn't come when I was ill, and she won't come for you. She thinks that she will never get old, never be ill, never need help. So I'm the one who will have to take care of you, the way I've always had to take care of everyone. Anyway, after this, for me she doesn't exist anymore."

My heart slams shut. I want to shout at Veronika: "Why are you telling me such things when I'm in this condition in the hospital? It's not true that B is indifferent to everyone's fate but her own. She did come back to take care of A—not right away, but she came. True, she didn't stay very long, but . . . And eventually she came for her father as well. Maybe not exactly for him, but . . . Some people just can't deal with death. Maybe B is one of them."

Of course I know what Veronika's reply would be: "You protect her. Why do you always protect her?" B would have an answer to that. She would say, "Protecting your friends is protecting yourself. After all, you chose them." Striking enough. And convincing, in a way. But since I have no answer of my own, I say nothing. I just listen and nod and am glad when Veronika leaves. There is no room inside of me for any more bad news. I see B from far away, through the wrong end of a telescope. From a distance I wave to her, knowing that I am waving goodbye.

That evening, I go looking for the surgeon who examined me in the morning, and find him in the lounge. I want to know more about what is happening to me. He invites me to have a cup of instant coffee with him, and apologizes for the lack of sugar. While he is pouring the water, he says, "You know, I can't count how many people I have seen die here. I've never worked in a hospital where so many people died. But there is a special atmosphere here, not like any other. Maybe some special kind of person comes to work here. I don't know which kind, but not like any other."

He stands, warming his hands on his cup of coffee, and looks out the window. His face is young and vulnerable. There is something shaky, uncertain about him, something almost desperate. "It's true our hospital doesn't have such a good reputation in our city," he says. "People are afraid of us, afraid of infections. But some people like to work here, and I am one of those people. You know, we are very close to Alexander Nevsky Monastery. Often I feel that there is some connection—some spiritual connection—between this hospital and that place. I don't know if this comes from heaven or from hell, but it is a connection. I have nightmares here, like I never had before. I dreamed a few times of some burning hill of surgical waste, and when I woke up I was so glad to be alive.

"In America, people don't lie," he suddenly adds. "We have heard about this here. They tell you the truth. They say what they really think. That's why I am telling you this. I was a doctor in Afghanistan. I was against the war. So they put me in a mental hospital, even though there was nothing wrong with me. My nerves have never been so strong, but I wasn't crazy. That was when I started reading the Bible. And from that, I began to understand everything. One thing about Botkin, there is no intrigue in this hospital. The doctors don't try to destroy each other. Maybe it's because they know that they are on the outside, that they have chosen to be. Do you understand me? It's not because they have to be. They are very good doctors. It is because they want to be. Victor Lazarevich, our chief, was first in his class. He could go anywhere. But he is here. There are others like him. That is the bond between us."

"Can you tell me what is wrong with me?" I say. "I want to know."

"We're still not sure," he says. "Probably a tumor, though it could be diverticulitis or colitis. Perhaps we will have to do a CAT scan, but we don't have that equipment here. It is very expensive to do. Every day here, our most difficult decision is whether or not it is necessary to operate immediately. If you have a tumor, we can't do the operation here right away. We have to send you to another hospital or wait to do it here. Transferring you to another hospital is complicated. There is red tape. It takes time. We are still trying to decide what is the best thing to do with you. That is the truth."

My mouth suddenly feels dry. B was right. I should have gone back to America.

"I could be wrong, though," he says quickly. "I am only saying what I heard the doctors talking about. I haven't looked at your chart. I could do that if you want me to."

He goes and comes back. "Actually," he says, "it doesn't look so much like a tumor. More likely just colitis."

I don't know whether to laugh or cry. I thank him for checking my chart. "But it might have been better to check first and then tell me," I say.

His face registers his confusion. "I wanted to tell the truth," he says. "The way you do in the West. Isn't that what you do in the West? A doctor must first communicate with his patients in a human way. We are all human beings. We are all going to die. That is the truth, after all. Isn't it the truth?"

"Yes," I say. I am unable to imagine a doctor in the West doing what he has just done. Doctors in the West don't tell you about their fears, their uncertainties, their mistakes. They are too concerned about being sued.

I accept his offer of a cigarette, even though I almost never smoke. We sit there smoking in silence.

On Monday, my surgeon gives me the verdict. What I had was a *kishechnaya neprochodimost*. My intestine stopped functioning. When he first listened to my belly, there was almost no sound. The barium X ray confirmed this. When peristalsis stops, death follows soon after. How soon after? Several hours. But I am still alive. That means he saved my life.

"You have to have surgery," he says. "We have a week or two in which to do it the proper way, without complications. We can do it here if you like, but there are also alternatives. We have already called another hospital this morning. The On-cological Institute. The chief of surgery there will be in on Wednesday morning at eleven o'clock. We would like to arrange a consultation."

The Oncological Institute! So it is a tumor.

The surgeon doesn't say anything about my leaving the country for the operation. He has already understood that my decision is clear. But in the evening, the question is raised again by Nadezhda Anatolyevna, another surgeon. "We once had a French patient," she says. "She was brought in an ambulance from the Hermitage. She was a tourist. It turned out that she had meningitis. A special plane came and flew her back to France. If you want to go out of the country, we can arrange that."

"No," I say, hardly even hesitating, "I think I'm going to stay."

She asks about my insurance. Do I have any? I explain to her that I changed my insurance plan shortly before starting to live in Russia, that anyway I am afraid this would be considered a pre-existing condition, not covered by a traveler's policy. I have to explain to her all of the intricacies of American hospital insurance.

"What foxes!" she says. "We have heard about such things in America, but I didn't know if they were true. Soon it will be the same in our country. Already some hospitals take money now, and there the atmosphere is completely changed. We recently began studying the chemical formulae for drugs among ourselves. Antibiotics, for example. The older generations aren't available, and the price is higher for the new ones. But the chemical formulae are the same." She looks at me. "By the way, the Oncological Institute also isn't a free hospital."

"How much does it cost there?"

"Can you afford one hundred dollars?"

"For what?"

"For everything. There is no charge for the operation, only for the hospital stay, either ten or twenty days depending upon your condition. Medicine would be included, of course. There are different prices depending on who you are. If you are Russian, it is one hundred dollars."

"But I'm not Russian."

"For citizens of the Union of Independent States"—the former USSR—"it is two hundred fifty dollars, for foreigners seven fifty. We already asked about trying to organize it for the lowest possible price. Can you afford two fifty?"

I am stunned into a silence that she misreads.

"You don't have to pay it right away," she says.

I am embarrassed. What should I do? Explain to her what such an operation would cost in America? Surely she already knows. Or should I offer to pay more? Even if I don't have more here with me, I should be able to find a way to get it. Maybe someone could bring it from America. Transferring money here is an almost impossible thing to do. People just carry it in sack-fuls aboard the plane. Who will be coming soon?

"Don't worry about it," she says. "Money isn't something that people in hospitals should have to worry about."

I hesitate. "I wasn't really worrying. It's just that . . ." Then I decide. The best way to deal with generosity is to accept it graciously. I go over to embrace her. "Thank you," I say. "For everything."

"So two hundred fifty is all right? We'll say two fifty, and we'll find a way to say that you are a citizen of the UIS. After all, you are working here. I know what salaries are at the university."

I don't mention that I haven't received mine in months. There is no need to. I'm sure she knows. Chances are that she hasn't received hers either. That is our common bond. It may also be the reason why my operation is going to cost $250 instead of $750. Unless? My brain starts clicking again, as the shadow of that reality which perpetually flickers here behind perceived reality glimmers for an instant, then, hiding its head in shame, vanishes.

f o u r t e e n

■

On Wednesday morning, the surgeon arranges for a car to take me to the Oncological Institute at Pesochnaya, north of the city. It takes an hour and a half to get there. I leave all of my belongings at Botkin. After all, I am only going for a consultation.

As soon as I walk in the door at Pesochnaya, I recognize the difference. This is a real hospital. The doctors stride around looking important. Even the woman who mops the floors does it briskly. And it seems to me that the patients are different as well. I recognize them from all of the bureaucratic offices I have walked into and out of over the past several years. These are the people who have the power to say no to everything but disease. They carry themselves with authority. They are authority.

I feel a pang of nostalgia for Botkin. I don't belong here, I think. I don't belong in this kind of world.

I sit on a bench outside an examining room whose doors swing open and shut from time to time, with patients and doctors entering and exiting. This time I am given two squares of sheeting; the second one is to cover my head. I wait. The driver, who is carrying all of my documents from Botkin, has disappeared. One of the nurses scolded him for coming onto the surgical ward with his shoes on and sent him back downstairs to get slippers from the cloakroom, and he hasn't come back. Probably he has gone shopping for meat, or butter. The woman sitting next to me on the bench asks whom I will be seeing. "Professor Bockmann," I say.

"A saint," she says. "A great man."

She points at two greatly enlarged photographs on the wall. They are of former chiefs of the hospital. Former great men. "His picture will go right up there beside theirs," she says.

Bockmann arrives. He is short and round, with a halo of short frizzy hair, obviously Jewish. I barely have time to reflect that I thought Jews were kept out of the top jobs in top hospitals before I am whisked into an examining room where two other patients are being examined by other doctors. Bockmann and another doctor, tall and imposing, examine me. Bockmann says to the other doctor, "Shall we take her?" The other doctor nods. They will check me in right away and operate within several days. Wait a minute, I want to say. What about Felix Emilianovich? What about all of my things, which are still at Botkin? I didn't have a chance to say goodbye.

When I mention Botkin, Bockmann looks scornful. "I don't know what you were doing there in the first place. You'll get proper care here. I can assure you of that."

I am whisked out of the examining room again. Bockmann follows me. He puts his arm around my shoulder, tells me that he has relatives in America, in Colorado, that he has been to America several times for conferences, that he is an associate member of the American Medical Association.

"Don't worry," he says. "This is a serious and difficult operation, but you will be fine. Believe me, you are in good hands."

My operation is scheduled for the following Tuesday. A young Georgian doctor, Yelena Vilievna Bachidze, is the surgeon responsible for my day-to-day well-being, and will also be one of four surgeons, headed by Dr. Bockmann, operating on me. She first meets with me on a love seat in the corridor outside of the room to which I have been assigned. Inside, a woman is taking her belongings out of the night table beside the bed near the window, and piling them on the windowsill. She is going home today, she says to me, trying not to reveal that she has been evicted in order to make a place for "the American," though this is plain from the resentment in her face.

I'm no saint. I surrender to what has been offered to me, my place at the table. It would do no good to refuse anyway. The place would only be taken by someone else like myself, another privileged being.

Would I mind if she kept a few of her things in the night table? she asks. She is postoperative now, and only comes to the hospital for chemotherapy. Two other women in the room watch the scene, anticipating the outcome. Territory, after all, can be defined in inches.

"Of course not," I say. "I don't have anything with me anyway. My things are still at Botkin."

"Botkin?" she says. "You were at Botkin?"

"Yes," I say, taking momentary pleasure in the effect the information clearly has on her.

"All right," she says, "I'll take one side of the night table. You can have the other side."

But Larissa Petrovna, whose bed is closest to the door, has decided to intervene. "My night table has two shelves," she says. "Yours has only one. Take mine, and I'll take the other one. That way, each of you will have your own shelf."

She looks at me as if to say, Don't be so quick to give anything away; it will be taken from you easily enough.

The night tables are arranged. A fragile peace is in place. And
I have acquired an ally.

Among the things I have left behind at Botkin is my roll of toilet
paper. Julia, a seventeen-year-old diabetic sitting on the bed across
from mine, strumming a guitar, lends me a roll. It is a given that
there will be no toilet paper in the "procedure room" across the
corridor, which is intended for the administration of an international variety of enemas—British, French, and Russian—but is in
fact the only bathroom at our end of the floor. I have never seen
toilet paper in any public Russian bathroom, aside from the
length of it given to you upon admission to public pay toilets. If
toilet paper were generally available, it would immediately disappear. Russians consider that whatever is not nailed down belongs
to them. After all, they are "the people," and, as every good socialist knows, everything belongs to "the people" except those
things that real people jealously guard for themselves.

I am unprepared, however, to see a toilet in the middle of
the procedure room, unprotected by a stall of any kind, and a
woman sitting there, groaning and farting. A second toilet, this
one enclosed, is occupied by a second woman. At first I think
that I have accidentally wandered into the wrong place, a room
that has been unintentionally left unlocked, and I begin to apologize. "Don't worry," the woman sitting on the toilet calmly
says. "We are all the same here. Everyone's body is the same."

But what about privacy, I think, the essential right to relieve
oneself safe from public view? My eyes take in the rest of the
room, the wooden bench covered with a rubber mat where enemas are administered, the bucket of grainy disinfectant with a
much-used rag hanging over its rim, the collection of half-pint

milk bottles on the windowsill for urine samples. My body is gassy beyond belief, uncontrollable and uncivilized. I try to restrain myself, knowing that in polite society this just isn't done, but it's impossible. A burst comes out of me. "Congratulations," the woman sitting on the toilet says. Suddenly my anxiety about privacy evaporates and I laugh, feeling like a toddler being praised for its first success on the potty. The world here is topsy-turvy. I will be "congratulated" often in the coming weeks, and will learn to congratulate as well. Success has acquired a new meaning, been turned on its head. Anything is possible here. In this nether world, I am to be cured.

Of my three roommates, Larissa Petrovna is the first to be scheduled for surgery, I am second, Julia third. Tamara Ivanovna, who was operated on three months ago, is here for chemotherapy, like the woman whose bed was vacated to make room for me. She is our authority on "what happens next." She lies on her bed, fielding questions, addressing Larissa and me by our names and patronymics, a formality that balances the intimacy of our relations, the rude but necessary exposure to one another's bodily processes. Pesochnaya is, after all, a cancer hospital, and everyone who comes here awaits a verdict: whether to live or to die, and if to live, for how long. This circumstance creates a collective concentration, a collective will, an almost superhuman field of energy that packs our room as tightly as a sausage casing. It is this energy that we must bring into the operating room, each life drawing to it another life, linking us like pins to a magnet. We are one another's teachers, nurses, confidantes. If we are a "good team," we will help each other to survive.

Tamara Ivanovna says that there are certain essentials I will have to acquire before surgery. The first is two bottles of Borjomi mineral water, from the high, snow-covered mountains of the Georgian Caucasus, water rich in mineral salts. One bottle is to go with me into surgery and will be the first thing I will taste when I re-emerge into consciousness. Second, a pair of *chulki*, elasticized stockings, which I am to put on just before the operation to keep my blood up where it belongs, circulating among my vital organs; and a waffled cotton towel, sewn with a series of hooks at both ends, to be wrapped around my abdomen after the operation to hold my organs in.

Where am I supposed to find all of these things? "Your relatives can find them for you," says Tamara Ivanovna. "An ordinary waffled towel will do. They can buy the hooks and sew them into the ends of the towel." She shows me hers. "And they usually have Borjomi at the kiosk across the road, because they know that everyone here asks for it. In other places, you can't always be sure it's really Borjomi." And what about *chulki*? She has heard they can be found at Gostiny Dvor, the main department store on Nevsky Prospekt. Once again, my relatives will have to look for them.

I cannot bring myself to say that I don't have any relatives here, that B is gone and I don't really know when she will be back. She has always been unpredictable, even under the best of circumstances. I will only be sure of her return when she actually arrives. And even if she does come back, it is impossible to say whether she will be willing to hunt for *chulki*. I have lied to the hospital already, claiming that B is my cousin living here in Leningrad. At the accounting office, they once again asked me for my propiska. There was trouble as before when I didn't have one. In a panic, I gave them Veronika's name and said that I came from the Baltics, which in a way is the truth. They called Veronika and told her that I would have to pay a quarter of a million roubles (the figure in roubles conveys its impact for a Russian far better than its conversion into $125) for the first part of my hospital stay; I started to tremble and then burst into tears.

The administrator exchanged glances with the other woman working in the office. "Don't cry," she said. "This isn't America. We're not going to throw you out of the hospital just because you don't have money."

I wiped my eyes with the back of my hand and said, "I don't want my cousin to have to pay."

"Sign this paper," the administrator said. "Then go back to your room. There's plenty of time to pay later. Your cousin said you shouldn't cry, you need to conserve your energy."

I asked to speak to Veronika. They handed me the receiver.

"We'll have it tomorrow," Veronika says. "I'll try to borrow it from my friend Nastya. Only don't cry. And don't talk to me about B."

So I didn't.

But what about *chulki*?

Tamara Ivanovna tells me that the date of the surgery has been determined not only by the need to "clean out my body," as Yelena Vilievna told me, but by other considerations as well. The hospital needs enough time to find the considerable amount of blood required for the operation; blood, like so many other things, is in short supply these days. Having surgery on Tuesday also means that my two days spent in postoperative intensive care will fall on a Wednesday and Thursday instead of on the weekend, when the hospital staff, or at least its finest practitioners, are radically reduced. If it turns out that I need an extra day in intensive care, Friday is a failsafe. No one wants the American to fall into the wrong hands.

Larissa Petrovna, like my father, comes from Vilna, only she calls it Vilnius, the Lithuanian name. My grandparents and all of my aunts and uncles on my father's side were "eliminated" from its ghetto in the fall of 1940, when the Nazis captured the city, and I have never been able to bring myself to sift among the mental ruins by returning to the scene of the crimes. The Vilnius which Larissa Petrovna recalls, however, and for which she has been unremittingly nostalgic since her move to Moscow, is full of churches and monuments, gracious and well preserved. She spends several hours showing me photographs and postcards of the old city, giving me an impassioned tour. There is a Jewish Museum in Vilna now, she says, fingering the Russian Orthodox crucifix around her neck.

Julia opens the drawer of her night table and takes out an insulin syringe to give herself a shot. She does this every few hours, and drinks Pepsi to raise her blood-sugar level. She has on hand an extensive supply of cookies, crackers, candies, and soft drinks for this purpose. I know by now that she was pregnant once and lost the baby, and that she will never be able to have any more children. The operation for which she is scheduled is never fully explained. She sings sad Russian folk songs, accompanying herself on the guitar, and then plays "Lucy in the Sky with Diamonds." No one makes any attempt to stop her when she goes out in the hallway to smoke, or sometimes even out to the street at night to meet her friends and drink. Life is life. What can you do about it, especially in times like these?

Larissa Petrovna wants to talk about the latest news. Boris Fyodorov, the finance minster who is the darling of the International Monetary Fund, a "reasonable Russian with whom it is possible to deal," is about to lose his job, signaling an end to the period of reforms. "It is a terrible mistake to lose people like this," she says, getting out of bed to talk to us about it, though, aside from myself, no one is listening. People don't pay attention to the news now. What is there to pay attention to? The entire country is still numb with shock over the death and destruction during Yeltsin's showdown and firestorm at the Parliament last October, numb from almost daily recalculations of the prices of staples, numb from the fear of unemployment and from not receiving salaries for months on end even when people do have jobs.

"We never had these kinds of problems before," Valery Nikolayevich, the head of my department at the university, recently said to me. "From democracy to bureaucracy. That's what your Yeltsin has done to us. By the time he finishes with us, our education system will have collapsed altogether. Democracy died here in October. And everyone knows who killed it."

Larissa Petrovna looks at me with intense, almost pleading eyes. I need someone to talk with about these things, her face says. Someone who's on our side, who believes in democracy.

I turn my face away. Which side *am* I on? Even I don't know the answer. Everyone except me has already gone upstairs to watch TV, where the final week of the Mexican soap opera *Second Maria* is drawing to a close. Apologetically (but grateful for the excuse), I pull myself away from Larissa Petrovna's expression and follow the crowd upstairs to find out what everyone in the entire country really wants to know: Will Maria finally marry or not? Will she find happiness? They are all holding their breath for the answer.

In the lounge, there is complete silence. Everyone is observing how the servants in rich Mexican families behave, how they dress, how "civilized" their relations are with their employers, what the furniture is like in their homes, how the social hierarchy operates. The universe on the screen represents the promise of capitalism, its glories. It is a universe in which Russians will never be in the role of servants, only in the role of masters. This, in a nutshell, is their dream. The single conundrum is, "Do these rich Mexicans on TV ever work? From where does all that money come?" But the series does not provide answers. Why should a catalogue of luxuries provide answers?

Late at night, after midnight, the little reading light beside Larissa Petrovna's bed is still burning, a glowing counterpoint to my own. The pages of her newspapers rustle. From time to time she stands up, walks around, stares out into space, and sighs.

From the enormous window of our room, the forest across the road stretches off into the distance, bisected by a snow-covered field. A footpath begins at the road and leads down to the railroad tracks just beyond a gully in the distance. Like the cancer hospital in Siberia where I visited A after his operation, this one has nature at its doorstep, nature consciously incorporated as an element essential to the well-being of the patients, who will naturally go for walks in the course of their recoveries. In the days before my operation, I too am free to go outside. When I do, the sun and snow glare in my eyes. The snow-covered spruce along the roadside, the still mounds of snow beneath them, the crows cawing in the treetops, the ice, dull and reflectionless underfoot, seem like the lynchpins of existence, an existence that has become more acute and precious now.

My first excursion out of the hospital is in search of Borjomi. Julia lends me boots to wear, and Larissa Petrovna lends me a parka, since I came to the hospital wearing a sanitation worker's coat borrowed in haste from Botkin when the ambulance driver was ready to leave for Pesochnaya and my own coat couldn't be located. The boots too were borrowed from Botkin, and went back to Botkin together with the driver. Will I ever see my things again?

I cross the road to the kiosk to ask about Borjomi. They don't have any. When do they expect to have it? I ask. Anyone who asks such questions is obviously a novice, a fool, or a foreigner, though it's not obvious which I am. The young man inside the kiosk decides to go along with me. "Maybe next week," he says, but his eyes challenge me to believe him.

I cross the road and start walking in the direction of the nearby stores. The sidewalk is invisible; there are just lakes of ice surrounding the trees, their trunks sunk so deep that they look like telephone poles. The paths are distinguished only by a series of ridges in the scarred black ice, frozen footprints where the ice melted and then froze again. It is almost easier to skate between the trees, as boys in a hurry do. Or else to pick your way along the cracked, uneven paths, or create new ones.

The Borjomi for which I am searching must be somewhere in one of the stores ahead of me and to my right. It is my job right now to find it. I don't bother to think about what will happen if I don't, or if others don't, or if Borjomi doesn't exist anywhere in all of Holy Russia, if it is yet another casualty of the breakup of the Soviet Union. I think only: I must, therefore I will, remembering the time in 1991 when almost everything was in short supply and people had coupons to buy the basics. B and I hunted for weeks for mineral water and one day came upon someone selling Borjomi in a doorway. It disappeared as quickly as the helpers were able to bring it up from their supply, hidden somewhere in back, and we bought as many as we could carry, a dozen between us, stuffing five of them into B's shopping bag and cradling the rest in our arms. When we reached her apartment, we set them all on the table and just looked at them; they were such a treasure, and we were so proud of ourselves for having found them.

This is different, though. I am convinced now, in a quasi-mystical way, that the key to my postoperative success resides in whether I drink of the ultimate elixir at the ultimate moment. This means that I am the essential accomplice in my own recovery, not only on a spiritual level but on a practical one as well. If I find Borjomi and *chulki* and can get my hands on a waffled towel with hooks sewn into the ends, I will exponentially improve my chances of recovery. The hospital's quest for the necessary blood to replace the blood I will lose in surgery pales beside my own quest, for no other reason than that it is mine.

First I try the Gastronom, where there is sausage and herring and jars of pickled tomatoes, but no mineral water. I go on to the next store, which supplies "Produkti," but I don't find any there either. I do, however, find a curtain rod in the store's annex, exactly the kind of wooden curtain rod B has been looking for for months. If I don't buy it now, I'm liable not to find it ever again: I buy it and walk out of the store with it tucked under my arm. Just wait till B gets back, I think excitedly, and then remember what has been happening with B. How easily I forget what I don't want to remember. Maybe I shouldn't have bought the curtain rod. B might not even be willing to sew the hooks into the waffled towel for me, so why should I be taking pleasure in finding things she wants?

I walk in and out of stores, stopping people on the street to ask if they have seen Borjomi anywhere. Sometimes I get a curt shake of the head, sometimes an inward, reflective "no," sometimes a faintly optimistic, "Try the store inside the housing complex over there." Finally, when I have already walked almost to the train station, a good mile or so, checking in every hardware store, clothing store, and odd-lot store along the way, I stumble upon ten dusty bottles, not of Borjomi but of another mineral water, Narzan. The bottles are brown. I scan the label, trying to determine if this will be an adequate substitute. Does it have to be Borjomi and only Borjomi? Will I recover too slowly, or not at all, if something else passes my lips at the critical moment when I return to consciousness? Is this an unpardonable compromise, or am I simply settling for "life" as it presents itself in all its complexity? My anxiety escalates. I ask the salesgirl if she has any more besides what is on the shelf. No, she says, this is the last. Okay, I decide. This is the moment of truth. I buy all ten bottles and rush back to the hospital.

Triumphant, or at least half triumphant, I show the bottles to my roommates. Is this as good as Borjomi? I ask. Can I be relieved that I found anything at all?

"Narzan is good water," Larissa Petrovna says.

"There is enough for all of us," I say. "Two bottles for each. Plus extras." I line up the bottles on the windowsill. I clean them off. How beautiful they are, these not-Borjomi bottles of mineral water. Now that I have mastered this essential step in the direction of our collective destinies, I am at peace. The ten bottles stand at attention on the windowsill, winking at me in the light as if to say, We, at least, are prepared. I take off Larissa Petrovna's jacket and Julia's boots. Back in my bed, I am happy at last.

In the ultrasound room, I am being examined using a sophisticated new piece of equipment that has just been installed here. Yelena Vilievna stands huddled together with a group of medical students, radiologists, and technicians. Everyone cranes to look at the image appearing on the screen, talking rapidly, enthusiastically, arms looped affectionately around one another's shoulders as they all point at the evidence and share perceptions, not bothering to repress their delight. Russians are wild about new technology, which they see as possessing the capacity to transform their lives; they respond to it like children presented with an especially longed-for new toy. And as the doctors crowd around me for my examination, I feel included in the circle of their absorption, as well as in the bonds of their friendship. I am proud that my body is providing an occasion for excitement, and relieved that what they see seems to be reassuring. Their enthusiasm is contagious. If only it could also be curative.

When I go back to my room, it is already time for me to have my shots. But the nurse who comes to administer them, the head nurse, Anna Nikolayevna, has a problem that is making her boil: she has run out of the day's supply of syringe number three, the one she needs for the injection she is about to give me. Each day she receives a fixed quantity. I vaguely recall hearing the number seventy-five, but if I calculate that there must be forty people on our floor and that we each receive several shots a day, this becomes highly unlikely . . . or perhaps very likely, I don't know. If it is the truth, then am I the only one who has been getting my shots consistently, or do people have their own syringes, which they reuse, or is the hospital reusing them? Anna Nikolayevna is upset about the situation. She can do the injection with syringe number two, but the results, for reasons I don't understand, won't be quite right.

Julia rummages in her drawer and takes out one of the syringes she uses for her insulin injections, sealed in plastic. "Here, take this," she says. I protest that I can't — she needs it for herself. She insists. It is, after all, the right size, and she has a lot of them. Anna Nikolayevna, embarrassed, takes it from her and loads it, then gives me the injection. "When I get back to America," I say, "I'll send a shipment of needles for the hospital. Think of it as humanitarian aid." Anna Nikolayevna's face turns bright red. "We don't need any of your humanitarian aid from America," she says furiously. "We're fine without it. We were before, and we should be now." From across the room, Larissa Petrovna pats her lips with her forefinger, and I avert my eyes as Anna Nikolayevna stalks out of the room.

It is Friday evening. B is leaving on a train from Moscow tonight and will be arriving in Leningrad in the morning. Veronika is coming to pick me up at the hospital and bring me back to the apartment for the weekend. This is my "furlough" before surgery. Yelena Vilievna tells me I am to eat nothing but clear chicken soup—from a fresh chicken bought, if possible, at the farmers' market, not those *"Bushovski lapki"* ("Bush legs"), American prepackaged chicken legs introduced to Russia during the Bush administration.

She also tells me that before I leave the hospital I should sign up for the *bolnichny list* at the hospital, the sick list. This means that I will receive my salary for six months even if I am unable to work. I look at Yelena Vilievna and start to laugh. I can barely wait to go back to work, can barely tolerate the thought of being absent all of this time from my students. Besides, if I and everyone else, including Yelena Vilievna herself, can't succeed in receiving our salaries for months at a time even when we are healthy and working, how will we ever receive them when we are debilitated and not working? Will I be like the *blokadnik*s and cripples at the Kirov, claiming my just deserts?

I remember A's hospitalization for cancer in Siberia four years ago, how confident he was then that, as a patient, he should have only one legitimate preoccupation: getting well. An administrator at the Theater Workers' Union would take care of everything else, all of the headaches that can sap a sick person's vital energies, anxiety about allocation of funds, arrangements at work, pre- and postoperative sick pay. I remember the late-night visits of his doctor to B and A's apartment, his staying to talk and drink tea with them and eat, seemingly unaware of the passage of time. I remember thinking, "Time here has not yet become money." Was the *bolnichny list* a phantasm even then?

"It doesn't hurt to get your name on it," Yelena Vilievna says. "No," I say, "I'm sure it doesn't hurt."

What do I care about the past? B is home and so am I. Time has squeezed itself so thin that there is no space in the interstices of memory for anything that might deflect the sheer will to joy, the sweet taste of life itself. I sit at my desk or at the kitchen table, touching and savoring familiar objects which have acquired an unfamiliar weight, while B takes photographs of me that, when developed, will show me looking serene and happy though much thinner than I realized I had become. We say nothing about what happened before her departure or about her failure to return sooner. I no longer know how to be anything but generous with life's smaller misfortunes, and, perhaps in acknowledgment of this, B bends over backward on my behalf. She buys the chicken and cooks it; she sits in the kitchen sewing hooks into a waffled towel. She hunts down a pair of *chulki* and shops for apricots and rose hips, which Yelena Vilievna has said are to be essential elements of my postoperative diet, in the form of quantities of rose-hip tea and equally large quantities of stewed apricots. Caviar, formerly considered a postoperative staple for its hemoglobin content, is no longer recommended because of the present vagaries of the packaging, sorting, distribution, and quality control that have sprung up since the collapse of the Soviet Union, not to mention the growing pollution of the Caspian Sea.

These two days at home are days of floating grace, luminous with the sense of their perishability. "Don't look at me that way," I say to B at one point. "I promise you I'm not going to die." She turns away and doesn't answer, and when the doorbell rings, she is obviously eager to escape from me.

I come out from the kitchen into the corridor to see who it is. "Allan! You're back," I shout, rushing to embrace our American pediatrician friend who shuttles between Leningrad, Yugoslavia, and the U.S. and has just returned from a week in Kosovo, Macedonia, where he has been struggling to give a name and a face to one of his latest projects: the construction of a multiethnic children's hospital on soil not yet bloodied by the nationalistic savageries which have begun to encircle it. The last time he was in Leningrad, he remained for only two days, and during those two days, when I was still at Botkin, he twice managed to visit me and talk with Felix Emilianovich about my decision to remain in Russia.

Now, worn out from juggling the multiple demands of crumbling, crisis-ridden societies, and trying to sustain his fast-eroding belief in the essential goodness of humanity, he sits at our kitchen table drinking tea, his gray hair, gray suit, and tie customarily rumpled, his thick black glasses constantly sliding down his nose and having to be retrieved.

"Did they send money for the curtains?" he asks. "Yes," I answer. "They deposited it in our bank in America for B. Now all she has to do is make them."

The curtains in question are a set of handpainted curtains, which, at Allan's recommendation, B has been asked to make for a children's clinic within a clinic here in Leningrad, which is being sponsored by the Children's Health Fund, for which Allan works, and by Merck, the American pharmaceuticals giant, which is donating half a million dollars' worth of free medicine to it. Allan is medical director for the project, and Merck and the Children's Health Fund are planning a publicity presentation in two weeks at the former House of Friendship Palace, trumpeting their contribution to the well-being of the city. A delegation has been monitoring the project, and they have decided that the clinic should not resemble a typical Russian clinic, that it should be more like an American clinic, selling the "American concept" to the Russians. The decor of the clinic is of great significance to them, and although they have considered the possibility of buying Mickey Mouse curtains, B's design of fish swimming in the sea appealed to them, and they have given her one thousand dollars in advance to make and paint the curtains for the waiting rooms. But B has already run into difficulties with the Russian side. Does she realize what the hospital could do with one thousand dollars? Why do they need fancy curtains? The director of the children's wing of the hospital in which the clinic is to be located is proud of what she has been able to do for "her children" over a period of many years. Fancy curtains are not on her list of priorities. But Merck is not only interested in providing medicine for the clinic. They are building their image, and curtains are part of that image. If the view out the window of the clinic, a view of factories in the distance, could be changed as well, they would like to do that too. With B's curtains, they can shut out the view of factories in the distance, at least during the presentation. Can they also shut out Russia?

Allan says that someone from the Hermitage will be coming over to the apartment to look at her designs for the curtains. B promises that she will paint and sew them during the next two weeks, while I am in the hospital. She will be very busy working on them, but will come to visit me every two or three days. They will be ready in time for the presentation two weeks from now. I think about Botkin, about the murals of birch trees and flying cranes, the worn linoleum, the lovingly tended plants, and admonitions not to worry, because everything at the hospital was free. I think about the cost of my stay at Pesochnaya, and about Merck's donation. How is it going to be possible to convince Russians that they should be grateful for half a million dollars' worth of free medicine when, until a few short years ago, it was all free or almost free? The Russian director of the existing clinic has said that B's curtains will be stolen within a week of being hung. But everyone knows that the potential theft of B's curtains is the least of Merck's worries. If they are up on the day of the presentation, Merck's image will be preserved eternally in the press.

I recall a job I had thirty years ago in New York, when I was nineteen. An advertising firm hired me in connection with the promotion of five new tissue-box designs that were to be presented at the Interior Design Center. Five rooms of the center were being redecorated to match the style of the tissue boxes. A breakfast was planned to which the press would be invited to see the new boxes in their matched settings. My job was to send out invitations to celebrities and journalists. The budget for the project was five million dollars. Everyone at the agency thought it was an exciting concept. I didn't last very long at the job. In fact, I quit right after the breakfast. But ever since then, I have always bought tissues in plain white boxes.

Allan's face is tired. Everywhere his idealism is under siege, with Russia's intrigues and Yugoslavia's savageries constantly dragging him through precisely that mire which he is intent upon sidestepping. I have sometimes heard people here whisper that he is a *sviatoi*, a saint, though like many saints he can be impatient with the human detritus that impedes his upward passage. Sometimes the word is said with a slight snicker, classing him with all the other fools and idealists for whom Russia remains the ultimate romantic magnet—until it becomes the ultimate betrayer of faith.

What are all of us doing here anyway? Russians ask. Why should Americans with enough money to do whatever they choose decide to come to Russia or the Balkans, when they could live in peace in America, or take vacations in the Bahamas like those promised on TV to Russians who put their money in the investment company MMM? Is America really so boring, and suffering in Russia and the Balkans so exotic? Or do we have a secret agenda? To strip poor Russia of its wealth? To steal and sell her children? To spy on her technologies? To divert thousands of needed dollars to the purchase of hand-painted curtains?

I go into the bathroom, and when I come out again I hear Allan telling B that she should be kind to me, that he called the Oncological Institute at Pesochnaya from Yugoslavia and came to the conclusion that I probably have no more than six months to live. Why make my short life unhappy? B agrees, and although I have not been consulted in the matter, so do I.

I make a lot of noise coming back into the kitchen, trying to prevent them from saying anything else I don't want to overhear. Anyway, I have just remembered about my boots and fur coat, which are still incarcerated at Botkin. B will have to retrieve them for me. In the kitchen, I bring this up. "Don't worry," B says. "In their condition, no one will want them."

I am too weak to react. Instead, I go into my study, lie down on the couch, and fall into a dreamless sleep.

I will never know what Yelena Vilievna is like in the operating room. At the moment of my most intense engagement with her, I will be unconscious, unable to respond as an individual, for even the most inquisitive or attentive patient, thoughts lulled into submission, knows nothing of the surgeon's performance. What I do know, however, is that Yelena Vilievna's skills are determined not only by what she will be able to accomplish then, but also by her ability to make me her accomplice in the process, her ability to create between us a kind of umbilical cord that will bind my unconscious self to her throughout the operation and will be cut only at the moment when I return from the womblike stillness of anesthesia to the light of new consciousness as a healthy or doomed individual. What stands between the surgeon as carpenter and the surgeon as savior is the condition of his or her humanity, the condition of relationship with the patient. It is this relationship Yelena Vilievna so assiduously cultivates, sometimes sitting with me on a couch in the corridor talking for half an hour or more, preparing me for what is to come, reassuring, explaining, putting her arms around me when some particularly devastating piece of information needs to be conveyed and evokes tears, or when my inability to comprehend in Russian some complex medical terminology reduces me to panic.

Today, Yelena Vilievna tells me that my operation has been rescheduled for Wednesday, Larissa Petrovna's changed to Tuesday. In two days, I will be wheeled into the operating room. In three days I will know everything.

The midday sun is bright on the fields. Larissa Petrovna and I go for a walk, the last walk for both of us before surgery, perhaps the last walk for a very long time. We cross the road to the big field and start walking on a path through the snow down toward the railroad tracks in the distance, away from the hospital. There is a crust of ice on the snow, but beneath it everything is melting. It is warm and springlike, the last day of deepest winter, making both of us jubilant. We have to step carefully, in order not to sink deep into the mush below the snow's crust. Water is rushing everywhere under the surface, and at any moment we could plunge through. We are giddy with the realization that our own last day of being able to go for a walk is the last day anyone else can go for a walk in the snow either. We walk for more than an hour, confiding our deepest thoughts to each other. We make plans for the future. We hand over our lives to each other. When we turn back, at the far end of the field, the hospital is way off in the distance. Returning to it, we feel refreshed, convinced of our invincibility. We promise each other to survive.

I want to tell them that I can feel pain, that the anesthesia has begun to wear off before the operation is over, but I can't seem to move or say anything. I feel them swabbing at something inside my belly. Have they already sewn me up, or am I wide open? The pain isn't excruciating, just annoying, a reality from which I am trying to flee. I am struggling to communicate. I can't. Then there is a gap, and I hear Yelena Vilievna's voice near me, feel her arm on mine. "It was ninety percent," she says, telling me that the dread procedures envisioned as a 10-percent possibility have not been necessary, telling me that life as I know it will go on. I want to kiss her, but I can't move.

I am wheeled out of the operating room and into intensive care. People move around me. The bed is covered with blood. It is my blood. I am awake. I try to ask the nurse to change the sheets. She doesn't pay attention to me. I feel as if I am swimming in blood. I try again to get her attention, but I am too weak. Maybe no one has told her yet that I am American. Maybe she doesn't know that in America everything is perfect. Eventually, she does change the sheets, but it seems to me that hours have passed before she does. They put a cloth dipped in Narzan to my lips, just wetting them at first, then telling me to suck on the cloth. My eyes are open. Yelena Vilievna comes in. Her face is glowing. "It was a difficult operation," she says, "very difficult, but we were successful." She is proud of herself and of their team. So am I. "Now you are going to stand up," she says. "Just for a second, to make your blood circulate." She holds me, slides me off the bed until my feet touch the floor, and then tells me to shift my weight so that I will be standing on my own. I do, for a moment, and then tip back toward the bed, exhausted and in pain.

Later, my first solid food is a raw egg which I suck through a hole in its shell. A young woman lies in a bed just a few feet away from me. She is naked, her skin luminous and transparent but frighteningly pale. Her lips and face are completely white. She looks bewildered by what has happened to her. She has been in intensive care for days now. Everything was supposed to be okay, but clearly it isn't. Her mother comes to sit beside her, to sponge her feverish body. She is thirsty but has no mineral water. I tell her that I have Narzan in the room, that she is welcome to a bottle. Her mother goes up to my room to get the Narzan and brings it back. The young woman looks at me with mute appreciation, as if I have given her something extraordinary. I am afraid that she is going to die.

Now I am lying in a clean bed. The night has passed. I am

able to turn over onto my side, with great effort. When I lie on my right side, I am looking right at the young woman with the bewildered, patient, suffering face. Her mother goes to get another bottle of Narzan from our room for her. Can her life be saved by Narzan?

Another day passes. I am recovering well. I eat kasha. Yelena Vilievna comes to ask me if I feel well enough to go back to the room. I hesitate. No, not really, I say. Can I stay another day? Dr. Bockmann arrives. He and Yelena Vilievna and the chief nurse of intensive care, the one who ignored my bloody sheets, are having an argument. The chief nurse wants to send me back upstairs to make room for someone else, who needs to be brought into intensive care. Yelena Vilievna and Dr. Bockmann insist that I remain. The head nurse is furious. "Don't make her angry," I want to say. "She will take it out on me for sure." The argument is settled, but the head nurse looks at me with hostility. A fourth patient is wheeled into the intensive-care area, which is intended for only three. We are all lined up together, our beds very close together. I can see the young woman's eyes in the bed next to me, frightened eyes, eyes resigned to death. I close my eyes and think, "Please, God, don't let her die."

The next day, I am wheeled back upstairs and welcomed to my room by Julia and Larissa Petrovna. B brings stewed apricots, fresh chicken soup, rose-hip tea.

Within twenty-four hours, I am on my feet, walking, being congratulated frequently. My lips are dry. Yelena Vilievna recommends dabbing the white of a raw egg on them. It works immediately. I feel almost no pain. But I am afraid to ask about the young woman in intensive care.

Now it is time for Julia's operation. She is terrified. The anesthesiologist spends a great deal of time with her, because of the complications caused by her being diabetic. Many specialists come to visit her. Her mother has come to visit only once. The night before her operation, she is supposed to take valerian and a sedative to calm her nerves in preparation for surgery. She doesn't want to take the valerian or the sedative, doesn't want to sleep. I sit on the edge of the bed, holding her hand, stroking her forehead, and singing to her the Russian lullaby my mother used to sing to me, the same one I sang to B the first time I met her, seven years ago, when she came up to the stage with Veronika and her niece.

Larissa Petrovna has just found out that she has cancer, not from her doctor but from a nurse at the nurse's station where she went for an injection and learned that she was about to have her first dose of chemotherapy. She wept. Why did she have to learn about it in this way? Telling her was a mistake, that's all. Everyone makes mistakes. But they shouldn't have made this one. Larissa Petrovna and I decide to buy Julia a new guitar as soon as we get out of the hospital. Even though Larissa Petrovna has cancer, we keep making plans for the future. I will come to visit Vilna. We will see each other again no matter what. I stay at Julia's bedside until, finally, she is persuaded to take the sedative and falls asleep. I hold her hand when the nurse comes to wheel her into surgery in the morning. Larissa Petrovna and I hover over her, kissing her and reassuring her. Larissa Petrovna makes the sign of the cross over her. Larissa and I have become her aunts. She is a good girl, just in need of love and attention.

After her surgery, Julia isn't taken into intensive care. She is brought back to the room immediately. Yelena Vilievna comes in, and once again I hold Julia's hand while Yelena Vilievna pulls bloody rags from between her legs and Julia writhes in pain. There is a seemingly endless amount of blood, and the rags pile up on the floor. Yelena Vilievna is brusque with Julia, as if to say that it is Julia's own fault for having gotten into this situation. I look up at Yelena Vilievna, trying to catch her eye, to ask her with my own eyes to be gentler. I have never seen this Yelena

Vilievna before. Is she the real Yelena Vilievna? The moment she sees me looking up at her, her expression softens. Yes, I decide. This is the real Yelena Vilievna. And so was the other. I am, after all, in a Potemkin Village. But it is here that life has been returned to me.

Yelena Vilievna is still cleaning up Julia when I notice B standing silently in the doorway. I motion to her to go away. She doesn't belong here now. This is our world, not hers.

A few days later, however, I am rejoining her world, having been released from Pesochnaya almost fully recovered, though still weak. As we drive off in the car, with me sitting in the back seat, I feel as if I don't belong in the normal world anymore, I don't recognize my place in it. My place is still back there, with all those women saying "Congratulations!" and Larissa Petrovna weeping and Julia playing her guitar. I look back, but Pesochnaya is already out of sight.

When we get to the apartment, I look into B's studio and see that she hasn't made the curtains for the clinic. She says that if she had her life wouldn't have been worth a rouble. We will have to return the thousand dollars, now in our bank in America, which she received for doing the work. A friend of mine has arrived from America, bringing one thousand dollars in cash for me. B says we will definitely need it. Tomorrow she has to go to the hospital to pay the outstanding balance on my bill. Whenever I start to say how wonderful my stay at the hospital was, she raises her eyebrows skeptically, implying, without saying so directly, that she greased a great many palms in order to make it happen. Knowing B, I think, Maybe she did, maybe she didn't.

The following week, I return to the university to teach one class a day. My students welcome me with flowers. They accompany me home, carrying my books for me. I ask them to tell me about their own hospital experiences. Was mine so unusual? Some say yes, some say no. I will probably never know the truth for sure.

f i f t e e n

■

These are my last days in Russia. B says: "Go home. Get out of here and don't come back. You don't know what kind of country you are in. You think you're in America, but you're not in America. Every day that you are here, the clock is ticking on your life. Do you understand that? The boys from the racket told me that if you didn't leave after the fair in Paris, if you didn't go back to America then, I would have to start to pay. And now, every day that you're here, I pay. When you came out of the hospital, they said that you'd better leave; they said that if you didn't it would be easy for them to send five guys over here to fuck you. Presto. Nothing. No problem. You don't believe me? It's because you're naïve. It's because you think people are good. They aren't. They want this apartment. They want you out of it. If I don't pay, they'll find me a husband, and then no propiska will help me. Nice and easy. The apartment is in my name. Then it's in his name. Presto. The apartment is theirs. I told you not to tell anyone about the apartment being ours. I told you it was dangerous. But you didn't want to listen. 'Ours.' You were so proud that it was 'ours.' But you didn't care about my safety. 'We' have an apartment in Leningrad. You were a fool. You didn't know when to keep your mouth shut. So now they're counting the days, I'm counting them. Leave, I tell you. Leave."

"I'm not afraid," I say, though it's a lie, and I'm already shaking. "They can't intimidate me." B looks at me as if she doesn't know me. I see in her eyes that I have become the stranger, the enemy, the other. I'm walking a thin red line. Which thin red line? I'm with the Whites. I'm with the Reds. I'm with the Americans. I'm with the Russians. I'm against the fascists. But which fascists? The Russians were on this side. The Russians were on the other side. Who was fighting whom? Which side am I on, boys? Which side am I on?

Is B telling the truth? Is B lying? Is B trying to frighten me? Is B afraid? I walk out the door to the street and suddenly remember that the house where Raskolnikov killed the pawnbroker is almost opposite me, just on the other side of the canal. I stand on the bridge that links one embankment to the other, and contemplate jumping in. But then I think that people who kill themselves usually do it because they want to kill someone else.

I go to the phone booth on the corner and call Vera Leontievna, who has been our friend for a long time. I know that B has often confided in her. My voice shakes on the phone.

Vera Leontievna says, "You shouldn't take it seriously. You know how B is. She never knows what she wants. Tomorrow everything will be fine. Just wait until tomorrow."

"But she's crazy," I say. "She's completely insane."

"I thought you already knew that," Vera Leontievna says. "She always has been."

"Yes," I say, my voice shrinking back into itself. "I know she always has been." And then, like water eddying at the moment when high tide starts to ebb, all of my rage at B moves off in another direction, and I am left with a sense of her ultimate fragility—with naked pity and love.

Things are often over at the moment when they begin, but it can take years for them to actually end. It depends on how good you are at lying to yourself. And the longer it goes on, the harder it is to abandon the lie. After all, it's your own life, and you're responsible for it. Knowing the truth doesn't mean that you can do anything with it. The mind is infinitely elastic. It can accommodate itself to anything. I've always been good at contortions. As a child, I could raise my leg backward up over my head and, holding my foot in my hand and arching my neck backward, bring my big toe as far as my mouth. In some ways, nothing has changed.

I walk back to the apartment. In the courtyard, children are picking up the bricks from the playground tower smashed last week by a gang of future racketeers. The bricks are strewn everywhere. The cement columns with their steel posts that held the archway entrance were uprooted and used to destroy the playground. The children are arranging the bricks in a circle. "This is ours," the circle says. They build up six levels of bricks and lay a board across them. Sasha, the son of our upstairs neighbor, shouts at me, "Are you going to build a new playground? Will the Americans pay for it?" We could rebuild it ourselves, I say. If everyone in the building did it together, we could do it. Sasha shrugs. "My father already built it twice," he says. His friend says, "My father helped. His father was the chief and my father helped." I look at them. This is their home, their playground, their lives.

I go upstairs, undress without turning on the lights, and fall asleep on the couch in the study. It occurs to me just as I drift off that madness is a contagious disease, and I have caught it.

B is right. It's time for me to leave.

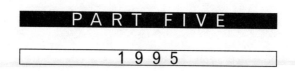

PART FIVE

1995

s i x t e e n

■

Five months later, I am back. Masha and Misha pick me up at Pulkovo Airport. The first thing they want to know is what is happening with the apartment. Obviously it can't be anything good—otherwise, why would I have had to call them from America and ask if I could stay with them when I got to Leningrad, a month, maybe two months, until I could find another place to live.

Misha sits with Liza on his lap in back. Masha smokes a cigarette before she gets behind the wheel. I climb into the passenger seat and congratulate her. She has just gotten her license. Misha says, "You shouldn't congratulate her. She is a terrible driver."

Masha slowly turns the wheel to the left in preparation for making a turn onto the main road leaving the airport, getting into the lane that logically, to her, seems to be the correct one, because no one is in it, but is, for precisely that reason, the wrong one.

"You will never be able to move from this lane," Misha says. "You cannot ignore the signs, drive at fifteen kilometers an hour, and expect to go anywhere. Shift! That's why we're always running short of gas, because you shift at the wrong time and stall. You use up all the gas. You have to listen to the engine, to hear the right moment when you have to shift."

Masha doesn't say anything. She knows that he is burning over the fact that she has a license now and he doesn't. They took his away for a year, with eligibility for appeal in six months. In Russia, there is no such thing as a little bit of alcohol in the blood. Masha shifts, stalls, restarts the engine, and stalls again. She is so small that she has to stretch upward, keeping her body absolutely straight, in order to see over the steering wheel.

"When women drive," Misha says, "they think only about themselves, about where they need to go. They don't care about anything that happens around them. It is female psychology. A man pays attention to everything. He knows if the person near him didn't brake soon enough. His instinct leads him to recognize what is happening with all of the other drivers."

Masha ignores him. She needs to move into the right lane. There is a space in the lane now, only one car in the distance.

"Go, Masha! Now!" I say.

She looks but doesn't go. The traffic thickens again.

"I'm sorry," she says. "I want to know about the apartment. But I can't drive and think at the same time."

My luggage is installed in the big second room of their apartment which has a green fold-out couch and two green upholstered chairs, an armoire filled with Masha's clothes, a chest of drawers filled with Liza's clothes, and two spare hangers. A bear bigger than Liza sits in one of the chairs. A big box holds her toys. There is no desk, or even a table, so I keep my typewriter in its case on the floor. The desk at B's and my apartment was so big that, when B called me that summer in America to tell me about having bought it for me (A's purloined desk had mysteriously vanished), she said it was big enough to sleep on, or under. She said, "You will love it. It came out of a ministry. Antique. It will fit perfectly in your study." "Go ahead, buy it," I said. So who is using it now? B's new American boyfriend? He's not so new anymore, almost a year now. Probably his computer is parked on top of it. My books are locked in the glass-doored bookcase there, unless of course they have broken the lock and thrown them out the window, or given them away, or sold them.

Masha unfolds the bed for me, unrolls a cotton-stuffed mattress on top of it, gives me sheets, a quilt, and a quilt cover. The sheets are freshly ironed, frayed at the edges. I look out the window at the elaborate cornices on the façade of the pale-rose building across the street, its eye-level medallion of a brooding, hooded head with downcast eyes turning its gaze inward. B wanted to get an apartment in that building before I found the one we finally bought on the Griboedova Canal. But the apartment on the canal was my destiny, just as B was, just as Russia was. I chose my fate while standing in the middle of the Lion's Bridge, where all four of its suspension cables meet. I pointed in the direction of the canal, where it circles back on itself like a serpent's tail, targeting the exact spot where our apartment would be, and said, "Here, right here, is where I could spend the rest of my life."

I don't intend to do anything but look, but my mind takes off like a disobedient child freed from parental constraints, heading down the street past the Theatrical Institute, which was, in its prior incarnation, the famous Tenichev School for cadets that Nabokov attended during his Petersburg youth, turning left onto the Fontanka Canal Embankment, with the golden-headed trees of the Summer Garden on its far banks, and then following the Moika River past the French consulate, all the way to the Potseluiev Bridge, the Kissing Bridge, where a left turn brings you out onto Theater Square and the Kirov Theater, looking straight on at the blazing domes of Nikolsky Sobor, brings you home. My heart wrenches at the sight of those domes, breathtakingly ethereal, shimmering in the near distance, but no longer, as they once were, mine.

I take a toilet kit out of my overnight bag, a towel, a nightgown, slippers, and bathrobe. I don't unpack anything else. There's no place to put anything else anyway, so what's the point. I am grateful to be here, to have a place, anyplace, to stay. How is it that I did nothing to protect myself against this betrayal? I knew I should, but even the thought seemed offensive, a violation of trust, in itself shameful.

B always told me that I was a mongrel, who loved the way dogs love, unconditionally, even if their masters are cruel to them. A case, I thought, of the weak controlling the strong. On the other hand, Nabokov wrote of his mother that she always heeded a simple rule, "to love with all one's soul and leave the rest to fate."

So who's right? This is a question I could conceivably spend the rest of my life asking.

At the end of that previous semester, a month after I was released from the hospital and just a week after B and I returned from working at the Paris Fair again, I was uncustomarily harsh in grading my students' exams. I could see the suffering in their faces, their sense of injustice and betrayal, but I was immovable. While I was sitting in the hallway of the philology department entering their grades in their grade books, my colleague Svetlana Semyonovna said, "You were in such good condition after you came out of the hospital. I was amazed when I saw you. But now what's happened to you? You look awful." Immediately I began to cry. "Come for a walk," she said. "Tell me about it." We walked, and I told her a lot, including everything that had been happening with B since my operation. I even told her about B's claim that the Mafia was trying to get the apartment and that they wanted me out of it.

"Are you sure she doesn't just want the apartment for herself?" Tatiana said. "Are you sure she isn't trying to get you out?"

"Yes, I'm sure," I lied. "She would never do something like that." I didn't say that I had confided in Tatiana just to check her reactions. I could see that she was worried. So was I.

Two weeks later, I left Russia for America. B had said she would follow me in three weeks, but she didn't come, though until the very last minute we collaborated in the deception that she would. I sent her the money for a ticket on Czech Airlines, which had to be paid for in cash. The day before her scheduled departure, Veronika called to say that B had gone into the hospital. No one would tell me what was wrong with her. A mixture of everything, Veronika said: stomach, heart, nerves. I was consumed with guilt for having abandoned her when in the midst of a nervous crisis, even though it was she who had abandoned me. I said perhaps when she was well she would use the ticket after all—but Veronika said that B hadn't bought one, she had kept the money instead. Still, by August, instead of paying my already overdue bills, I scraped together another $250 to send back with a friend who was going to Russia. After all, how could I leave B to her own devices when she had absolutely no resources and was ill? What if she really had had a nervous breakdown? What if it was my fault?

I had taken out a fifteen-year mortgage of $40,000 on my house in Maine to pay for B's and my apartment in Leningrad. At the end of August, faced with a mountain of debt and no way to pay any of it, I sold my mother's summer cottage for a quarter of its appraised value. My mother's memory was in rapid retreat, and I had to have the money to pay for the help she increasingly needed. But, almost as soon as the money was in the bank, it struck me that I really should send some to B to buy more Orenburg shawls. It would help her to get back on her feet again and give her a sense of purpose. I wrote to her suggesting that when she recovered she could come back to America. I would send money for shawls. A week later, she called. She apparently was recovering from whatever it was that had afflicted her (I still didn't know precisely what it was) and agreed to come to America in October and stay until January. In the meantime, she would use the money I had sent to buy shawls.

She was very thin when she arrived, though it had seemed impossible for her to be any thinner than she already was. She said that she had to go back to Leningrad for a couple of weeks at Thanksgiving, because she had been offered an important consulting job there. Over the phone, from Russia, she had mentioned that she was embarking on something new, something "very important for Russia." "What is it?" I asked. "Dry cleaning," she said. "Russia desperately needs dry cleaning." "Oh," I said, "I see." I wondered with whom she had fallen in love. She must be smitten, if she had developed a passion for dry cleaning, even though, in a way, she was right. Russia did desperately need dry cleaning.

Not to my surprise, the consultant job and the dry-cleaning job turned out to be one and the same. I encouraged B to return to Russia. It would be an opportunity for her to establish herself on her own. She said that she had "found someone" to take care of our apartment while she was away, an American who just happened to be the person who wanted her as a consultant and also happened to be starting up a dry-cleaning business.

She was alternately sullen and excessively gay. I decided that she really had had a nervous breakdown, and that the dry-cleaning infatuation was a sign of her present fragility.

We were accepted to participate in a crafts fair in Minneapolis with our shawls. The fair was a success. Or, rather, we sold a lot of shawls and received a lot of money, though by the time we had paid all of our expenses there wasn't much left. B spent a long time talking on the telephone with the Dry-Cleaning American who was living in our apartment. By prearrangement, she called him at our neighbor's apartment, since she had only just been officially registered with the new propiska that would allow her at last to get a phone installed in ours. One day when she called him, he told her that the phone company was ready to install the phone in a few days. Now all she needed was five hundred dollars to pay for the installation, plus another five hundred dollars to buy a fax machine for the Dry-Cleaning American, who would return the money when she got back to Russia. He was going to help us by staying in the apartment until February, when I was coming back to teach for the spring. Having a man in the apartment would be good protection against the Mafia. He had at one time worked as a detective, and understood her fears. He knew that she couldn't go out alone, because she might be killed. Of course, it was possible that he might be CIA, but that would be all the better. What more secure protection could she have than CIA? The fax would stay in the apartment, and when he left in February, she would make sure that he didn't take it with him. I bought the fax, charging it to my credit card. She said that the money could come out of her share of the profits from the sale of shawls. Then, of course, she needed to borrow some more money to pay for the Thanksgiving trip back to Russia. He would also refund that when she got there. I gave her another thousand dollars from my share to buy more shawls, and she put in another thousand dollars from her share. By then, everything we had made in Minneapolis was spent. But she was in a good mood. Why wouldn't she be, with the Dry-Cleaning American waiting for her in our apartment?

"I'm surprised you came back," I said, when I went to pick her up at the airport in New York after Thanksgiving. "I didn't think you would."

Her eyes were metallic. "I came because I need money," she said. "That's the only reason."

I didn't offer to help her with her bags. But as it turned out, all she had was an elegant little black suitcase I had never seen before.

"That's all you brought with you?" I said.

"I told you," she said. "I came for money. I don't need anything else."

By then, of course, I just wanted the whole thing to be over with. I kept asking myself whether it was possible that, in the end, things had really boiled down to this, to the money that "Russians didn't care about and never would"?

When the Golden Horde under Genghis Khan came galloping across the steppes, civilized Russia was plunged into darkness and remained there for four centuries. Give people who have been schooled in brutality their freedom, and they'll use it to be brutal. B had said that I was naïve, that I believed people were good but they weren't. Had she also meant herself?

We did the fairs, even though we didn't have enough shawls to make it worthwhile. B said that she hadn't had time to find any more that were of good enough quality. She had kept the money in Russia, she said, to use later on, when she could be more selective. "We're still partners, after all," she said. "Aren't we?"

Eventually, we sold almost everything we had. In between fairs, I overheard her whispering in a strangled voice over the telephone to Russia, long expensive calls dripping with the urgency of her return, the impossibility of remaining without the Dry-Cleaning American. Once I heard her discussing shawls with him, and realized that B had used our money to buy shawls she wasn't telling me about, that the dry-cleaning business was being transformed into a shawl-buying business.

We worked. We made more money, we spent more money. B decided to visit friends in New York for Christmas. She packed a bag for the trip. It was huge, but I was too embarrassed to ask her what was in it. We agreed to meet for New Year's in New York. I took her to the bus station, kissed her goodbye, and said, "Call me when you get there. Let me know what's happening." Then she was gone.

Just before New Year's, I received a brief note in the mail. It said, "As of January 1, I am terminating all personal and business relations with you." That was all. I learned that she had gone to Boston to meet Mr. Dry-Cleaning American, who had come back from Russia for the holidays. She was with him now. I knew she couldn't have written that letter by herself. I wondered what was going to happen with the apartment. Obviously, I wasn't going back to it. Or was I? After all, I would be paying the mortgage that had financed it for the next thirteen years. A week later, preparing to do an inventory for taxes, I opened the cedar chest where I stored the shawls. They were all gone. And so were most of the photographs I had taken in Orenburg.

A month later, I got a letter from Mr. Dry-Cleaning American. He wanted to help B settle accounts with me. How much did she owe me? he asked. I wrote back and said: Nothing. The only thing I cared about was the apartment, and I was sure she and I would work things out as far as that was concerned. I had decided not to return to Russia for the spring term, but would instead be coming in May. By then, things should be clearer. I did not say that I thought he was probably a temporary infatuation, linked somehow to B's nervous breakdown and her recurrent need to "start her life all over again from scratch." Nor did I say that this wasn't exactly starting from scratch, though I did emphasize that the apartment belonged to both of us, and that I had paid for it. I said I would of course appreciate his willingness to act as an intermediary who would understand my point of view and hers as well. I thanked him in advance for his willingness to settle things fairly.

Things heated up fairly rapidly after that, and after I had faxed them reams of documents, I somehow found myself in the position of the guilty party who had shamelessly exploited B. How I arrived at this situation I could not figure out, but I decided that there must be a communication problem, that for some obscure reason my message just wasn't getting across. I explained to the Dry-Cleaning American what I was sure he already knew, that we had bought the apartment in B's name because it was illegal for foreigners to own property. I had paid for it but always considered it ours. I really don't want anything, I kept reiterating, but the apartment belongs to both of us.

By May, after trying to explain everything in a new and original way so many times that I knew there were no new and original ways left, and after offering at last to let them have the apartment if they would take over my monthly mortgage payments, I suddenly found myself at a loss. Paralyzed for want of new ideas, and with the knowledge growing inside of me like mushrooms after a rain that something was going horribly wrong in these "negotiations," I finally turned to a lawyer. He read all of my calm letters and all of my desperate letters and all of my enraged letters and said: You need a lawyer to tell her that you want to settle this in a civilized way. Tell her that you're coming to Russia in May and want to meet with her to discuss things, and that if she doesn't cooperate you'll have no choice but to go to court, though of course you would prefer not to.

"To court! I can't do that."

"Yes, you can," he said. "But go to Russia first. I'll write a letter to her on your behalf. See if you like it."

He sent the letter. It sounded very humane and understanding, but of course B didn't answer it. When I arrived in Russia, I called, but got only her (our? my?) answering machine. I left a message saying that I was in Russia until May 10 and would like to get together with her and her lawyer to discuss things. She didn't return the phone call until two days before I was supposed to leave. She offered to meet the following week, after the fiftieth-anniversary celebrations of the end of World War II, known in Russia as the Great Patriotic War. That meant I would have to change my ticket. I did.

It was unusually hot in the city. Even along the canals, the air was stifling. I was glad that I had come. I had felt starved for Leningrad. On the day of the fiftieth-anniversary celebrations, it rained. Thousands of people stood patiently in the rain for hours on the Neva Embankment, even though they couldn't see anything but the umbrellas in front of them, to wait for the flotilla of sailing ships coming down the Neva. It was the first time since the collapse of the Soviet Union that a Soviet holiday, usually accompanied by a display of military might, had been celebrated with anything resembling true patriotic feeling. Young girls repeating the ritual of fifty years ago went up to veterans who had dozens of medals pinned to their chests and kissed them on the cheek. Old men wept for joy that their country hadn't forgotten them altogether. And in Palace Square crowds of young people stood quietly and sang together with their parents and grandparents the old Soviet songs that everyone had known since childhood. It was the first time that I had felt Russia loving itself, proud of itself, felt the self-hatred and misplaced grandiosity slipping away, displaced by simple national pride over what had been sacrificed and what had been gained by saving the Western world from the Nazis at the cost of twenty million lives. Old people who had survived the blockade were everywhere in the streets. Russia at its best was in the streets. They were heroes, and I loved them for it.

The next day, I went to the Memorial Cemetery at Piskarevskoe, to the wall commemorating Leningrad's war dead, buried there in *allées* of mass graves. All around the memorial were huge wreaths of exotic flowers sent by the governments of Denmark and France and Germany and Holland and Thailand and South Africa. There were thousands of people at the cemetery, long lines of them filing past the official wreaths, looking at all of the flowers and reading the inscriptions. I was shocked not to find any flowers from America or Great Britain. How was it possible? In the morning I called the consulate. "Of course we sent flowers, lots of them," I was told. "They were laid on the memorial at the cemetery the day before yesterday." Someone must have stolen them. Who would steal wreaths from a cemetery? Nothing ever changes in Russia.

B and the Dry-Cleaning American met with me at the newest office of their lawyer, who just happened to be B's and my former lawyer. He seemed uncomfortable with the entire situation. B sat there stony-faced, not saying a word. What did I want? the lawyer asked. Why were we meeting?

"I was just hoping to come to some sort of agreement," I said. I considered that the apartment belonged to both of us, half and half, and wanted to get something in writing to that effect. I didn't want to sue, I said, but would if I had to. The lawyer was surprised. He said, "Oh, I'm sure we can decide something very quickly, within twenty-four hours." I canceled my flight again and decided to wait for their decision. They never called again, and neither did their lawyer. I went back to America worried that I might never be able to return to Russia, and filed a case in court. I knew as well as anyone that it wouldn't get me anywhere.

s e v e n t e e n

■

Y
ou don't need a lawyer, you need bandits," Misha says
when I have finished telling the story. "We know some
nice intelligent ones who will tell you exactly how this
should be handled, and take care of it for you. You'll be back in
your apartment in no time."

"But it's not my apartment, it's ours."

"The Soviet Union stopped giving medals to Heroes of Socialist Labor almost five years ago," he says. "No one respects a
fool. Especially now in Russia."

I turn away, avoiding his eyes, and look out the window just
as the last lights in the apartment across the street flicker out. It
is already three o'clock in the morning. We are planning to go
mushroom-hunting at five, and everything we need for the expedition is already gathered in the hallway.

"Give me time," I say to Misha. "Let me think about it."

———

In the back seat of the car, Liza squeezes in beside me with family friends Rita and Igor and their ten-year-old son, Antosha. Igor and Misha went to theater school together and worked in the same theater together (as have their wives) as part of the same collective for almost twenty years. Liza is stroking Antosha's face with both of her chubby hands, leaning her head against his shoulder, smiling radiantly at him. She is two years old and in love. Antosha accepts her love patiently. He leans into the curve of his mother's arms, entwining the fingers of both of her hands with his.

The road runs parallel to the Gulf of Finland. On both sides the forest is golden; the sea and specks of rose-granite shoreline are visible from time to time through a cleared forest path. In my mind's eye, I experience it all again: just beyond the Z——sk train station, past the apartment building where B's older sister and mother live, I smell lilacs and apple blossoms. The petals are falling onto the spring grass that undulates on the far side of the apartment complex. A crisscross of footpaths leads down to the white Russian Orthodox church with its three sky-blue domes, and from there to the park with its *allée* of flower beds descending to the sandy beach, where broken-down dressing rooms stand tipsily in the sand, and the calm, algae-filled sea is flat and silent. When everything goes to hell, all of the remembered beauties of the world go to hell with it.

Along the road now, people are coming out of the woods with mushroom baskets, grandmothers and grandfathers, children and teenagers, all who have the national passion in their blood, the love for the hunt without murder or blood, the hunt made contemplative. They are everywhere, cleaning out everything worth gathering from woods that in a few short weeks will be touched by first frost.

"There won't be anything left by the time we get started," Misha says. "It's not like in America, where people won't even touch mushrooms, they're so afraid of being poisoned, and you can fill your basket in half an hour. Remember the day before the coup, when we brought mushrooms back to the people with whom we were staying in Maine, and everyone watched us for signs of convulsions?"

I remember the hurricane warnings that day, how all the fishermen were hauling their boats up out of the water, taping their windows, stocking up on kerosene and drinking water and enough food for a week. Then, at seven in the morning, the phone rang. It was Misha, calling from their host's house on the other side of the bridge. I listened and then woke B, knowing it was dangerous to talk to her in the morning.

"There's been a coup in Russia."

"Go to hell," she said. "Leave me alone."

"A coup, don't you understand? There's been a coup in Russia."

"What do I care? What do you care? We're in America."

She put the pillow over her head. I went downstairs to turn on the television, but the power was out. I tried the shortwave, but the batteries were dead. The wind was blowing a gale, and the water was rising fast in the street, almost at flood tide. I ran out to the car and drove to the store in water almost a foot deep.

The store was out of batteries. I said, to no one in particular, "There's been a coup in Russia. Does anyone know anything about the coup?"

"What coup? We're in the middle of a hurricane, and you ask about a coup? There's no coup here, there's a hurricane."

By the time I came back to the house, B had gotten out of bed and tried to call Veronika in Russia, but the phone lines were dead. By then she believed me.

I asked her, "If the coup succeeds, would you want to stay in America?"

"Of course not," she said. "For what do I need America?"

That night, we drove across the bridge and sat together with Masha and Misha watching the junta's press conference. Yanaev's hands shook, giving it all away, the way Yeltsin shaking his finger in Gorbachev's face that following Christmas would tell us it was all over and the Soviet Union was in shreds. By then the electricity had come back on. The hurricane had passed. We were in the eye of the coup. It passed too.

"Sometimes now I wish that it had succeeded," Misha says. "Sometimes I wonder what life would be like if it had. You don't have to worry about the Communists' winning the elections for Parliament. Before catastroika, we couldn't have a car, couldn't travel to the West, couldn't do a lot of things. But life was interesting. The theater was interesting. Every word counted. What have we gained? The right to pleasure? Maybe life will become interesting again. I think I'll vote for the Beer Lovers' Party in the election. Everyone agrees on beer."

A train whistles in the distance. Dachas are almost always "within walking distance" of a train. Misha and Masha are the only people I know who have a car.

The road makes a ninety-degree turn, and a phantasmagorical jumble of dachas suddenly sprouts up out of the forest, one right on top of another, hundreds of houses, each on its own tiny rectangular plot of land, a regular frontier town carved out of a chunk of forest given to members of the Theater Workers' Union during the early Gorbachev years. There is hammering everywhere, the whine of chain saws, and as we bump our way along the rutted road, dotted with puddles the size of small ponds, a brigade of actors and directors and their friends appears alongside the car, carrying a log the length of a tall tree. The land here has been dug up every which way by bulldozers engaged in strategic advances and rapid retreats, and the houses are a mishmash of pitched roofs, multiangled roofs, tarpaper roofs, metal roofs, wooden roofs, roofs like little party hats with pieces of salvaged glass for windows, hand-hewn door- and window frames. Some of them are narrow and straight-sided and three stories high, some look like sheds or log cabins, *izbas*, some have started going up but haven't quite taken shape, as if they are being improvised along the way, dwelling in a thoughtful twilight of the imagination until money and inspiration can get the show on the road.

For seventy-five years, Russians were told the exact permissible dimensions of every living space they inhabited, based on government calculations of what is essential for the needs of the average human being. Now, suddenly, they have been set free by the revolutionary cry, Build whatever you want! They are drunk with the sense of possibility. No one is going to tell them anything anymore, even if the result is a monster of chaos. The wilder and more fantastic, the better. The sky's the limit. All of the old rules have vanished anyway—new directors, contract systems, the prospect of losing their jobs, of there being no money for theaters at all. The theater workers are waiting for their particular ax to fall, the ax of freedom. For now, though, this yard, this window, this chimney are still theirs.

When we have finished unloading the car at Rita and Igor's dacha, everyone gathers around the chimney Igor and Misha have just finished building together. They examine it carefully. Igor traces the mortar around the bricks with his finger. Misha opens the firebox and looks inside. Their eyes travel up to the ceiling, checking for flaws. Tonight the chimney will have its baptism. Tonight they will test the draft.

We get back in the car and drive along the woods road, then park in a rough grassy area at the edge of the forest. Just beyond are red-spruce trees with smooth trunks going straight up as much as a hundred feet, spreading branches and needles only at the top, a canopy that light rarely penetrates. We head into the woods. There are delicate traceries of footpaths everywhere through the forest, an infinite menu of choices curving around this side of a tree or another, this patch of lichen or that mossy bit of swamp, a map of reassurance that, no matter how vast this forest, you will not lose your way if you only follow the footsteps of those who have preceded you.

In *Anna Karenina*, Levin's repressed, intellectual brother, having planned his marriage-proposal speech, finally faces the woman he loves (who also loves him) while they hunt mushrooms together in the forest. He struggles to speak, loses courage, and says nothing. The moment passes. The opportunity is lost forever.

The history of Russia is the history of lost opportunities, the history of nostalgia for lost opportunities.

Misha's basket is full. Everyone else's but mine is almost full. We drive back to the dacha, then walk through the woods behind the dacha down to the swimming hole, which they call "the lake." We walk around the lake, then turn back to the house as the sky is darkening. None of the dachas have electricity. There are no power lines. Darkness is swift and total. We climb up to the second floor with bottles of champagne and vodka. We sit together on a plank in front of the chimney while Igor and Misha start a fire in the firebox. The draft is fine. We applaud and toast the chimney, Misha's and Igor's skills in building it, their friendship.

"I was right to have Liza when I did," Masha says. "I could have had her in Finland. I was on tour there a week before she was born. But I prayed to make it home on time, and I did. If you're born in France, you're French. It's the same in America. I even know someone who deliberately went to America when she was nine months pregnant, just so her child could be born an American. Now they won't let you into America or Europe if you're pregnant. But even then that wasn't what I wanted.

They say that you'll be a worse actress if you have children, but it's not true. I'm a better actress now. Aren't I, Misha?"

Misha isn't listening to her. He is holding his head in his hands. His mind is elsewhere, absorbed in his chimney.

"There is a woman in our theater who is eighty-seven years old," Rita says. "She's been with the company for more than sixty years, since 1931. She's played every role from Chekhov to Shakespeare, from ingenue to babushka. We've all worked together our whole adult lives. We've never done anything else. What else could we do?

"If you work in the same theater all your life, that theater is your life. But if you lose one generation, it's finished. The old ones die out without passing it on. Someone takes the tradition out with the garbage by accident, and then, when they go to look for it, they can't find it anymore, because it's disappeared."

"Maybe I should learn something about administration," Masha says. "Actresses have to be optimistic, especially after forty." She smiles at me brightly, the way women in the West smile, with their mouths but not their eyes.

We sit in silence, looking at the fire. Rita says, "It's a known fact that looking at a fire cures the soul. So does looking at waves."

I go downstairs and outside to the outhouse. It is pitch-black in the dooryard. Nothing but darkness, a starry sky, and an even deeper darkness where everything merges into the forest. By the time I get back, they have all come downstairs and are setting the table on the veranda. A kerosene lamp is burning on the table. They are talking about someone's problems with his propiska.

Igor says, "They don't have residence permits in America. Foreigners don't even know what they are. They only exist in our country."

"I know about propiskas," I say. "In fact, I know a lot about them."

"She does know," Misha confirms. And he tells them about the apartment.

"We have connections with good bandits," Igor says. "I wouldn't recommend anyone with whom I didn't have experience. These are civilized bandits. They'll weigh the evidence. They'll even have a trial. It will be completely fair, more so than in the courts. Some of them are former law students. They know what to look for. You don't have to like it, but that's the reality of conditions here."

"Sure," I say. "First I'll send my bandits, and then she'll send her bandits, except her bandits won't be civilized, and that will be the end of it. And even if that doesn't happen, I would still have to live with my conscience. Me and Raskolnikov."

Igor shrugs. The momentary sense of my being one of them vanishes.

Back in Leningrad, Masha answers the phone and says, "It's for you."

The voice on the other end is rough. "Grigory told me to call. He said you got a problem."

"Me, a problem? What problem? You mean Grigory from New York?"

"You got a problem, or you don't got a problem?"

"Well, maybe. Would you mind calling me back tomorrow?"

"What time?"

"This time is fine."

He hangs up. So do I.

"What's the matter?" Masha asks. "Is something wrong?"

"No. Nothing. Everything's fine." Imagine my Russian friend Grigory in New York deciding to do something like that. I call New York and say to his answering machine, "Grigory.

Some guy here just called me on your behalf. Who is he? Please call me back."

Grigory doesn't call back. Of course he wouldn't. There are some things you just don't talk about over the phone. B always said that I didn't know when to keep my mouth shut. I have just proved her right.

But the bandit does call back. His name is Yura. I suggest that we meet—on a purely informational basis, of course. What do I have to lose? I can just listen to what he has to say, get another point of view, look at it from his perspective. "Where?" he asks. "Dom Knigi," I say. The House of Books. It's the most obvious place I can think of.

"Where's that?" he says.

Not knowing where Dom Knigi is, is like not knowing where the Hermitage is. What kind of bandit can he be?

"The bookstore on Nevsky with the glass globe on the roof," I say.

"Yes, but where?" He pauses, his mind overstrained. "Never mind," he says. "I'll find out. I'll be in a blue BMW."

We arrange to meet the next day, at two in the afternoon.

I wear heels, lipstick, and a dress for the occasion. I want him to know that I'm a respectable woman. I am curiously detached about the whole thing, as if I am going to a seminar that has nothing to do with real life, and isn't even remotely connected to B or to me.

I spend an hour walking up and down Nevsky. I go to the theater kiosk. There is a performance at the Maly Theater on Friday of Dostoevsky's *The Devils.* It is in two parts and takes eight hours, but it's already sold out. I stop at the Philharmonic to look over the schedule for the coming month. Temirkanov. Sotkilava. Stadler. Then I walk toward Ploshchad Vosstaniya, to the crystal-and-porcelain store, to see if they have any cobalt teacups, the ones with the elaborate gold filigree rims that I bought four years ago, and which are still in the apartment. I stand for a long time looking at the cups. Before, you couldn't find them anywhere, but if you did, they were cheap. Four years ago, I found three of them, and then, six months later, another three at a kiosk on Prospekt Bolshevikov. After we moved into the new apartment, I placed them all ceremoniously on the dining-room table, setting it for the guests I dreamed of inviting. They were my treasured discoveries. Now they're available but unaffordable. And anyway, simply buying them in a store would never give me the same feeling.

It's bad enough that B has the apartment, but somehow the question of the teacups bothers me more than anything else, even all the antiques I bought and the desk. Well, maybe not the desk. The desk rankles, especially since my typewriter is on the floor now. By the time I walk back down Nevsky to meet the bandit, I'm not so detached anymore. Murder has entered my heart.

The BMW is parked at an angle near the corner of Nevsky, with its nose pointing out at the Griboedova Canal, where a tour boat is passing under the Kazansky Bridge, going toward the Cathedral of the Spilled Blood, which rises up out of the gray canal waters like a mirage of resurrection gone wild, as if the very force of its excess, its glittering gold domes, its profusion of mosaics, all doubled by their reflection in the waters of the canal, could compel Tsar Alexander II, murdered on the site, back to life.

Yura is standing alongside the car, wearing a suit that looks as if he had to force his shoulders into the jacket. Evidently he too has decided to look respectable. He opens the car door for me, and I climb in, suddenly scared. Have I already embarked on a road with no return? What if he decides to drive off with me in the car instead of talking to me right here? Would anyone even notice if I screamed?

He settles back in his seat, and doesn't turn on the ignition. Instead, he asks me to tell the story. He already knows that it has to do with an apartment, but he wants details. I am struck by the fact that his eyes are very large and very blue, and protrude ever so slightly, giving the impression that he is absorbing things beyond the normal field of vision.

At first I look directly at him as I talk, but then I start looking straight ahead, through the windshield, where my eyes meet those of Prime Minister Victor Chernomyrdin, facing me from the election poster for his party, "Russia Is Our Home," which is pasted on a billboard in front of Dom Knigi on the opposite side of the canal. Chernomyrdin's avuncular face is grave, determined. His hands are raised, fingertips touching to form a roof. The poster says, "Everyone Needs a Roof. Russia Is Our Home." In Russia, the word for "roof," *krysha*, is slang for Mafia protection.

"Do you have any documents?" Yura asks. "Anything to prove that you paid for the apartment?"

The question jolts me. He thinks we're going ahead with this. He doesn't realize that I'm just a tourist in the world of banditry. He should check my references with the bandit at the Kirov Theater, who could tell him I'm a fraud. That bandit is probably a millionaire by now, living on the Côte d'Azur, drinking Dom Pérignon by the magnum. Or maybe he's dead, knocked off like a bowling pin by one of his competitors. How innocent I was then. How innocent we all were then. Even B? That's what I don't know. That's what I wish I could figure out.

I think nostalgically of B's upstairs neighbor, the one who was in the militia and proud of it, who kept his meat in B's freezer compartment and was dazzled by the beauty of American police cars. Where are people like him now? They probably don't even exist anymore. They're all on some bandit's payroll.

"Documents?" I say. "Yes, I do have some documents. Bank documents."

"Good. We'll ask her if she has any too."

I'm getting nervous. "I don't want anything to happen to her," I say. "I couldn't live with myself if she was hurt."

"She won't be hurt if you don't want her to be. We won't even touch her little finger if you say so. We have experience with this kind of thing. I work for Panam. One of our clients had a problem with an apartment. We got it straightened out for him right away. We'll talk with her. She'll understand what we mean, what's in her best interests. No one will get hurt."

"You said you work for Panam. You mean the American airline? I thought they went out of business years ago."

"Not the airline," he says. "The country. We have a trading company with Panam." Panama! That's where money gets laundered, where ships are registered that eventually sink or spread oil leaks over the surface of the planet, where crimes take place in dark alleyways, and the canal, the vital link between East and West, is everything. Panama, which was once Peter Lorre land and then became Noriega land.

I want to get out of the car already, but instead I say, "How much will this cost?" Not "would" but "will." I am starting to sweat.

"Ten percent," he says. "We take care of everything. When the apartment is sold, we get our ten percent. Nothing up front. You don't have to worry about dealing with anything yourself."

I look at him intently, and then look at Chernomyrdin again. "I don't think I can do it," I say.

"It's not as bad as it seems," he says kindly, and smiles at me. I try to smile back, but can't. My face slides into a grimace. My teeth are starting to chatter. What is happening to me? I've only been back for a few days, and already the immorality, the undertow of "life as it really is," has started to pull me down, suck me in, toss me around.

Already everything that I know to be abnormal is starting to seem normal. Already I am starting to think the way they do. It's a sign of some dreadful weakness of character, this inability to resist a mass mentality, this inability to separate myself from it.

Once, almost ten years ago, I met someone else in front of Dom Knigi, a man who had arranged a rendezvous with me there. He talked to me in a whisper, in English, looking around to be sure that no one was watching or listening. He was sweating because he knew he was doing something that could get him into serious trouble: he was speaking English with a foreigner. What have things come to? How is it possible that I am even having this conversation under the benevolent gaze of Chernomyrdin, who has given it his seal of approval?

"Think about it," Yura says. "I'll give you my phone number. You can call me anytime." He writes "Yura" on a slip of paper with his phone number, and gives it to me.

"Thank you," I say. "But I'm really not ready for this. I'm going to try to get a lawyer."

He looks at me pityingly. "If you change your mind," he says, "you know where to get in touch with me."

I crumple up the paper and put it in my coat pocket, but when I get back to the apartment, I smooth it out again and slip it into one of the transparent plastic sleeves of my business-card portfolio, together with cards from the real-estate agent who sold us the apartment and the American consul general. Just in case.

e i g h t e e n

■

Constantine Kirillovich is a very busy man. He has agreed
to spare some of his valuable time for me only because
he has known Masha and Misha for so long. He is doing
them a favor. But on the phone he speaks so fast that I can hardly
understand a word he says, and I have to pass the receiver to
Masha. The upshot of the matter is that there is no reason to talk
with me until I can show him documents. Lawyers and documents go together like tea and jam, their destinies intertwined.
When I have gathered together all of the documents and had
them translated into Russian, he will look at them and tell me if
there is any hope for my case. "Which documents in particular?" I ask. He can't tell me which documents, because he
doesn't know anything about the case, and when I tentatively
open my mouth to tell him about it, he says he doesn't have time
to talk with me. Clients are demanding his attention. There is a
call on his pager. I hear him shouting, "What the hell do you
want me to do about it?" and then he slams down the receiver.

The point is that you have to have a good lawyer for things like this. Grigory said to me in America that what it would cost me in stress trying to deal with Russian lawyers was more than the apartment was worth. His wife, Raya, said that if B did what she did, it probably meant that God was finding a way to make me pay for my sins. What sins? The sins in the Bible, of course, all of the Biblical sins. "Consider it as a gift from God, who is choosing to make you suffer as a means of getting closer to Him." Raya's and Grigory's daughter stood on a little chair three times a day, facing the corner icon in their kitchen and saying her prayers—*"Bozhe pomiluiy"*—in a small, slightly quavering voice while her nanny stood next to her, praying as well. Raya thought that I should be baptized in the Russian Orthodox Church. Baptism would help me more than any lawyers in Russia possibly could.

So really I have three choices—bandits, lawyers, or baptism—a pretty broad spectrum if you think about it. For now I decide not to.

Instead, I decide to follow Constantine Kirillovich's advice.

The first thing I do is go to Ulitsa Antonenko, to the office where we originally registered our joint venture. There I am told that the office moved a year ago to Smolny, but the more efficient system that was put in place a year ago wasn't yet in effect at the time of our registration. "You know what can happen to documents when they are moved," the woman in the office says, assuming that the answer is obvious. The documents may or may not be at Smolny, may or may not be possible to find at all.

I go to Smolny, wandering through labyrinthine corridors and looking in on a series of people who all tell me that I need to speak with someone else instead. Eventually, I find the office of the person with whom I need to speak, but she has already left for the day and won't be in again until the end of the week. When I come back at the end of the week, I am told that, be-

cause of an illness in her family, she won't be back until the following week. When I come back the following week, she tells
me that, since it is a joint-venture agreement, I can't get a copy
without the agreement of my partner. I explain that, since I am
planning to initiate a suit against my partner, who is no longer
my partner, she will never agree to my receiving the documents.
In that case, I need to file a petition explaining my reasons for
needing the documents. The petition will be presented to the
person in charge, who isn't in today. It should say everything
that is necessary to say. What is necessary to say? If I don't know
what is necessary to say, why am I filing a petition? Why don't I
have the documents in the first place? If I am really the company
president, why does my partner have them instead of me? Why
don't I have the company seal? It is useless to say that I never
really took the documents seriously, that I only got involved in
the first place because I wanted to help my friend, who is no
longer my friend. She has the stamp because it gave her a feeling
of power, and I didn't need a feeling of power. Ditto the rest. All
of this is far too confusing. Documents are documents. Friendships are something else. People shouldn't sign documents they
don't take seriously. A joint-venture agreement is a legal document. What do I mean that "I didn't take it seriously"? Don't I
realize that I am dealing with the city administration, that I registered a company in Russia and didn't take it seriously? No
wonder I am having problems with my partner. I deserve to have
problems if I don't take documents seriously.

I don't answer any of the other questions she has implied but
hasn't asked, because I know that answers will only make things
worse. I don't know what to explain and what not. I only know
that I need these documents for what are apparently bad reasons,
and that if I confess to these reasons no one will give them to
me. If my lawyer were to request the documents, they would
give them to him, but the lawyer won't request documents un-

til he has already seen documents. Without documents you are shit, but with documents you are a human being. I am shit.

Eventually, I solicit the sympathies of a subaltern in the regional division. I think that I am probably supposed to pay her a bribe, but I don't know how. Should I delicately slip some money into her pocket, or frankly put it into her palm? How much? What if she's offended and tells me that I have no right to bribe a city official? That's ridiculous. No one in Russia is above receiving a bribe, it's only a question of how much. I finally say to her, "Thank you for your help. How much do I owe you?" She seems to find the question odd. She looks at me carefully. I have told her that I teach literature at the university, that I was cheated out of my apartment. She knows the story. "Nothing," she says. "Nothing?" I say. "Nothing." The next time I come, I bring chocolates, flowers, a tablecloth, and place mats, a pot holder. "This really isn't necessary," she says, but with a little bit of coaxing she takes them, making us both happy.

When I finally receive the documents, she makes an official copy, sews the pages together, glues a patch of paper over the thread on the back side of the last page, and seals the thread and patch with red sealing wax. This makes a dramatic impression on me, and I wonder why it didn't make the same dramatic impression when I signed the documents in the first place. I know why. Because then I was thinking only about B, and not about documents. Now this ceremony has the gravity of historic ritual, of permanence, the backing of civil servants whose place in history has been guaranteed by the likes of Tolstoy, Gogol, and Dostoevsky. This is not mere paper drawn up by mere lawyers, this is paper with a red wax seal on it. Now I know what she meant about taking things seriously.

I read over the agreement. It says right here that we have the right to acquire property, and since we are fifty-fifty partners, obviously the property must be fifty-fifty too. Only one thing surprises me. Although both of our signatures are on the joint-venture agreement, it seems not to have been stamped and registered. So why did B bother with it in the first place? To protect herself from me? Already then? Or was it only in order to be able to show people a document that would raise her in their estimation from shit to a human being, a full-fledged partner in a full-fledged Russian-American joint venture? It probably didn't matter who I was or what I did, or what the joint venture did. Only one thing mattered, the crown of glory conferred upon her by her formal association with a real American, a glory that has since faded along with all of the country's other illusions about the life awaiting it on the fast track to capitalism.

I was useful then. I ceased to be useful. My personal trajectory corresponded to the trajectory of America in the national consciousness, from the bearer of a superior civilization to the harbinger of cultural collapse. The Russians thought that the West was offering them freedom, but it turned out to be just another form of slavery.

So Americans aren't fashionable anymore. In fact, they've become a nuisance, an obstacle to a success that often depends upon a wild and heartless capacity for improvisation, which B possesses in spades.

Brutal, yes. But when has Russian history ever been kind?

Another question, a piddling little detail, remains. If our company was never registered, why has it remained in the city's files without a registration stamp? Does it exist or doesn't it?

I look at the stated "initial capital investment" of eighty thousand roubles—twenty-five hundred dollars at the time, about twenty-five dollars now. The figures carry the nostalgic weight of historic transformation. In 1992, we didn't have twenty-five hundred dollars. My typewriter, a fax, an answering machine, and her sewing machine were considered equity enough—the fax and the answering machine in particular, rarities of infinite

value. Is it possible that was only three years ago? B was in ecstasy, and I was proud to think that my fax and answering machine could be the source of it. I had already forgotten that a
year earlier a pair of Italian high-heeled shoes produced the
same effect. The barest knowledge of human nature should have
told me that the ecstasy over Americans, joint ventures, and
apartments would be as transient as the ecstasy over shoes and
fax machines.

I take my documents to the offices of Intourist to have them
translated. There I am told that unless I wish to pay triple, the
translation will take two weeks. The translator looks in horror at
my papers: a copy of the mortgage loan negotiated on my house
in America in order to pay for the apartment, my bank state-
ments showing debits for the apartment, wire-transfer slips,
withdrawals from my credit line, and a home-equity loan taken
out in order to pay off the credit line.

"I'm a translator, not a bookkeeper," he says. "What is a
'mortgage loan'? What is 'home equity'? I can't find these words
in the dictionary." His suspicions have been aroused. Why am I
connected to such things in the first place, if not for some foul
purpose? How can I possibly begin to explain all this to him
when I myself am just being introduced to the wonders of borrowing and the nightmares of repayment? I try, knowing that it
is futile. "It's borrowed money," I say, "but you have to pay it
back." I show him my checkbook and explain how a checking
account works, but it means nothing to him. No one in Russia,
aside from bankers and the bandit owners of banks, has a checking account. If I have one, I must be like all other Americans,
and must be able to pay fifteen dollars a page for translation, or
any other figure that strikes his fancy. Rich Americans are clever.
They know how to get their money's worth. When I try to explain to him that I'm not a rich American, that, on the contrary,
I'm an *idealistka* who has just lost the one material thing that

meant anything to me in Russia, this confirms his suspicions that I am not only rich but cheap, and probably used the documents I am asking him to translate to swindle my innocent Russian partner, who, like all Russians, was of legendary generosity. He looks at me with distaste. Anyone connected to words that don't appear in the dictionary is a swindler for sure.

"If you want me to translate this, write it out in plain English for me," he says roughly.

"But I can't," I say. "These documents have to be used in court. I came to Intourist because your translations are official, and I need an official translation. Sworn to. Notarized."

A cold glint comes into his eyes. It is a glint that I recognize. "I'm very busy," he says. "I can't solve your problems for you."

"All right," I say, seeing my authority slip away from me like a mirage, leaving behind a person who grovels before bureaucrats, a slug, a shit without documents. "I'll put it in plain English."

I muster the kind of smile for which Americans have a lifetime of training. "I'll pay fifteen dollars a page."

"In cash," he says. "In advance."

"I don't have that much money with me."

He looks at me contemptuously. Americans always have money that they don't admit to having. "What do you expect?" he says. "That I should work for free?"

"I'll have to come back in a few days," I say.

"Suit yourself," he says. "It's up to you. In a few days, I'll be too busy. By the way, can you please tell me what a legal guardian is? I have a document I'm supposed to translate that refers to a legal guardian, but that's another one of those words I can't find in the dictionary."

Two hours later, I bring him $150 in cash. He knew I would.

While I am waiting for the documents to be translated, I am also looking for a place to live. Each time I go to see an apartment and have to calculate that I cannot afford it because I am already paying for the one in which B and the Dry-Cleaning American are living, Yura's stature grows in my eyes. Every few days, I take out his phone number, look at it wistfully, and put it back in its elastic sleeve. I keep remembering how he looked at me sideways when I told him that B was very delicate. "She stole your apartment," he said. "What's so delicate about that? Why are you protecting her?"

"Stole?" I said. "Well, not exactly stole."

"Stole," he repeated calmly. "It's up to you, of course. It's your money going down the toilet."

My money down the toilet! Sometimes I see it floating in the canal, nestled in a curve along the embankment where Raskolnikov thought of ending his life. At other times, it foams up out of the toilet, bills stuffing up the bowl, spilling out everywhere as I try to grab them. But they are soggy now from their life in the sewers. When I squeeze them in my hands, they disintegrate. What use would it be to get back money in that condition?

I can't afford an apartment in any of the neighborhoods where I would want to live. Not even one room, which would satisfy me if only it didn't look out on a blank wall and allowed a few rays of the pitiful late-autumn light to penetrate. I can't stay with Masha and Misha forever, no matter how kind they are. But where am I to go if I can't afford what is available? Maybe in the end I will have to rent a room in a communal apartment. Half the city's population lives in communal apartments. What makes me so special?

I walk along the Griboedova Canal in the direction of our apartment, but cannot bring myself to approach it. What if the two of them walk out the door together, or she walks out alone? What are you doing here, spying on us? I'm not spying. I have every bit as much of a right as you do, if not more . . . And then there would be shouting and accusations in the middle of the street, and someone would call the militia, and I, just to escape from my own fury, would throw myself into the canal right at the spot where Raskolnikov imagined he heard the words "You murderer."

"You murderer." I would never escape from it, never escape from myself. Oddly enough, I can more easily imagine myself killing her than I can imagine walking up to the door and demanding that she move out.

The golden domes of Nikolsky Sobor dream beneath the clear blue sky, and below the domes, the even more delicate blue of the cathedral itself, and the surrounding park with its scattering of newly bareheaded trees. I go into the cathedral and find the icon of Jesus in which he looks like a soulful Jewish artist. I light a beeswax candle before it and press it into the candelabra, where the light wavers among those of a dozen other confused souls. I pray for B, and for myself. Then I pray for the holy impulse that keeps us from killing our fellow human beings.

When I walk out of the cathedral, a claque of beggars standing in front of it cross themselves fervently and stretch out their hands. I want to look at them kindly, but I can't. I don't want to give them anything. I don't want to give anyone anything. That's how much good praying has done for me. Nothing can help me now, not even Yura. I have started down the slippery slope, and there is no turning back.

The last leaves are still falling golden from the trees when the first winter snowfall begins. It lasts for three days. As the air warms, and the snow turns to slush, it is continually covered by a fresh layer of snow, giving the city a perpetual air of renewal. The first of October is when the city usually turns on the heat in its apartments, but this year, because of a crisis in the city's accounts with its providers of natural gas, by the third week of October many districts are still without heat. It is cold in Masha and Misha's apartment. Authorities have proposed a temporary solution to the crisis until a long-term solution can be found: city residents might receive heat but get along without hot water. On the tramway, there are vigorous protests and reminiscences of the blockade. "It was never like this before. This isn't wartime, after all. Why are we living this way during a time of peace?"

The transition from the nonheating season to the heating season roughly corresponds to the transition from the season of productive labor to the season of consumption, the season of need. It is in this season that people expect something from the government, and it is precisely during this transition that Yeltsin enters the hospital with what is described by the press as ischemia, a condition that stops the flow of blood to the heart. The words "heart attack" or "stroke" are not used. Television cameras show him sitting up in a hospital bed, his face puffy, his words slurred. Who is in charge here? No one seems to care. "We have our own problems. Let him deal with his."

By November 7, Revolution Day, which is being celebrated for the first time since 1991, it has turned cold again. There is a thick layer of ice underfoot. Thirty-five thousand people gather in Palace Square to urge the overthrow of the current government and its replacement by patriots who will restore order to the country, get rid of foreigners and Jews, and make sure that apartments that are being taken over by foreigners are restored to the possession of "true Leningraders." I imagine trying to explain my case against B to a people's court. Poor B, exploited by yet another foreign Jew. Just look at Yeltsin's Cabinet. It's full of them. Filth! Scum!

A TV reporter and a cameraman stand in the midst of a circle of people who are pressed tightly together. The reporter is asking questions about Russia's future. He is not looking for sound bites but for thoughts, ideas, feelings. He knows how to listen; he doesn't cut anyone off.

A heart surgeon in the circle says, "At my level of professionalism, in the West, I could be making two hundred fifty thousand dollars. I don't need to tell you what I make here, if I get paid at all. I'm just like the rest of you. But what I have is worth more, a good collective and the knowledge that I am doing something for my country. What's more important, money or a sense of purpose?"

"It's absurd to think of going back to what we had before," someone else says. "There's no way to go back."

"Comrades! Who says we have to go back?" the heart man answers. "You can't step into the same river twice. We'll learn from our experience to create something better."

"Sure," says another. "Why can't we just create what everyone else is creating? Why do we always have to be better? What's wrong with being like the rest of the world?"

"Who should we vote for? Lebed? Zyuganov?"

"We don't need all this garbage from the West. The television is filled with it. Nothing but advertising, sex, and violence. How does the Snickerization of the economy improve our lives? You TV people have been bought. It's all about money, nothing but money."

That evening, the discussion is shown on TV in its entirety. The heart surgeon speaks without interruption. There are long, nostalgic interviews with people who still have fond memories of what Revolution Day was like "before." *Chapayev*, the classic film of the Revolution, is aired at prime time.

I can't help wondering whether it is my destiny to love those for whom I am the eternal enemy.

n i n e t e e n

■

S hortly after the demonstration in Palace Square, I wake up one morning to a St. Bernard eagerly licking my face. I have finally found a place to live, a room in the apartment of an actress friend of a friend of Masha and Misha's. "It will either be wonderful or terrible," I say to them, after meeting her and taking weeks to come to a decision. "She's complicated. We will be friends or enemies. Nothing in between. The apartment is a mess. But it's all I can afford."

There are no surprises. Things quickly turn out to be terrible. There are dog hairs everywhere, such a quantity of dog hairs that I should (but don't) sweep my room three times a day, and in the kitchen, dog saliva spreads from the dog dish to the floor and the open wooden shelves that hold all of the dishes, pots, pans, and silverware. On my first day in the apartment, while Nadia is out walking the dog, I remove everything from the shelves and scrub it thoroughly. I exhibit an uncustomary domestic vigilance. When Nadia returns with her dog, she is quietly outraged. I have just moved in. What right do I have to take over her kitchen?

I don't say, "It was filthy, so I had to clean it." Instead I am conciliatory, saying that I am a terrible housekeeper myself and understand how difficult it can be for someone else. "I just decided to help."

Her eyes are icy. She closes the door of her room and keeps it closed. I do the same with mine, though she has to walk through mine to get to the bathroom. From the window of my room, I see a long *allée* of snow-covered locust trees. Children are playing on a snowy slide in the playground. Babushki are standing in the snow watching them. I decide that I was wrong. I should have left everything as it was, and washed only what I needed to use, instead of trying to teach a complete stranger by example. Russians detest reformers. Someone once said to me that no reformer in Russia ever lasted more than twelve years. But what about Peter the Great? He, like Gorbachev, was oriented toward the West, which means being sensible, having perspective. These are foreign virtues. They have nothing to do with Russia.

"I'm sorry if I offended you," I say in a voice I recognize as ingratiating, intent on peace at any price. "I didn't mean to."

"You're a phony," Nadia says. "If there's one thing you learn in the theater, it's how not to be phony. I hate phonies."

I retreat to my room and write a letter to my mother, whose memory has so radically deteriorated recently that she has to be told every five minutes that I am in Russia. I don't say anything in the letter about housekeeping, or about the St. Bernard's saliva or the accumulation of vodka bottles in the kitchen (which I had the good sense not to remove), or about Nadia's telling me that I am a phony. I don't ask her why I grovel instead of saying, "Fuck you and your dog hairs." Why am I polite when I should shout? Why do I shout when I should be polite?

I don't say that I rented this room because it was the only one I could afford and there was a fifty-fifty chance of its turning out to be terrific instead of terrible, because I inherited my father's irrational optimism about anything that has a fifty-fifty chance, instead of her pessimism about the same odds.

I don't tell her about the hot-water heater in the bathroom, which is a miracle of complexity: you have to turn on the hot-water tap in the kitchen before returning to the bathroom and lighting the heater with a long wooden match and waiting for the hot water to flow. I don't say that, as a result of two small explosions that scattered soot all over the bathroom, I practically never turn on the hot water anymore, since I have a congenital inability to follow instructions on a repetitive basis and prefer the *banya* anyway, for the intimacy, the heat, the conviviality, the earnestness with which we beat ourselves with birch branches, steam ourselves until we can't stand it anymore, then throw ourselves into a freezing swimming pool. I do say that: that I love going to the *banya*.

I also say how happy I am to be back in Russia, where contradictions are the norm. I write about a concert of classical music played by children between six and sixteen, at which the audience consisted largely of girls with big bows in their hair and boys in bow ties who never squirmed in their seats. I say that I am rereading *Crime and Punishment* from a new perspective, and that Dostoevsky was right when he said that beauty will save the world. There is enough beauty in this city, I write, to last me a lifetime. Anyway, I am my father's daughter, and as all Russians know, hope dies last. It hasn't died yet, I write. I don't write about bandits. I don't say that there is murder in my heart.

When I finish the letter, I look around the room. Even with all of the dog hairs, it is a lovely room, with its rosy wallpaper and an antique ceiling fixture that casts a warm golden light over everything.

"And by the way," I write in a postscript, "if anyone wants to know what I am doing in Russia, tell them that I am waiting for beauty to save the world, that if it happens anywhere, it has to happen here."

The fax from my friend and next-door neighbor in Maine who frequently visits my mother at her retirement community apartment, half an hour from where I live, is dated November 14.

> Your mother had a rough, disoriented weekend. She wandered time and time again into a large private luncheon being hosted in the dining room. She wanted to eat (although she already had) and couldn't grasp the fact that she wasn't included in the party. On Sunday, the electricity was out from morning until night. Although a generator lights the halls and community rooms, the apartments have only an emergency night light. I spent the night on the couch in her apartment, and we had fun together, but she was pretty thrown by it. The administration has suggested that your mother have a medical reevaluation.

I stand by the window, my hands on the radiator, which is generating no heat at all. The radiator under the other window is only slightly warmer. What is happening to my mother? For the past seven years, her mind has been clouding over, a slow attrition, like drops of water wearing away the original contours of her mind, leaving a smooth and sometimes even glassy surface in its place. She isn't aggressive or peculiar. She just remembers a little bit less from one week to the next, a drop less of what happened in the past, a gallon less of what happened yesterday. She still likes to dance. She still has the ladylike graciousness and generosity of spirit that are the hallmarks of her generation of prerevolutionary Russians, who were dumped out on a world reluctant to receive them, a generation that understood better than most the meaning of Dostoevsky's belief in redemption through suffering.

Mama, I came here for your sake, to repair the holes in a past that is vanishing along with your memory, faster than I can salvage it. I didn't say that in my letter, but it's true, though perhaps meaningless to an eighty-six-year-old woman whose daughter has vanished across an ocean and a continent.

I reread the letter for hidden meanings, but there are none. The meaning is all too clear: Your mother needs you. A decent daughter doesn't tell lyrical tales about nostalgia for the homeland and recovering her roots while leaving the real human being who is the incarnation of those roots to fend for herself. Even as I am writing letters to her about the Russian soul (which everyone but myself, with my immense capacity for romantic self-deception, sees as being in practically irreversible decline), she is wandering the hallways of a retirement community we can't afford, trying to figure out whether it is winter or summer, whether she should go downstairs to eat or has already eaten. Russian daughters don't abandon their mothers. Only American daughters do that.

I shuffle through the growing pile of apartment-related documents on the mirrored vanity I use as a desk. A picture has begun to emerge from them, a paper trail. All I need now is the original sales agreement with the escrow number on it that corresponds to the escrow-account number of the California bank to which I wired the money. If I had that, I could prove that I paid for the apartment. If I had that apartment money now, I could get all of the help for my mother that she needs. I could even bring her here to live with me. I wouldn't have to sit around figuring out how to sustain her, choosing between my life and hers. I wouldn't be a perfect daughter, but I wouldn't be a heartless one either.

For weeks now, I have been trying to cajole a copy of the contract out of the real-estate company that sold us the apartment, but have gotten nowhere. Even if I had all of the documents now, it would be months before the case would go to court, and even longer before something could be decided.

"She stole your money, it's your money down the toilet."

"Not stole. Not really."

"Stole."

"Yura, tell me please, are you a hundred percent sure that nothing would happen to her?"

"Nothing. As I said, we wouldn't even touch her little finger if you said so."

"But what if B dies of fright? What if she has a nervous breakdown?"

"Your money down the toilet. What if you have a nervous breakdown?"

"I won't. Why should I? Money is a vulgar concern. This is only a question of money. Money should never control your life. No one should have a nervous breakdown or die of fright just because of money."

"Just?"

"Yes, just. It's just . . . but what about my mother? What should I do about my mother?" There is no reason to panic, absolutely no reason at all.

I pick up the phone and call Masha. I tell her about the letter from America. It's not necessary to tell her about the panic. She can hear that for herself. "Come over," she says. "Come now and spend the night."

Outside, it is snowing, as it has almost every day since the beginning of November. I decide to walk. Snow always calms me.

It is densely packed now, and beneath it is a thick layer of black ice, worn so smooth on the streets that if the snow were cleared off it would be perfect for skating. My boots squeak against the packed snow. It sounds like a chorus of crickets. You only hear that squeak when the temperature drops to zero. The snow must be perfectly dry, the air so cold that even in bright sunlight there is no possibility of its softening. It is the sound of real Russian winter. On days like that, everyone looks more beautiful than usual, especially the women in their fur coats and hats and shawls wrapped around their heads, and the swaddled children. They all look as if they have just come running out of a *banya* to roll in the snow. And at night, as soon as that early darkness comes over the city, the snow becomes brilliant, the single natural source of light in a darkened universe.

There's a solution to everything. Of course there is. On nights like this, it's not hard to believe.

In the end, I decide not to stay overnight at Masha and Misha's. But by the time I leave, it is after midnight, and the metro and trams have stopped running. The only people on the street are people like myself, who left wherever they were too late to catch the last metro, people who are walking their dogs late, people who are walking other people home. I start walking back to the apartment, feeling just a little bit nervous. Women don't usually walk alone here at night. Misha wanted me to stay. He was adamant about it. And I was just as adamant about leaving. I wanted to have that feeling again, to hear the squeak and feel that happiness. I wanted to sleep in my own bed. Sometimes there is nothing more important than a squeak and sleeping in one's own bed, even if it isn't really one's own.

The streetlights shine on the snow. As I walk, I check to see if there's anyone behind me. There isn't. But then, suddenly, soundlessly, there is. I see a shadow behind me, but almost immediately, as soon as I realize that it is mine, I see a second shadow in front of me. How is this possible? How can my shadow be in front of me and in back of me simultaneously? I look down at the ground again. The shadows are multiplying as I walk. They shift places, so it isn't so easy to identify them, but I am sure that I have seen as many as four. I count again. No. There are only three now. And then again four. It is an eerie feeling. I have never seen four shadows before. Is this an optical illusion, or has my imagination gone wild? I concentrate, trying to separate imagination from reality. But there is no denying it. I have sometimes two, sometimes three, and sometimes four shadows, which move closer together and farther apart as I walk. Is one of them Yura? Is he following me? If I called him, if I said, Okay, go ahead with it, would he follow me forever? I would never be able to walk alone again at night. I would live in fear. And what kind of life would that be?

There are four shadows again now. I can't keep track of them, they shift so often. Maybe sinners have more shadows. Maybe Raya was right.

In the distance ahead of me, I see three transport workers in bright-orange jackets. I want to ask them about the shadows, but by the time I get to where they are, they have already flagged down a car and gotten in. I look up at the street lamp and see that the snow is descending in a long, delicate, silver cone beneath the street lamps, drifting very slowly, very distinctly, like silver New Year's confetti. I am quite sure that I have never seen snow look like that before. Then the streetlights go out. That means it is already one-thirty in the morning, and I have been walking for more than an hour. The street is completely dark now—nothing but two widely spaced traffic signals along Ligovsky Prospekt, blinking yellow on and off in the distance, and beyond them, near the Ligovsky metro, a single street lamp. I have never walked alone this far in the middle of the night. With the street lamps off, I can no longer see the four shadows or the silver cones of snow. It occurs to me that in the morning I have to ask someone if they have ever seen themselves with four shadows, if they have ever seen snow falling below street lamps in long silver cones.

In the morning, I will find out whether or not I am going mad.

Another argument with Nadia has erupted—this time over politics, over Russia's "Western lapdog" foreign minister Kozyrev and shock therapist Gaidar, both of whom Nadia adores, and I despise. "Look what shock therapy has done to you," I say. "Do you like going out to find jobs that involve turning your kitchen into a tile factory, or selling Herbalife, or Scientology? Do you like the idea of being Blanche du Bois with a tile factory in the kitchen? Kozyrev is a spineless, ingratiating character, a phony. Remember how you said that you hate phonies? Well, look at him bowing and scraping before the West, a man absolutely without backbone."

She says, "Shock therapy is exactly what we Russians need. We are naturally lazy and don't understand anything besides shock. Men like Gaidar and Kozyrev are our only hope for a civilized future. If people don't vote for them in the elections, the elections should be canceled."

"I thought you were for democracy," I say. "How does canceling elections fit in with democracy?"

"If people are too stupid to know what's good for them, then they don't deserve democracy," she answers.

After that, she looks at me with permanent suspicion, as if I am one of the conspirators plotting the overthrow of her gods. Maybe she's right. Maybe I am.

On December 5, there is another fax from America. It says that my mother woke up two mornings in a row at 5 a.m. The first time, she wandered down to the nurses' station in the assisted-living unit. The second time, she went into another apartment, where the door had been left open, walked into the bedroom, and stood over the woman who was asleep in the bed until the woman woke up. At the administration's insistence, my mother now has an appointment with the doctor. This is beginning to look like a pattern.

My knees go weak when I read the letter. What if the woman had woken up and died of fright? I write back to apologize for my mother and say that I have a return ticket to America on January 18, when the university semester ends, but I can't come sooner. I only pray that by then I can figure out what to do next.

I write to California again. I have already sent three faxes, directing all of my queries to the wife of the president of the American real-estate company here that sold us the apartment. The people who work at the company here say that they don't have the documents, they are kept in California. The company president's wife in California is the keeper of the documents. In reply to my faxes requesting them, she has first answered, via a phone conversation with their secretary here (nothing is ever put in writing), that they will send them out immediately, then that, in order to send them out, they need an official letter of authorization from me, then, when they have received the letter of authorization, that her husband will bring them back to Russia with him after Thanksgiving, then that, for some unexplained reason, they can't be found. "If they're not here, and they're not there," I ask in my next letter, "then where are they?" Hedging her words, the secretary tells me that they appear to have temporarily disappeared, but will surely be found. A few days later, when I call their office, no one answers. Not that day or the next or any day that entire week.

I write to my mother:

I miss you and think about you a lot. I wish it were possible for you to be here with me. I went to a lecture last night given by a woman whose family left Russia at about the same time as you did. During the lecture she said, "We didn't consider ourselves emigrants, because we didn't leave our country, our country left us: it was taken away from us." I couldn't help wondering whether you feel the same way.

Living here helps me to understand my childhood. I keep thinking about what happens to families when they immigrate to America for the sake of their children, but then lose those children to America, as the children become Americanized. A few weeks ago, I went to a piano competition, and during the break, I heard one of the jurors say of the only pianist whose playing had moved me, "He has the Odessa sound." I didn't even know that there was such a thing. Did Granny's brother, the one who was a pianist and composer, play with the Odessa sound too? When guests at the dacha played the piano before the Revolution, did they play with the Odessa sound? If our family had stayed in Russia, would I have kept on playing the piano with the Odessa sound? Did the fact that the first thing you bought when you came to America was a piano have anything to do with the Odessa sound?

America is oriented toward the future, Russia toward the past. Maybe that's why I feel at home here. I know that there is so much you don't remember now. If you don't remember, I will try to remember for you. That's my real job here.

Maybe in the spring, if we have enough money, you can come here and we can go to Odessa together. I hope so.

Love,

When I reread the letter, I understand that it is a miracle of evasion, in which, aside from avoiding the subject of her present circumstances (discussing which would accomplish nothing aside from scaring her), I have also done everything possible to

lend legitimacy to my desire to remain in Russia not mention-
ing that I have abandoned her in order to do it. Of course, "I
wish it were possible" for her to be here with me, as if some dis-
embodied agent were responsible for its not being possible, as if
it had nothing at all to do with me. Of course, I have found nice
locutions for everything. In the end, however, I have said absolutely nothing.

Logically, though, it really would be impossible to bring her
here. Black ice would cease to be beautiful. She would freeze to
death on the streets or even in this apartment, which in any case
has only one bed. We would live together in one room, with an
angry Nadia in the next. The St. Bernard would constantly be
knocking her over. There would be quarrels. She would have to
climb four flights of stairs. We would be just like . . . just like
everyone else in Russia.

I put my hands on the lukewarm radiator again, wondering
whether or not to send the letter. In the end I send it. Nothing
has happened yet to change me. I still want to believe that black
ice is beautiful. I still want to live certain lies. I want nothing to
interfere with their perpetuation.

The real-estate company that sold us the apartment has apparently vanished, at least temporarily. I call Constantine Kirillovich to explain the situation, but his telephone is always busy, or
else he's with a client or in court. Time is running out. I have to
do something. There are daily desperate faxes from America, and
equally desperate faxes back.

I no longer look at families on the street and think about the
differences between my life and theirs. Now the only people I
notice are babushki. Getting on the trolley, I mentally measure
the distance between the steps, watching how old people grasp

the handrail and hoist themselves up or down, strangely suspended in relation to the bottom step, which is so high off the ground that even I have to mobilize my energies for it. I watch waitresses in restaurants giving free bowls of borscht to rheumy-eyed babushki in shawls and *valenki* who are obviously unable to pay, and just as obviously humiliated by having to admit it. I listen to the sclerotic tirades of babushki on the tramway. I see babushki with canes and blind eyes and swollen legs walking up four or five flights of stairs in their apartment buildings, see them in line at the stores trying to buy the smallest and cheapest possible piece of meat, or no meat at all, just a single carrot, or two potatoes. The younger ones, more energetic, always have their grandchildren in tow, and are always carrying heavy sacks of produce. They live in communal apartments. They don't complain. There are no babushki here who live in retirement communities, wear lipstick, go to the hairdresser once a week, invest in stocks, have financial advisers, and take vacations.

People in America don't address old women whom they encounter on the street as *Baboulia*, "Little Grandmother." One of my students at the university who has visited America once asked me, "What do they do with old people in America, hide them?" If my mother came here, she would be like an heirloom exhibit in a museum.

I have to stop thinking about bringing her here. It's obviously out of the question.

On the trolley, the windows are completely frosted over. People scratch out tiny peepholes in the glass with their fingertips in order to get some idea of where they are. If you know the route, you can figure everything out. If not, not.

It is remarkable how much you can see through a peephole the size of your fingertip: the entire panorama of the street in front, alongside of, and behind the tram. If you adjust your vision slightly, you can see the tops of the buildings as well. If you are standing up, you can't see out the windows at all. All you can see are other people's peepholes at random levels on the window. Maybe that's all you can ever see anyway. You just have to keep changing your perspective.

t w e n t y

■

Decemeber 17 is election day. I go with Masha to the polls. There are forty-three different parties and candidates for the Duma. I am allowed to go into the voting booth with her. She has decided to become what she calls "an activist." This means voting for the first time in her life, but she can't decide for whom: maybe Yavlinsky's people, maybe Gaidar's. Someone democratic anyway. I help her decide. (Is this what they call "vote tampering"?) It definitely isn't Gaidar.

The lobby bar of the Grand Hotel Europe is crowded with foreign tourists and the criminal elite, who sit in deep leather chairs at round tables in a mahogany-paneled room with three immense tiled Russian fireplaces, racks of foreign newspapers, and a pair of floor-to-ceiling stained-glass windows framing the bar. The criminal elite wear leather and shearling jackets, or long black leather coats. Their bodyguards, former students at the Institute for Physical Culture, former KGB men of the lower sort, and common criminals, pace the corridors just outside the bar, walkie-talkies pressed against their ears. Their bosses carry cellular phones that ring constantly, into which they bark commands. The bosses are almost all accompanied by exceptionally young and lovely Russian women who look like schoolgirls but wear long fur coats.

The headquarters of the EC observers of today's elections are upstairs in the business center adjacent to the Atrium Café. The offices are empty: the observers have scattered about the country to keep track of the polling. Security is tight at the hotel. I am carrying a suspicious container: a bright-yellow plastic egg-container with a handle. The security guard has seen thousands of these all over the city, but people who come into the Grand Hotel Europe aren't usually carrying them. Who knows what could be in it? He tells me to open it for inspection. I do, carefully, not wanting my eggs to break. He peers inside, tells me to close it up, and lets me pass.

In the lobby bar, a pair of Americans ask the waiter to write down the name of the Russian champagne they have been drinking. Another bottle of champagne is uncorked at the table next to mine, where six Russians have just polished off two bottles. There are two women in the group. Their furs are tossed lightly over the chairs. A man with a Clark Gable mustache and slicked hair comes in, wearing a black leather jacket lined in white shearling. With him are six lackeys, four bodyguards, and a restless girl in blue jeans who paces the bar and answers a series of apparently urgent phone calls. The waitresses, usually slow-moving, rush about anxiously, taking their order. One bodyguard stands outside in the corridor, his legs planted wide, his arms akimbo. Another paces back and forth, and a third stands near the second exit, checking his boss's every movement, and the movements of everyone else in the room. The boss orders Johnny Walker. I order cappuccino.

I open the *St. Petersburg Press*. On page four, my throat constricts: GANG OF SIX CHARGED OVER "KILLING FOR FLATS" SCHEME. I keep reading.

> Police have charged a gang of six men with murder after finding a severed human head and hands dumped in a city sewer.
>
> Detectives believe the suspects, aged between 22 and 34, are also guilty of at least two other killings as well as a series of property extortion bids. . . . A police spokesman said the gang was suspected of targeting alcoholic apartment-owners with a view to appropriating their property through a network of bribed officials. Posing as down-and-outs, the mobsters stalked their victims in cheap bars and cafés around the city. Toward the end of last year, one of them befriended V, 34, who was proposing to sell his one-room apartment. Three members of the gang later tried to force him to sign over the apartment to their boss, a 31-year-old city businessman. At this point a friend of the victim's arrived at his apartment and urged V to resist their demands. However, the gangsters allegedly attacked the newcomer, strangled him, and slit his throat before hurling his blood-spattered corpse into a sewer.
>
> The three men were subsequently arrested but released after a three-month investigation failed to produce sufficient evidence to convict them.
>
> The Kalininsky District Police Department reported that over one-third of the 93 murders committed in the area last year were motivated by property theft, particularly related to transactions involving real estate.

So what B said about the Mafia wanting the apartment could have been true. And I didn't believe her. Once again, the evidence against me for the crime of naïveté is on display. I believed "them" and didn't believe her, just the way everyone she met in New York in 1993 wanted to know what was happening in Russia and then became detached and skeptical when she told them, because the *New York Times*, which surely could be believed, had said exactly the opposite. After that, she stopped answering questions.

The problem with B was that so many of her most extravagant opinions turned out to be true. Sometimes it seemed to me that her craziness was nothing more than a consequence of her refusal to knuckle under, one more element of the craftiness that had enabled her to elude all of her potential captors. And in the end I betrayed her, became one of them, went over to what she surely considered "the other side," those who read and believed the *New York Times* and looked askance at her grandiose judgments.

"Russians are an ungrateful people," said Dumas or the Comte de Custine or Brodsky or someone else altogether. B refused to be grateful. For what? she said. For making her a prisoner of my mentality instead of hers? Was that something for which to be grateful?

I was the International Monetary Fund writ small: Take this help. That's what we're here for, to bail you out of this mess you're in. We see the larger picture. We understand that you're on the right path, that if you follow our instructions, and change your ways, exchange your truth for ours, your rose-colored glasses for our rose-colored glasses, in time you'll get to where you're going. Big Brother and Sister have your interests at heart. We'll drive you mad with helpfulness, we'll destroy you with love. We're keeping an eye on you. Every minute of every day, we're keeping an eye on you. Nothing to worry about. No need to be grateful. Leave that to the next generation.

Thank you, thank you, thank you, thank you.

"I spit on your money, but I'll take it anyway. Just for spite, I'll take it."

Who created this monster? Where's the surprise that it bites?

It's probably a good thing that I left Russia when I did. When I could. Before they found my head and hands in some city sewer.

I look up from my newspaper.

At the table next to mine, four men are conferring, two Russians, an Englishman, and a Californian who has come to Leningrad to buy real estate. The Russians tell him that he will have difficulty buying buildings on the private market, but that the city has a great many for sale. What does he have in mind? "Prime," he says. And how much is he willing to pay? I can't hear the answer, but see his informers exchange glances that say, "Real business."

"Are there people living in these buildings?" he asks.

"Yes, of course, but this is not a problem."

"Do you mean there is no law regarding tenants?"

"We can take care of it. You don't have to worry about that."

"I was afraid you'd say that. It makes things worse."

"In central London," the Englishman says, "if someone lives in an apartment, there is no way to get them to move."

The Russians confer in Russian. "Don't worry," one says to the other. "They just want to protect their image. It's nothing serious."

Then he switches back to English. "Actually," he says, "we find new apartments for everyone. They are much happier with the new ones than the old. How do you visualize these apartments?"

"Luxury. Two bedrooms. Two baths. Separate showers. Westerners won't get along without separate showers."

Only half an hour ago, on the tramway, I heard a pensioner say, "Why should our signs be in English when we don't speak English? Why should we have to worry about making things comfortable for them instead of for us? Whose country is this? They'll see. Wait until tomorrow morning."

Tomorrow morning is now. The figures start to come in. The television festivities are suddenly sodden. The popular TV announcer Svetlana Sokolova looks like a woman who has lost a pocketbook containing her life's savings. It seems that the Communists have won. Zhirinovsky is in second place. I find the latest edition of *Moscow News* on the newspaper rack. In it is an excerpt from a new book by Professor Alexander Yanov, *After Yeltsin: A Weimar Russia*:

Russia is currently going through a collapse of a centuries-old imperial civilization and the disintegration of all traditional values. . . . The real choice will be the same for Russia as it was in the 1920s for Germany: which of the two ways, civilian or military, will the defeated, humiliated, and agonized country opt for in endeavoring to assert itself as a great world power. . . . Fascism has by no means become an anachronism in Russia. . . . On the contrary, only now has this formerly marginal movement started to develop into a real political force. . . . If the communists return, who will surface on the crest of the new anticommunist wave? It won't be the democrats who are called back to power . . . but, rather, a global network of right-wing extremists . . . the financial pillars of the world conservative revolution whose goal is the destruction of world civilization. . . . Truly Russia is a gift from heaven to the international fascist capital that has for decades vegetated in the forgotten backyards of world politics. Although an armed coup is possible, the best way to power is through elections, through inculcation of ideology among the broad masses of the population.

Someone uncorks another bottle of champagne. The tourists are laughing and chattering. The deals are entering their next stage. It occurs to me that there is remarkably little difference between communist thugs, capitalist thugs, and fascist thugs. I listen to the sound of the piano in the alcove near the corridor where one of the thug bodyguards is standing, straining for, but not hearing, someone starting to play the "Marseillaise."

t w e n t y - o n e

■

There is a note from Nadia on the kitchen counter. "I have gone to Pskov for a few days. Please feed and walk the dog." I am outraged. I look at the dog. The dog looks at me. There is no love lost between us. He is too big and this apartment is too small. There isn't enough room here for both of us. And he slobbers. I don't care if he is gentle and has soulful eyes. I don't want to be responsible for him. How can she have done this to me? She didn't even ask. What if I had other plans? I do have other plans. My plans do not include walking the dog, whose name I never pronounce because I have all along been struggling to deny his presence in my food and on my clothes. Now we are alone together, locked in unholy matrimony for who knows how long.

I call Masha. How far is it to Pskov? How long does the trip take? Most of a day there. A day back. She won't be home for at least three or four days. It is snowing. I grudgingly feed the St. Bernard and avert my eyes from his slobbering. It isn't his fault that Nadia went off and left him; a dog is like a child, you can't just let him fend for himself. She is always talking about how much she loves him, but what kind of love is this, going off and leaving him in the hands of someone with murder in her heart, a heart that has been only temporarily subdued by a sweet surge of righteousness. He is an innocent. I know that. But still I look at him with distaste. "If I walk you, you'll drag me all over the place," I shout at him. "I already told her once that I can't do it, that I have a weak ankle that has already broken twice. I told her! How could she just leave us alone with each other like this?" He keeps his head down as if he is ashamed of the answer.

I get the dog's leash and hook it onto his metal-spiked collar. I wrap the leash three times around my wrist. We walk down the stairs, with me holding on as tightly as I can, propelled rapidly forward against my will, struggling for control, and knowing that one good yank will topple me down the stairs on top of him.

"You bought me," B said almost two years ago. "Now I am like a dog on a short leash."

"I didn't know that you were for sale," I said.

But she was. She had calculated the price and decided that it was worth it, that she could sell herself and come out ahead on the deal. If all of Russia was on the block, grabbed up by whoever had nerve enough to steal it, why should she be at any lesser advantage? Life was a tactical maneuver, and you had to seize the moment.

But if she sold herself to me, then who was I in her eyes? The person who could save her from the disaster of her life when the floodwaters were creeping higher and higher, drowning out not only her personal universe, but the entirety of the universe in which she had, until now, lived? It was like the last days of Pompeii, people frozen in flight, their mouths open, as ash came hurling down on them. But there was no ash, no fire, no flood, only the familiar oxygen suddenly vanishing, and in its place nothing at all, no way to keep on breathing. And in this moment, B found me.

In 1991, B and I were eating treasures from the farmers' market, but in the stores there was nothing. Absolutely nothing. I thought I understood what was going on then, but I was wrong. I had a "false experience," one that was rich in detail but so colored by the absence of critical information that I failed to grasp the essentials. I assumed then that empty shelves were the norm, because I had never seen them full. I understood that food was acquired in "other ways," or at the very least that it disappeared before I ever laid eyes on it, because those who needed to know where and when it would appear knew, and were there when it did. It was obvious to me: people got the things they needed not because they simply walked into a store and bought them, but because they had connections that bound them together in a web of interdependency of which I would never be a part. I adapted to this, coming to understand that everything that wasn't, was; and everything that was, wasn't. It never occurred to me that for B, I might be just another connection.

The blockade of Leningrad by the Nazis lasted nine hundred days—almost two and a half years. A million and a half people starved to death, a quarter of the population. The memories of those who survived were branded into their skin, shaped into their modus vivendi, their methods of thinking, feeling, and simply being. Watching your child starve to death, or seeing yourself or your neighbor resort to cannibalism, is not a memory, it is an illness, a virus that remains forever in your system. It affects your perception of the nature of hard times. Anything short of the blockade isn't hard times, and it would be petty to complain about such things as mere shortages, mere coupons, when the coupons guaranteed the possibility of having something rather than confirming the presence of nothing. Besides, anyone who survived the war learned that it is always wise to have enough food on hand to last for at least two years. And they did. B's mother's pantry was full even if her refrigerator was empty. The stores could be empty, prices could skyrocket, and all of it would hardly touch her; she was prepared for the siege, and so was anyone else who had been alive during that "Great Patriotic War." You survived by planning ahead and curbing your expectations.

Still, in 1991, just as the Soviet Union was sliding into extinction, there was nothing in the stores. Any normal Russian with a memory would say, *"Vy pomnite, v' 1991 godu vobshe nye bilo nichevo v' magazinakh"*—"You remember, in 1991 there was nothing, absolutely nothing in the stores." Not "on Friday there was nothing" but "in 1991."

Wasn't I here in 1991? Wasn't I sitting at a table loaded with food, talking with Dostoevsky's great-great, wasn't I carrying a fruitcake along Nevsky Prospekt? The fruitcake, after all, was in a store. How, then, could the stores have been empty? What country was I in? What was going on? Living within that moment, I was unable to grasp it. Russia is a land of illusions, of circles within circles, of multiplying mysteries. What I remember is no proof of accuracy. The past is infinitely crafty in its ability to metamorphose.

Do you remember Dyadya Petya, the old man standing in the ticket line for *blokadnik*s at the Kirov in 1993? I thought I understood him too. I thought I understood the situation. But almost a year later, I saw him sitting off to the side, behind the columns at the Philharmonic, listening to Mahler's Third Symphony with a rapt face. His sweater was as worn and ragged as before, and he remained toothless. But his face was rapt. He didn't look out of place there, among the newly impoverished Russian intelligentsia. There were many others like him, the kind of people who are sometimes sponsored to important conferences in the West because they are unable to pay their own expenses, and wander into stores in New York or Paris looking sufficiently battered by life that they are identified by salespeople as potential thieves. Maybe that's why I misunderstood the situation at the Kirov. Then I still looked at Dyadya Petya with Western eyes. I didn't understand what Misha later told me, that Russians are often gray on the outside but brightly colored on the inside, whereas in the West it is just as often the opposite. Appearances are more deceiving in Russia than in any other country I have ever known.

After that evening at the Philharmonic, I saw Dyadya Petya over and over again. At the Small Hall of the Philharmonic. At the Big Hall. At the ballet. At the opera. He was always there. I saw him in line for tickets several times, but never again under the watchful eyes of the Mafia, just among his friends who had passes that allowed them to sit in any seat that was vacant at the start of the performance. As he listened to the music, I watched him, his sparse hair flying about his head in gray wisps, an aura of angelic sweetness hovering about him, his love of the music palpable. Once, during April, when the sun doesn't set until after nine o'clock, I saw him sitting in the orchestra. Suddenly, in the middle of the playing of Shostakovich's Tenth Symphony, with Temirkanov conducting, a shaft of sunlight pierced one of the arched windows set into the Philharmonic's mansard roof, bounced off one of the eight fantastic birthday-cake chandeliers that dominate the hall, and lit up the orange sweater of a woman standing in the balcony. In another minute, it moved past her and suffused the adjacent marble column with light, and then, in some peculiar leap of optical faith, landed on the left lens of Dyadya Petya's eyeglasses, which instantly beamed the light back toward the stage. You don't get messages from God like that every day.

I also frequently saw someone else from that 1993 Kirov Theater line, a woman with long, slightly disheveled gray hair wound into a bun and thick bifocals, who was always smiling an otherworldly smile and hunted for empty seats at concerts like a warrior woman, pouncing on the best she could find and enduring repeated evictions when the real ticket-holders arrived at the last minute. Once, in the buffet at the Philharmonic, I bought an open-faced smoked-salmon sandwich and a piece of cake during the intermission. She sat down next to me at one of the small round buffet tables and stared intently at my food. Then she said, "Do you mind if I have a bite?" and when I, startled, said, "Please go ahead," she took the entire piece of cake. Until that moment, it had never entered my mind that she or Dyadya Petya might be hungry. It was easier to perceive them as marginally mad or just plain eccentric.

Now I know that those concerts were their life, their sustenance. They went the way Russians went during the blockade, when friends and family and neighbors were dropping dead of starvation on the streets or freezing to death on their way home from work, because a life in art was what kept them going.

When I realize this, I feel ashamed of myself for standing in line in 1993 and trying to buy tickets that should have been theirs, even if the Mafia, with its Roentgen vision and golden talons, was minding the nest. I didn't belong in that line. The weasel was right, and so was his boss. A few days ago, I saw Dyadya Petya in the underground passageway of the Gostiny Dvor metro, selling newspapers. His new Mafia boss was screaming at him about something, but he still had that calm, beatific, toothless smile on his face, a smile of inner resourcefulness that said, "As long as I have music, you can't touch me." Oh, Dyadya Petya, I beg your forgiveness. I see now that I was wrong about you, and about all of the others too. I am only grateful for the mercy of your having no idea who I am, and for the fact that both of us can now sit in the same hall, listening to the same music, with what might be the same degree of joy.

In 1991, there was nothing in the stores, and I understood nothing. But B understood. She saw the handwriting on the wall. On her first trip to America the previous winter, she looked at the meat hanging from ceiling hooks on Ottomanelli's Prime Meat Market on Bleecker Street in Manhattan, the finest cuts arranged in a clean, well-lit case. Beautiful meat. Fantastic meat. She came out of the store, sat on a bench, and cried. "Why do you have things like this, and we don't?" She saw fruits in the middle of winter that she couldn't even identify. She walked into an Ames department store and thought that it was like a museum. It's easy to develop an appetite for such things, and then the appetite turns into a craving, and from there into an obsession. The All-American Smile is always looking down at you from some poster advertising L&M cigarettes, Coca-Cola, or Miller Lite. Why are Americans always smiling? It must be because they are so happy. Until B visited America, she didn't think of herself as poor. She was the privileged wife of a conductor. People usually don't feel poor until they start to make comparisons. But by the time she left America that first time, the worm was already in the apple. "Here, taste it, you'll like it. Here, have a little more." And before you know it, it's too late, you're all the way at the bottom of the stairs, a dog on a short leash, yanked along by its temptress.

We are at the bottom of the stairs, Nadia's dog and I. He is eager to get out into the snow. He strains at the leash, pulling me out the door behind him. The decision about where we will go has almost nothing to do with me. He knows his routines. I just go where the thrust of his weight tells me to go. Even if B was on a short leash, it was she who controlled the direction, not I. It was obvious to anyone who knew us that she was the Blue Angel, even though B had never heard of the Blue Angel.

The St. Bernard and I are walking on the tree-lined boulevard outside the apartment. He is strolling, sniffing, pissing. I give the leash a little slack, thinking that maybe this won't be so bad after all. The snow is falling heavily, masking the dust and debris on the street, turning all the detritus of the city into softly sculpted hillocks. Silence. Serenity. We turn around and walk back into the courtyard, along the alley. An elaborate wrought-iron gate is ahead of us on the left. There is a wide gap in the spiked fence to the left of it, where a section has been hack-sawed away, doing away with the inconvenience of simply open-ing the gate or even breaking its lock. Quick solutions can always be found to imponderably difficult questions. I barely have time to register the presence of a man and his dog in the distance when I am jolted fast forward. I grab the leash tighter, straining against it, my feet sliding in the snow as the St. Bernard plunges in the direction of his pal. I am just hanging on now, praying that my faulty ankle won't collapse beneath me. But suddenly, for no apparent reason, he veers quickly to the left in the direc-tion of the gate, and I am swung around so that my chest slams hard against it. I drop the leash and the St. Bernard runs off. My chest is throbbing. I fall to the ground, stretching spread-eagled in the snow. Let the damn dog go wherever he wants to. It has nothing to do with me.

I lie there looking up at the gray sky, big flakes of snow falling on my face. The man with the dog whom I saw at a dis-tance appears above me, together with another man who is holding the St. Bernard. They look down at me. The owner of the other dog says, "A dog like that is no dog for a woman. I've told Nadia that a hundred times." He helps me to my feet, and offers to walk the St. Bernard back to the apartment for me. I gladly accept.

When we get upstairs, I put the dog in Nadia's room and shut the door. Then I go to my room. A newly arrived fax is ly-ing on the floor.

It is from my mother's doctor.

At the Residence's request, I have recently seen your mother for an evaluation. As you yourself know, she has progressive dementia and will require increasingly more sophisticated, or at least readily available, care. I could foresee, for example, a situation in which she might be lost for several hours in the housing complex. Even worse, she could stray outside and be unable to find her way back in. This suggests that she would most benefit from someone taking the responsibility to know exactly where she is every minute of every day and night.

I have told the administration at the Residence that I do not consider your mother's condition an emergency. The decisions on what to do next can easily wait until your return in January at which time we should have a family conference to consider your mother's best options. The financial calculations are beyond my area of expertise.

I lie down on the bed. My chest hurts. So does my ankle. I try to feel reassured. I now have until January to figure things out. But what if I can't figure things out by then? What if the financial calculations are beyond everyone's area of expertise? What if they are so simple that they are insoluble? "Every minute of every day." That's (I calculate it rapidly in my head) almost fifteen hundred minutes of someone giving her their undivided attention. What if they have to go to the bathroom or brush their teeth or have a cup of coffee alone or just think of something else for a moment or two? What if, when those pesky financial calculations turn out to be beyond anyone's area of expertise, the only possible someone available to do the job is me?

I get up from the bed and go into Nadia's room, where the telephone is. The St. Bernard is lying on her bed, his paws crossed over his eyes. He looks up at me woefully. I refuse to make eye contact.

I call my friend Vadim and ask him to start hunting for someone to come and help with my mother in America. It shouldn't be so hard to find someone who wants to go to America for six months, he says. The problem will be what happens when the person gets there. Vadim is a mathematics professor who lost his job when his family decided to immigrate to Israel in the seventies. He stayed behind to take care of his aged mother. When she died, he stayed behind to take care of his eleven-year-old dog. He never really wanted to leave anyway. He can't imagine how anyone who has spent a lifetime in this city, whose heart and soul are wedded to it, can leave. For a while he was responsible for the cultural program at the Russian Museum High School, but when the special programs in the educational system started to collapse, his job went along with them. He sold almost everything he owned in order to buy a car, which he now uses as a taxi. He has gotten very thin over the last few years. And, like the rest of the Russian intelligentsia, he is sure to know a lot of people who are desperate enough that, even with their doctorates in physics, they might be willing to help out with my mother. In this sphere, his connections are vast.

I hang up the phone. Next to it is a short list of phone numbers. I call the first one that doesn't have a family name or patronymic attached to it. It's "Katya." Luckily for me, Katya has an answering machine. I leave a message saying, "Someone needs to take care of Nadia's dog until Nadia gets back from Pskov. I am going out of town. I will leave the key at Misha and Masha's." I recite their phone number and quickly hang up. Still not looking at the dog, I walk out the door.

Vadim says that Vica, a former computer programmer in the military-industrial complex whose present dream is to start a Montessori school of her own, is probably the person I need for my mother. Her husband is a former leader of expeditions to the Antarctic, whose present dream is to find a job. The most overused word in Russia today is *bivshe*, "former." Together, Vica and her husband have opened a café in the basement of a school, but it isn't earning any money yet because they consider it immoral to make a profit from schoolchildren.

They would like to set up an after-school program in the café, oriented toward Montessori and mountain climbing, but so far they haven't been able to get either project off the ground. Getting things off the ground takes money, and they don't have any. Neither does anyone else they know who's trying to get something off the ground.

We meet at their apartment. Vica sees me as the Statue of Liberty incarnate. She says that she has always dreamed of going to America. Is it true, she asks, that the sidewalks in America are covered with green plastic? Astroturf is an interesting variation on the theme of streets paved with gold. How far the gods have fallen!

I tell her no, it isn't true, but she's not quite ready to believe me. In America, everything is possible. I try to tell her about my mother, but she doesn't believe me about that either. I emphasize that my mother lives in Maine. "How far is that from New York?" she asks. "Far," I say. "And, anyway, my mother has a memory problem. She can't be left alone. She needs a constant companion. There wouldn't be time to see New York."

"What about Brighton Beach?" she says. "And the Statue of Liberty? Could we at least see them?"

Then she tells me that she has a friend, an old woman, a former actress, now bedridden, who lives alone, and that she constantly runs back and forth to the woman's apartment in order to help her out. "There's nothing so strange about having a memory problem," she says. "Most people have it. It's just old age."

I want to believe her, so I do. Anyway, at this point, what choice do I have? Vica speaks English (a little) and drives a car (or says she does). She does not, however, have a passport or a visa. I say that I will write an invitation to America for her and arrange a visa consultation for her at the consulate. Maybe she's right. For Russians, life is just reality, not something to be tinkered with in order to get a prettier result.

For all I know, Vica will be just the kind of person my mother needs.

All right. So I won't murder or maim B. Beauty will save the world, yes, but each moment is a struggle to sustain that knowledge, to drag beauty out of the swamp in which its mirror image festers. I understand B, but I cannot forgive her. The link between the two has nothing to do with will in any case. "The quality of mercy is not strained." I do not feel mercy. Should I? Should I simply say, philosophically, that there were "extenuating circumstances"? That B was a mutation spawned by the world that produced her, and that all of the rest could therefore have been assumed?

I am in a serious jam. I have to get out of it. Recovering the apartment is my only out. Just because the Mafia was involved in a "killing for flats" scheme doesn't necessarily mean that they were after our apartment. The article said that they focused on alcoholics and down-and-outs. B and I weren't down-and-outs. Anyway, although she is capable of divining some ultimately hard-to-swallow truths, she is also capable of the outrageous lie. The hardest thing for me was figuring out which was which. One of her former lovers once said to her that she should have been a terrorist. She herself told me the story, saying the word with pride, as if it had inspired his tender affection (it probably had). Instead of seeing that as a warning, I interpreted it as a sign of her frailty, the pose of a weak creature aspiring to phenomenal powers. Of course, like everyone of my generation, I read *The Little Prince* at a formative age. I knew why roses have thorns, knew that they are in need of protection even if the thorns draw blood. As Freud taught us, it is just a matter of compensation. Does this mean that the moral peak of our capacities is the comprehension of evil, not its amelioration? If all is to be forgiven because of understanding, what happens to our moral criteria?

Another question: who are the victims in this case? I am already implicated as an accomplice, which disqualifies me as a victim. I can only ask myself, What did I know and when did I know it? This is the question that prevents a safe escape into the protection of naïveté. I knew. I was not naïve. I didn't want to know. I was naïve. Did. Didn't. Did. Didn't.

The commercial section of the U.S. consulate, referred to as the Business Center, is on Bolshaya Morskaya Street, formerly called Herzen Street. A few doors away from the Business Center is Nabokov's former family home, and just beyond it, the ornate Italianate palace designed by Rastrelli and converted by the Soviets into the House of Composers, where B's former lover (the one who said that she should have been a terrorist) composed some of the Soviet Union's best-loved melodies. Composers who work late in the upstairs studios sometimes camp out on the couches for indefinite periods of time.

I have called the Business Center in advance for an appointment with the vice-consul to get his advice on "an apartment problem." I have not yet decided which tack to take, but have noticed with some irritation that the temporary reprieve from my mother's doctor and the article about the apartment murders have combined to diminish the force of my will. There are even days when I say, "The hell with it, just get on with this life," but then I start to think about my mother, and the process starts all over again. I seem to be constitutionally incapable of sustaining a thirst for vengeance long enough to do anything useful with it, and keep being distracted by some small and unexpected daily pleasure (a shaft of light in some side street, an elaborately tied ribbon in a child's hair, snow, a radio program devoted to Akhmatova) that makes me forget there is still murder in my heart. I think this is what Dostoevsky meant about beauty saving the world.

Today is a half–working day just before "Catholic Christmas" (so-called and therefore unobserved here) as opposed to Russian Orthodox Christmas (observed), which falls two weeks later, and the vice-consul, who meets me downstairs wearing blue jeans in acknowledgment of its being "almost a holiday," is so young and attractive that he would fit right into a Pepsi ad. We walk up the grand staircase of the Business Center together, and he leads me into a conference room occupied entirely by a conference table. He sits at the head of the table in a swivel chair, and I sit near him, observing the appropriate physical distance (close but not too close, with an escape route available for both of us). He crosses his left leg over his right knee, revealing the intricate pattern of the sole of his Reeboks, grips his left ankle in one hand, wagging his foot at me, and smiles.

"Well," he says. "So how can I help you?"

I surprise myself by focusing on the problem with my documents and the real-estate agency that seems to have vanished. I tell him that when B and I bought the apartment the president of the company assured me that they kept all documents in California for safety's sake, but now they can't be found either here or there. I need advice on what to do next.

"What you're telling me is very interesting," he says. "I don't know why this hasn't gotten into the news yet, so it isn't public information at this point, but, just between you and me, the president of the company is in very hot water. He is being in-vestigated by the tax police, which just raided his offices here. That would explain why your documents disappeared. Of course it doesn't explain why they disappeared from California, though, who knows, maybe it does."

I'd met his predecessor during the prehistoric Russian wild days of 1992, when B and I had been invited to the Business Round Table he'd set up to forge links between Russians and Americans. It didn't draw a single bona-fide businessman (in-cluding B and me), and the question that generated the most heated discussion at the first meeting was about where to get business cards printed. B and I were a unique phenomenon then, an authentic Russian-American joint venture, an object of envy. It didn't occur to anyone to ask what we were doing, or what kind of business we had. A Russian-American "joint ven-ture" meant free passage into the inner sanctum of connections. When I asked the vice-consul why there were so many weird Americans drifting around Russia, trying to cash in on the Klondike, he said matter-of-factly, "They're attracted like flies to shit." The list he printed out of Russian-American businesses in the city was less than a page long, and there wasn't a recogniza-ble American name in the bunch. The real-estate agency was al-ready established in the city by then, but they weren't looking for business cards or coming to round tables. They were too busy making deals and raking in the money.

A year later, B and I were no longer invited to the Business Round Table. Bigger guns had started moving into Russia. Small fry were just in the way.

"So what do you suggest?" I say now, to the vice-consul's more politic successor.

"I wouldn't recommend your focusing on the real-estate agency," he says. "It would be expensive and wouldn't get you anywhere. You'd be better off trying to solve matters with your former friend. She's the one who's after your apartment. Who is the American living there with her?"

"Dry Cleaning," I say, and tell him the name.

"Doesn't ring a bell," he says. "But if you'd like, I could give them a call, as a good-faith intermediary."

"I doubt it would do any good, though it might scare them, and that wouldn't be so bad. You're welcome to try."

"What's her name?"

I stumble and can't get the words out. If I tell him her last name, she probably won't get another visa to America. It would go on the record, and that would be the end of it. I can't bring myself to do even that. Whatever has happened to that thirst for revenge? Why has it abandoned me when I need it?

I tell him her first name, and nothing more. He doesn't seem to notice the omission.

"Okay," he says. "I'll try to talk to them. It upsets me when things like this happen, especially when Americans are involved. By the way, the story on the real-estate agency should break any day now. Keep your eye out for it."

He shakes my hand and goes downstairs with me. A marine guard at the bottom of the stairs lets me out. As the door is closing behind me, I see the vice-consul running back up the grand staircase, taking the red-carpeted stairs two at a time in his Reeboks.

In anticipation of coming to America, Vica has started taking driving lessons from Masha and Misha's friend Feodor, a professional driving instructor who taught Masha to drive when Misha lost his license. Feodor also works as an ambulance driver for the city's cardiology-reanimation team and is a part-time unpaid theater administrator, the usual story. After Vica's first lesson, Feodor says that she's a terrible driver.

"She'll learn," I say. "It doesn't take that long."

"I'm not so sure," he says. "Of course, almost everyone can learn sooner or later, but when did you say you're leaving for America?" I call the visa section of the consulate to make an interview appointment for her, but they aren't doing any interviews until after New Year's, and even then the schedule is backed up. The best they can do is the 6th. I have to pretend that the 6th is fine. But the 6th isn't fine. Even tomorrow is too late. What if Vica doesn't get the visa? Then the only alternative would be to bring my mother here, and find another apartment for both of us. I should start looking right away, just in case. I check the ads in the paper, but everything listed costs five hundred dollars or more. Where am I going to come up with five hundred dollars when I'm paying fifty now for Nadia and her St. Bernard? Then I notice an ad for an apartment on the canal near Theater Square. Four rooms. Two thousand dollars. Now, wait a second. Our apartment is near Theater Square, and it's four rooms. No. B couldn't possibly have decided to rent the apartment—my apartment—for two thousand dollars. Where would she go? Maybe she and Mr. Dry-Cleaning American are planning to leave for America. Who would pay two thousand a month anyway?

A year ago, I did everything possible to avoid our old neighborhood, starving myself for the beauty that had made me choose it in the first place. I had dreams about Nikolsky's domes and the Lion's Bridge and the curve in the canal that loops around so that you don't know if you're going backward or forward. This year it's the opposite. Like a person with a toothache who can't stop probing the place that's in pain, I always end up on Theater Square, beside the canal, thinking about Raskolnikov.

Today, when I turn the corner onto Theater Square, Nikolsky's domes are blazing in the bright midday sun. Suddenly I remember when murder first entered my heart. It was after a performance of *Giselle* at the Kirov when I was still living at Misha and Masha's. I was standing in front of the theater in the pouring rain, waiting for the number-five tram to take me to the metro together with a throng of people who never had the luxury of living around the corner from the Kirov and wouldn't have considered it a luxury anyway, because it was too far from everything else that counted. No tram came. I was drenched. Finally a number forty-two arrived. Everyone got on for one stop and then got off again. The options were now greatly expanded: there was hope for the number fourteen, or the fifty-four. People peered into the darkness, hoping to catch a glimpse of headlights in the distance, but gradually they gave up and started to walk to the metro—fine, except that my leather boots and jacket were already soaked. At the corner of Rimsky-Korsakov and Sadovaya, I looked down Rimsky-Korsakov and remembered the piano store where Leningrad musicians often came to buy pianos. Once, I'd heard someone there play Rachmaninoff's First Piano Concerto on an 1880s Blecher and then on a 1920s Pleyel. People stood around and listened. This often happened. But by 1993, the musicians had stopped playing the pianos in the store; they only came in to sell their instruments before emigrating. And there was no one buying, because whoever was staying couldn't afford to buy a piano anymore, never mind that having a piano—and piano lessons—had previously been considered more or less a basic human right. The store had switched to selling antiques and bad landscapes.

I stood on the corner with my wet feet and wet jacket and kept looking into the darkness at the piano store. And all at once, a sense of outrage plunged into me from the street, the stores, the sky, the trees. How could B have taken all this beauty from me?

That was when murder entered my heart, taking root there

like some jungle plant, sending out tendrils that entwined with each other until they formed a matted nest no light could penetrate. And in this darkness, something stronger than thoughts or feelings began to proliferate, spreading outward until it consumed my consciousness. No matter what I have to do, I thought then, I will prove to them that I can't be manipulated and humiliated without consequence. No matter what I have to do.

"I have good news for you," the vice-consul says. "I've spoken with your former friends."

"Both of them?"

"No, actually just with him. At first I didn't remember him. But I have met him before. He says that it's true, you paid for the apartment, but there were other issues involved. He said that he realizes this problem won't go away and that they have to negotiate with you, if only you would be reasonable."

I laugh. "Reasonable! I suppose that over the last year and a half I haven't been reasonable. How much more reasonable could I get?"

"Why don't you give them a call? Try once more. They may be ready to negotiate this time."

"I won't call. They can say anything over the phone and deny it afterward. I'll write to them again and ask them to respond in writing."

I thank the vice-consul for his help and then say, "By the way, about the real-estate company. I've written them a letter, but I haven't sent it yet. I wanted to discuss it with you first. It could be . . . well, dangerous. I mean for me. Can I come in to talk with you again?"

"Sure," he says. "Anytime."

By the time I do come in, it is after New Year's and I still

haven't heard anything from B. I lead with that piece of information, as if to justify what I am about to show him. "I told you
the last time we met that my problem isn't just with B. It's with
the real-estate agency too. I understand that they have their own
problems right now, but I've done a little bit of digging into the
situation since we last talked, and it seems that the president is
defending himself to the tax police over the absence of documents by saying he has a right to keep them in the U.S. rather
than here. But as you know, my documents aren't here or there.
They're gone."

I hand him my most recent letter to the real-estate agency.
He reads it over quickly, and when he raises his eyes from the
page, his expression has completely changed. He doesn't look
like the Pepsi generation anymore. He looks like a grown man
who knows a tough corner when he sees one, and has experience with getting out of it.

"What does this mean here, when you say that you would
cooperate with the tax police?"

"Just what it says. I need those documents. If I don't get
them, I'll tell the tax police about not being able to recover
them. If they are trying to prove that he evaded taxes, missing
documents would be important for them to know about.
Wouldn't they?"

His face isn't so friendly anymore. I can tell that I have
stopped being the kind of woman to whom you give your arm
when she needs help getting over a puddle. "I don't think that
would be a very good idea," he says, his voice dropping to a
darker register.

"Why not? You yourself told me that the president of the
company is in serious trouble. He may have defrauded the Russian government out of millions in taxes."

He looks at me as if he is trying to fish for an object that has
fallen into a black hole of uncertain dimensions. "We're talking

about an American business," he says. "The United States has a very big investment in this country, and when the U.S. government is doing everything it can for American business here, when we are pouring billions into this country, we have to protect our interests. The Russians have to know that they can't have tax inspectors rushing into American companies with guns and seizing documents."

"Guns?"

"Yes, guns. That's what they do. If you cooperate with the Tax Inspectorate, it would be very bad for the American government, which is involved in this case at a very high level. Congressmen are involved, the ambassador is involved. The role of American business in Russia is at stake. As I said, this is being handled at the very highest levels of government, it is not public information, and you could endanger critical negotiations aimed at protecting American business."

It is obvious that I have missed something along the way, that since our last conversation something vital has changed.

"What about me?" I say.

"This is Russia," he says slowly, talking now to someone who must be either completely naïve or an idiot. "Do you know how valuable it would be for them to have an American testifying about having trouble with this company? They would use it against us."

"But an American *is* having trouble with this company," I say. "Why are you protecting people like that? You yourself think he's probably dishonest. If I understand things correctly, I'm probably not the only person whose documents are missing, and it's not just a random event. I've had to take out a fifteen-year loan on my house in America in order to buy this apartment here, and I need proof that I paid for it. Forty thousand dollars isn't small change. It's a lot of money."

His eyes go flat, and I can hear the answer he doesn't give.

His mind is crunching numbers, and I am being crunched in along with them.

I look him straight in the eye with what I intend to be defiance. "I'm a very stubborn woman," I say. "I'm not about to protect an American company that's withholding vital information just because they are American. I came here to talk to you about sending this letter because I recognized that it could be dangerous for me. Not because of the American government, or American business, but because I know where I am, and I know that wounded animals bite. I have to find a way to resolve this problem. My mother—"

He cuts me off, adjusting his face as he might straighten his tie. "I do understand your problem," he says. "And I am sympathetic to it. But I repeat to you, with emphasis, that what you wish to do would be very bad for the American government." He knows now that he made a mistake telling me about this situation, and that this mistake has given me power, which he has to neutralize as quickly as possible. The last thing he needs is an angry woman screwing up the works. "Do I need to say more?"

"No, not really."

He stands up. "I'm sorry, but I have to be going. Please excuse me. If there's anything else with which I can be of help, don't hesitate to let me know."

We shake hands, and when I try to catch his eye, he looks away.

"You don't know where you are. You think you're in America, but you're not in America," B repeated, over and over again. My absence of fear, she said, was what made me dangerous. The vice-consul would no doubt agree with her. It doesn't matter which side they're on, people like me are always dangerous. They end up in jail or at the bottom of canals, or go berserk in some noisy way or another, or write unpleasant books. They won't go away quietly. Well, at least one thing is clear. I would make a lousy spy, because I never know when to keep my mouth shut. That's one of the few characteristics B and I have in common. Both of us are wild cards. I start thinking about Yura with nostalgia. It's true: the Mafia is simpler than lawyers. Politics is the hardest of all. What am I doing now, messing with the Congress of the United States, when I could have had that money months ago?

I walk from the Business Center over to the Moika River, crossing the Fonarni suspension bridge, which bounces as I go, giving the usual impression of its imminent collapse, and continue along the embankment, past the Yusupov Palace with its baroque gilded interior and perfect miniature theater. This is where Prince Felix Yusupov, depicted in the splendid uniform of the Preobrazhensky Horse Guards in a Serov painting that hangs in the Russian Museum, hatched the plot to murder Rasputin, finally dumping his body into the canal. The great anomaly of this city is the way in which beauty and evil are so inextricably linked. You turn to admire one and watch in horror as it mutates into the other, though it could just as easily happen in reverse. Little by little, drop by drop, being in Russia gets to you, so that eventually you almost but not quite merge with it, almost but not quite become indistinguishable from it. No melting pot this, but a cauldron in which everything fantastic burns and bubbles.

In the end, maybe that's the reason why I love this place—because beauty here has so much with which to contend. Maybe I loved B for the same reason.

Just when you're ready to acknowledge that you're being paranoid, it turns out that your fantasy was right.

"It wasn't even an interview," Vica cries. "They looked at me through a glass window and spoke to me as if I were a criminal. They didn't ask me anything. They just read your letter and said no. They said I had no right to go to America to be a companion. They were mean."

She had never expected them to be mean. Everyone in Russia wants to live the way Americans live, or at least the way they think Americans live. How is it possible for them to treat her that way? Only Russians are cruel like that. Americans are kind; they are always smiling in the advertisements. They are always happy. They smile even when they just met you. Why are they against people like herself, who just want to have a taste of their life, to walk down their green plastic streets in peace?

I don't tell her about my meeting with the vice-consul. Surely one thing has nothing to do with the other—these are different departments, not even in the same building. What possible reason could they have to exchange information? Besides, the vice-consul didn't know that I was doing an invitation. There must be some other reason.

There is another reason. When I talk to someone I know who works at the consulate, she asks to read the letter I wrote and says, of course they turned it down. I'd said clearly that Vica would be a companion for my mother. That meant work. Anyone but a fool would have known that. I should have said that she was coming as my guest, to visit me in America for a month.

I request that the application be reviewed. I write another letter, correcting all the errors of the first. This time I go to the interview with her, thinking that I will be able to help explain. But they won't let me anywhere near the interview booth. I just stand at the entrance to the processing area, where I can hear Vica's voice getting louder and louder, becoming shrill. "How could you possibly think that I would abandon my husband and children just for a chance to see America?" she screams.

Gradually I manage to snake my way to the window where Vica has once again been rejected. I ask to speak to the visa officer personally. After all, I am an American citizen. Even if

Russians don't have any rights, I do. Reluctantly they let me approach the window, where the visa officer looks at me across the barrier of glass and says in a cold voice, "I interview fifty thousand people a year. I can tell the ones who aren't coming back in a second. She's not coming back."

"But her family is here," I say. "Two young boys. How could you possibly think that she would leave them?"

"Strange things happen to people when they get to America," he says. "They lose their values, their sense of proportion. They're ready to give up everything just to stay."

I admit that he's not completely wrong. After all, look what happened to B.

"But Vica isn't like that," I say.

He looks at me impatiently. "That's what you think. I'm sorry, but I have other things to do." For the second time in a week, I am dismissed.

I can't look at Vica when I go back to the reception area. What upsets me most of all is my sense that the visa officer has a better handle on things than I do, that he would have seen through B right from the start. He wouldn't have cared that she looked like Akhmatova but refused to accept the poster of Akhmatova I wanted to give her because she thought hero worship vulgar and considered all posters to be a form of propaganda ("Isn't that what marketing is?" she once asked). Or that her way of talking about Repin's *The Father Returns from Siberia* was unlike the point of view of anyone I had ever known. Or that in the beginning she gave me the stockings her husband had brought her from Paris when it was unlikely she would ever possess another pair like them.

He wouldn't have been impressed by the Little Prince's theories about the rose and her thorns. On the other hand, they did give her a visa, not once but five times. And continue to. Why?

"America is such a beautiful country," Vica says. "How could there be people like that in such a beautiful country?"

Of course I don't mention anything to her about my recent meditations on beauty and evil in Russia. I just say, "Life is full of surprises."

PART SIX

Meeting with

Raskolnikov

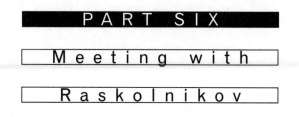

O nce again, I feel the heaviness in my bones that is the prelude to extreme rage. In six weeks, my mother will come back to Russia with me. I will figure out how to take care of her, even though I still don't know where we are going to live. Vadim has found two rooms in a communal apartment on Vasilevsky Island. If only I had that forty thousand dollars. Yura's phone number is now taped to the edge of the mirror in the bedroom. Maybe I should talk things over with Raskolnikov.

I walk, knowing exactly where to look for him. I follow the Griboedova Canal along the embankment, starting at Nevsky Prospekt, and where the canal bends sharply to the right, at the Sennoy (Haymarket) Bridge, I walk across the wooden footbridge, as delicately arched as a dancer's foot, to Ploshchad Mira, Peace Square, recently reverted to its historic name, Sennaya Ploshchad, the Haymarket. No matter where Raskolnikov was going, his path always seemed to take him to the Haymarket.

During the 1960s, when it was still called Peace Square, the cathedral in the square was blown up by the city administration to make way for a new metro station. The sixties were a relatively peaceful time, as peaceful times go. Still, I can imagine the shudders behind curtained windows as the dynamite blew the delicate onion domes to smithereens. People who lived on the square pretended that nothing was happening as church dust drifted into their windows, pretended that the gaping hole that remained there after the fearful detonating blast was perfectly normal, and that the absence of the cathedral, which had been there throughout their lives, was normal too. But if this was peace, what was war? If this was normal, any derangement could be normal too, and to some extent, still is. Now, more than thirty years later, the entrances to the metro are where the entrance to the church once was. In the middle of the former square is a huge hole in the ground, with cranes like fossilized dinosaurs standing idle there, surrounded by corrugated metal construction sheds on stilts with long catwalks joining one to another. I have never seen anything at all in motion here. The entire area is deserted, like a frontier ghost town abandoned as soon as the gold ran out, a permanent memorial to unfinished projects. This is the nature of dreams of glory, doomed to end in ugliness and sorrow. The hole in the ground is encircled by a wooden fence with cyclone wire on top of it. Tramway tracks wind right alongside the fence. The open plaza in front of the metro is densely scattered with kiosks of the less attractive variety. Between the kiosks, lines of women whose imaginations have been taxed to the limit by searching for what to sell stand patiently, displaying on the snowy ground pieces of stuff needed to repair other stuff (a lot of that), odds and ends of clothing, a cup and saucer with a small crack in it, the lid of a teapot, a pair of children's mittens, a short length of electrical wire.

On one side of the steps leading up to the metro is a stand

selling *shaverma*, or souvlaki, cut from a shapeless hunk of meat on a skewer. I once heard of someone killing a woman, cutting up her body, and selling it, neatly packaged, as fresh meat. Cats and dogs are fair game these days. It's hard to know what you are eating anymore. This guy's *shaverma* is suspect. I bought it once and, after wolfing down half, threw the rest away. Nothing was wrong with the taste. It was just that suddenly I had a funny feeling. I never bought *shaverma* from him again.

A flock of bedraggled Gypsies crosses the square, headed for the metro, dragging their children with them. I recognize one of the Gypsy girls. She was at the *banya* with her friends last week. In the dressing room, as soon as they came in, everyone started trying to find a place to hide their belongings while the Gypsies were in the *banya*. The *banshchitsa* locked the door of the cloak room, which was usually left wide open. She checked the amount of sugar in the sugar bowl next to the samovar. It's not so easy to protect things when you are stark naked. The Gypsy girls chattered like chipmunks. They were polite when they took water for tea from the samovar.

On the edge of the square, a young girl is singing to an accordion, but no one is paying much attention. But then the shade of Raskolnikov slips into the square and stands in front of them, watching. The scene hardly shifts.

"Do you like street music?" asks Raskolnikov, addressing a middle-aged man standing idly by him. "I love to hear singing to a street organ. . . . I like it on cold, dark, damp autumn evenings—they must be damp—when all of the passersby have pale-green sickly faces, or better still, when the wet snow is falling straight down, when there's no wind—you know what I mean, and the street lamps shine through it. . . ."

"I don't know . . . excuse me . . ." mutters the stranger, frightened by the question and Raskolnikov's strange manner, and crosses over to the other side of the street. Raskolnikov

walks to the other side of the Haymarket, where the huckster
and his wife had talked with Lizaveta, but they are not there
now. Recognizing the place, he stops, looks around, and ad-
dresses a young fellow in a red shirt.

"Isn't there a man who keeps a booth with his wife at this
corner?"

"All sorts of people keep booths here," answers the young
man.

"Is that a tavern at the top there?"

"Yes, it's an eating house and there's a billiard room and
you'll find princesses there too . . . la, la."

I listen closely to the conversation. Of course, I already
know every word of it, and am not at all surprised when
Raskolnikov stands there, thinks a little, and takes a turn to the
right, in the direction of what Dostoevsky referred to as "V," the
newly renamed Voznesensky, which I always knew as Maiorova.

These days when people give each other directions, they say
things like, "The place you are looking for is next door to where
the Russian Samovar used to be," or, "Keep going past the store
that used to sell stationery on what used to be Maiorova until
you get to what used to be the street where the nursery school
was before." "Before" was permanent. "Now" is not.

Sadovaya, however, has always been Sadovaya, the neighborhood's spinal cord. Here there are sunken entries smelling of
swamp water, swarming with winter mosquitoes, the houses
neglected, decaying, decayed, subject to flooding, mold, infesta-
tion. Raskolnikov's room is nearby, and no doubt it is as grimy
and miserable as before, though in his time people rented out a
corner of a room in which to live, whereas the Soviet system,
being more rational, entitled each person to his twelve square
meters. You've heard all this before, and even from me. Still, it
might be news to know that Raskolnikov's room is now part of
a *communalka*.

Out of curiosity, returning again from Sadovaya to the canal, I open the main entrance door to one of the buildings along the canal, which has a particularly impressive façade. Inside is a broad, elegant spiral staircase of marble with a broken iron railing, and a marble mantelpiece over a half-smashed fireplace in the former lobby, which has been painted over with blue paint. A pair of Grecian plaster caryatids with inclined heads and legs broken off help to hold up a pair of pillars flanking another stairway at the adjacent entry, where blackened walls behind the elevator shaft testify to a garbage fire.

In a few years, the neighborhood will alter, and the building will be restored. As of now, however, there is still no need to create a "Dostoevsky zone" for aficionados; the old one has never vanished. First one redistribution of wealth, then another, then it is all turned around again, like those glass eggs with snow scenes inside of them, the snow falling upside down when you turn the egg on its head. The word "gentrification" hasn't entered the Russian language yet. It will. Dostoevsky will be out. Ostrovsky will be in.

Raskolnikov is walking in the same direction as I am. Do we have a common destination, or is he simply taking his customary route, with me following behind, anticipating his every step? He knows everything except the eventual outcome, which I know better than he. For now, he is in no hurry. Mostly he pays no attention to me, and soon wanders off on his own, going into a restaurant where (upon information and belief) he reads the newspapers of the last five days and finds the news of the pawnbroker's death. He anguishes with himself. He sweats. He is delirious. He confesses, but no one believes him. Zametov thinks he may be mad. He comes out on the street again after a while, pretending (we have this much in common) to an artificial calm, and I continue to follow him again, this time daring to walk closer to him, only a few paces behind. We are almost there now, and I can hear his heart beating in my throat as we walk together along the canal embankment. Deliberately, I stay on the side of the canal opposite the apartment, rather than risk walking directly past it, where I would be more likely to run into B.

As we approach Theater Square, I want to walk faster, but Raskolnikov is taking his time. I suspect he is doing this so that nothing will be lost on me, so that I won't think it is merely a literary excursion that has brought us together. "Hope dies last," he suddenly whispers, half to himself and half to me. Then he turns around, looks me straight in the eye, and winks. "Yes," I say. "Of course you're right." Hopelessness isn't part of the Russian character. Suffering, yes; but hopelessness, no. The point of suffering is always redemption. Maybe Raskolnikov just wants to reclaim my soul from B, to restore my sense of proportion through the negative example of his own extremity. "B claimed it long enough," he mutters. "It could be my turn."

As we walk, I keep my eyes focused on the street in front of me, refusing to let them wander across the canal to the opposite embankment, which is a mere twenty yards away. I need to concentrate on one thing at a time now. I check the numbers on the buildings, as if I don't know exactly which one it is. It's been two years since I walked on this particular block. I always walked on "our side" of the canal, the other side. What is strange is that I knew from the very beginning that the apartment where Raskolnikov killed the pawnbroker was right across from us. Then it was part of the backdrop, evidence that we were surrounded by Dostoevsky's universe, that literature lurked right in our very own backyard. Somehow, in the course of things, I became sufficiently absorbed in my own life that I stopped being aware of it, at least until the moment when the building stopped being part of literature and began its invasion of life, like blood seeping out of the confines of the courtyard onto the surrounding streets. How could I forget? The answer is obvious. There was love in my heart then. I saw the Lion's Bridge. I saw Nikolsky Sobor. I saw the Kirov Theater. I saw the looping curve of the canal. Because there was no murder in my heart then, I saw no murder.

I am standing right under the number now: 104 Griboedova Canal. I turn to look behind me. Raskolnikov was ahead of me all of this time, but now he has vanished, evidently having decided to leave me temporarily to my own devices, not to interfere in my rendezvous with destiny. And there's no doubt in my mind that this must be my destiny, a destiny delayed or diverted, but finally come round to fetch me. What else could it be? It is a plain and simple fact that ten years ago, when I was a tourist here for the first time, the first walk I ever took alone in this city was to exactly this place. I even had a piece of paper in my hand with the address written on it. So why did I come here, instead of going to Palace Square and the Hermitage or to pay a visit to Pushkin and the Bronze Horseman? Does this mean that this meeting has always been my destiny? If so, why? Ten years ago, I had no thought of living in this city. I knew nothing of this neighborhood, aside from what Dostoevsky had told me. Why, at that very moment, knowing nothing of B, nothing of Theater Square and the Kirov, nothing of buying apartments, did I go on a romantic quest for literature, when I must have been aware, even then, that literature always leads right through life, that, in the end, it takes no shortcuts?

Just past the building number, there is an archway that leads into the yard, just as Dostoevsky described it. The archway is in fact more like a tunnel, with the pavement sloping down from street level toward the courtyard beyond. Standing there, I am suddenly overcome with terror. How can I possibly walk through this archway into this yard? How can I search among all of the entrances, look for the right stairway, climb the stairs, and try to find the apartment? Is this real, or am I imagining it? Am I actually standing on that fatal spot where Raskolnikov made his fatal choice? Did I actually live in such proximity to this? And forget about it? I close my eyes for a moment, still keeping my back to the canal, then open them again and blink. On the very periphery of my vision, I see a sequence of light, like the flashing number lights in a casino. At first I can't make out the numbers, though I instinctively recognize them without knowing what they are. Yura's phone number. I hadn't even been aware of memorizing it. So it is too late to gain anything by throwing it away.

It occurs to me as I stand there that if I actually try to go into the building someone could stop me, someone could ask what I am doing there, whose apartment I am looking for. On the other hand, they must be used to furtive-looking people here, who lurk around the courtyard as if trying to find something, going up and down various staircases, and finally leaving, unsatisfied. I can't check every apartment in every stairwell. There are at least half a dozen entrances, and Dostoevsky never said exactly which one it was.

I walk through the tunnel. A sign is painted on the wall: "It is forbidden to leave garbage here. Fine: 200 roubles." Directly across from the sign is a pile of garbage. The yard is grimy. I look up at the windows. Inexplicably, a dirty curtain is hanging on the outside of one of the windows, not as if it had been washed and hung out to dry, but as if it has always been that way and belongs there. Another window is partly covered with a page of newspaper on one side and a square of green mosquito netting on the other. There is an assortment of bottles and large jars on the windowsill. When I look up at the windows on the opposite side of the yard, I see an old woman peering down from the fourth floor. She sees me looking at her and shuts the curtain. I can't decide which stairway to try. I thought they would have entry codes, to discourage people like me from snooping around, but only two of them do, and a third has a square empty space in the door where one of the code panels has been ripped out by someone who was either too drunk or too impatient to bother with pushing all the buttons. None of the other entries have codes. The doors open directly onto the stairs. I open one and go up a flight. There is the smell of piss in the entry and on the stairs. An empty bottle of Stolobovaya vodka is standing in a corner on the second-floor landing, surrounded by cigarette butts. Carbolic acid is sprinkled in the corner. That's what happens when there's no code. On cold winter nights, there is no better place to drink and piss.

This isn't the right entry. I don't know why, but I'm sure that it isn't. I go back down the stairs and walk into the entry on the opposite side of the yard. Yes, this one feels right. I climb the stairs. My heart is hammering. The stairway curves steeply upward. Part of the railing is gone. On the third-floor landing there is a pile of scrap construction lumber. This can't be. This is impossible. Dostoevsky imagined *Crime and Punishment*. What is this pile of lumber doing on the stairwell? I close my eyes again, afraid now that the two painters who were working in the apartment below the old woman's, and who may have seen Raskolnikov leaving the building after he murdered her, might come out again, and catch me standing there. I am going to have to race up to the next floor, wait for them to come out, then rush into the newly painted apartment and hide. What newly painted apartment? The door is obviously new, but what's to say that it is freshly painted on the inside, or that the door is open, or that it's just been sold to some rich New Russians? I go up another flight of stairs. Another new door there, this one wooden and carefully varnished. This must be the apartment. This has to be it. But I can't imagine that anyone could actually live here. There isn't even a bell. Suddenly I hear a dog barking wildly in the apartment on the floor above me. Then I hear the voice of a child and her babushka as they start to climb the stairs from below. Now I am trapped. I panic. I close my eyes and open them again. I am still here. I am really here. This is an actual place, and I am an actual person. It is just that I am inside of a novel that has accidentally, or coincidentally, or perhaps fatally spilled out into life. There is only one thing to do now, go back down the stairs as if I'm not in a novel at all, as if this is simply life. After all, nothing has happened that couldn't actually happen anywhere except at this time and in this place. I mean, it could, but it shouldn't, in terms of credibility. I go back down the stairs. The child who is coming up as I am going down is struggling to conquer the stairs. I try not to stare at her, try not to ask, "Can it be that you really live here?" She is an ordinary child. She doesn't belong in *Crime and Punishment*. The painters do. Raskolnikov does. But they aren't here. And she is. I have been seen. The child or her babushka could remember me sometime in the future. They could point me out in a lineup. I run down the stairs as fast as I can.

The yard is empty. I notice that in one corner of it there is a rickety old kitchen chair leaning up against the wall, as if waiting for the return of its customary occupant. How many of us are there, wild ones who need to sit in a corner and recover from the experience? A man crosses the yard and goes into another entry. I can't just stand here like this. It's too conspicuous. I start walking back toward the archway when I see an old woman coming into the yard from the other entrance, on the Rimsky-Korsakov side. I stop. "Excuse me," I say. "Is this really the building in which Raskolnikov killed the landlady?" She looks at me in fear. "How the devil should I know?" she says, and hurries away from me, as if from a purveyor of evil. So—a murder has taken place in this building. An old woman like herself has been murdered. What a state Russia is in. You're not safe in your own home anymore. Obviously, the killer has been caught. But who knows? Maybe I was only asking in order to find out where she lives. She glances back at me, then ducks her head and disappears into an entry on the far side of the yard.

I walk back out through the archway onto the street and stop, looking across the canal. It's remarkable. I can actually see right into the yard of our apartment, can even see the entry. It's so close. It always was and still is.

On the corner, three people are standing close together. Drunks, a woman and two men. One of the men is wearing a blue woolen cap. He has a puffy black eye and, below it, a little slit encrusted with blood. They are having a conference. Oh yes, of course there is a bar here, right in the basement. I had forgotten about that too. I turn this way and that, undecided which way to go. Then, suddenly, I see the silver-blue domes of Nikolsky. They were there all along. It's just that for a while I forgot about them, forgot that only a few steps away, across the bridge, was the cathedral, that I could be there in a minute. Dostoevsky must have forgotten too. He never mentions in *Crime and Punishment* that if you come out of the pawnbroker's yard on the Rimsky-Korsakov side you are in sight of Nikolsky Sobor. The very same things that made me forget that the pawnbroker's house was directly across the canal from our apartment are the things that made Raskolnikov unaware of Nikolsky Sobor. Or, rather, not the same things, but their opposite. When there was love in my heart, I stopped seeing the pawnbroker's house. When there was murder in Raskolnikov's heart, he didn't see the cathedral, or the Kirov Theater around the corner, or the Lion's Bridge a few hundred paces away.

At precisely this spot on the canal, there is a complicated little bit of geography. Along much of its path, the canal winds along gently, but here, beginning at the Lion's Bridge, it makes a large loop that brings it back on itself. If you walk along the embankment from the Kharlamov Bridge, which crosses the canal here, to the Podyechaski Bridge, you pass the Lion's Bridge, which is only a hundred yards from where you started out, and then start back again in the direction from which you came. In effect, this micro-neighborhood is a mini-peninsula. If you don't know where you are, walking along the embankment, you can quickly become disoriented, thinking that you are walking in one direction when in fact you are walking the opposite way, because within a distance of five blocks you have walked around the entire peninsula, back to where you were.

Perhaps this too contributes to the hallucinatory effect of being in one place and another at the same time, in another time and space, in which what is highlighted when there is love in your heart vanishes altogether when there is murder in your heart, and the other way around.

Suddenly a great lightness comes over me. Dostoevsky said that beauty will save the world. He just forgot to tell Raskolnikov. I cross the Kharlamov Bridge. Now I am on "our side" of the canal, just steps away from our apartment, and an equal number of steps to Nikolsky. I stand there for a few minutes, making up my mind. Then I start walking in the direction of the domes, silver now in the graying sky. I wish Raskolnikov had come all the way with me. We could walk hand in hand to the park that surrounds the cathedral. We could sit on a bench and watch the cathedral. We could watch the light changing. We could walk through the park to the cathedral, and past it to the bell tower. We could walk along the Kriukov Canal, to the Krasnoguardeiski Bridge, from which it is possible to see seven other bridges. I know that because Zina, who owned the apartment we almost bought a year before we bought the one on the canal, told me. She stood there and said, "I could never live happily anywhere else. Where else could I see seven bridges? Look. Count them." We could walk along Sadovaya, where the Griboedova Canal intersects with the Kriukov Canal. Then we could double back to the Kirov Theater. The performance schedule is posted outside. A week from now, Prokofieff's rendition of *The Gambler* is scheduled. Who will sing the role of Polina Suslova? Dostoevsky's infernal woman from whom he could not escape will take over the stage. But beauty can still save the world.

I look into the canal at my reflection. "Beauty will save the world," I shout at my own image. Then I throw a stone into the water, fracturing my face, which disappears in ripples of water that eddy outward and are stopped by the cold, unyielding hand of the embankment.

But what if it doesn't?

Acknowledgments

■

I t is impossible for me to assign rank to the various influences that made this book possible, but I would like to thank above all Andy Reiss and the Fulbright Committee, which provided me with the time and space to write this book while living in St. Petersburg, and in particular Inme Gosnell, Vice Consul for Cultural Affairs in Petersburg at the time, who encouraged me to apply for that grant; Michael Ruhlman, whose essay about me in *Saveur* precipitated the book's publication; Jack Scovil, for consistently believing in me and providing the kind of moral support every writer needs from an agent; Becky Saletan, for reminding me that the tradition of great editors is still alive and well in America; and my husband, Edouard, for loving me.

Acknowledgments

∎

I
t is impossible for me to assign rank to the various influences that made this book possible, but I would like to thank above all Andy Reiss and the Fulbright Committee, which provided me with the time and space to write this book while living in St. Petersburg, and in particular Inme Gosnell, Vice Consul for Cultural Affairs in Petersburg at the time, who encouraged me to apply for that grant; Michael Ruhlman, whose essay about me in *Saveur* precipitated the book's publication; Jack Scovil, for consistently believing in me and providing the kind of moral support every writer needs from an agent; Becky Saletan, for reminding me that the tradition of great editors is still alive and well in America; and my husband, Edouard, for loving me.